Afterlife,
Interrupted

BOOK THREE

3

**A CATHOLIC PRIEST EXPLORES
THE INTERRUPTED DEATH EXPERIENCE™**

Afterlife,
Interrupted

BOOK THREE

3

Please Let Me Explain

NATHAN G. CASTLE, OP
WITH A SPECIAL SECTION BY JIMMY AKIN

FIRST EDITION, DECEMBER 2023

Published in the United States by Fluid Creations, Inc. d/b/a C2G2 Productions, 2023.

The Library of Congress has cataloged this edition as follows:

Castle, Nathan G., 1956, March 12 -
Afterlife, Interrupted, Book Three: Please Let Me Explain
A Catholic Priest Explores the Interrupted Death Experience[tm]/by Nathan G. Castle, OP
— 1st U.S. ed.

ISBN: 9798871037614

Section Two guest essay by Jimmy Akin
Book cover and interior design by Doreen Hann
Illustrations by Stefan Salinas
Cathryn Castle Garcia, publisher

Disclaimer of Liability
The author, Fluid Creations, Inc. d/b/a C2G2 Productions, the editors and designer shall have neither liability nor responsibility to any person or entity with respect to any loss or damage caused or alleged to be caused directly or indirectly by the information contained in this book.

Gratitude

Lots of people in the Catholic Church, which is my spiritual home, are understandably guarded where dealing with spirits is concerned. Sometimes I'm asked, "What does the Church say about the work you're doing?"

The Catholic Church has nearly 1.4 billion members. Within that large body, I live a vow of obedience to my religious superior, Father Christopher Fadok, OP. He is the provincial of our Western Dominican Province.

I'm very grateful for his fraternal support, as expressed in the following statement:

"Pope Francis refers to the Church as a field hospital to express his vision for the care of the wounded among us. He says, 'The thing the Church needs most today is the ability to heal wounds and to warm the hearts of the faithful; it needs nearness, proximity. I see the Church as a field hospital after a battle.' I know of few priests as dedicated as Father Nathan to serving as a medic at the battlefront. His faith in God Who is Love, and in God's promise of eternal life, leads Nathan undaunted to bring healing to those whose wounds menace them and their journey home."

Very Reverend Christopher Fadok, OP
Prior Provincial, Province of the Holy Name of Jesus
Oakland, California

Dedication

Our prayer partner, Linda Quinn, died on December 6, 2023.
We love you, Linda.

Table of Contents

Nathan, O.P.

Preface

Why the Subtitle: "Please Let Me Explain?"

This is my third book in the *Afterlife, Interrupted* series. In Book One, I explain to the reader the basic phenomena of receiving dreams from those who have died, whom I call my night visitors and, with the help of my prayer partners, assisting with their afterlife movement. If this third book has somehow crossed your path but you're unfamiliar with the previous two, I'd suggest you stop now and begin at the beginning with Book One. [ed. note: all books in the *Afterlife, Interrupted* series are available on Amazon. See QR codes on page 12] Think of the streaming shows that are so popular online. Would you begin watching any of them in Season Three with no knowledge of what has come before? I wouldn't.

In Book One, titled, *Afterlife, Interrupted: Helping Stuck Souls Cross Over*, I focused on the metaphor of being stuck. It seemed to me that the people we were being asked to help were spinning their wheels and getting nowhere in their afterlives. They had been through some trauma that continued to define them in ways that impeded their progress. That book came out in 2018.

By the time Book Two was released in 2020 I'd begun to realize that some of those we were invited to help really weren't stuck. They had moved through a healing process that was mostly complete. I began to compare my prayer partners and myself to the discharge staff in a medical facility. We were helping people gather themselves up and prepare for a move to some place better, happier, and freer. On the cover we struck through the word "stuck" to illustrate that point. We were growing to a deeper understanding of our work as we assisted more people.

For Book Three, I'm choosing this subtitle: "Please Let Me Explain." We are very task-oriented when we are in a session. Someone has brought me a story in a dream and it's time for them to make a significant crossing. We are only there to help them do that. We don't ask a lot of unnecessary questions. We're just trying to be helpful.

Sometimes we decide that this person's story would be one we'd like to tell publicly, either in book form or on my podcast, *The Joyful Friar*, or in some other way. We wouldn't do that without asking their permission because it's their story, after all. So, we go back a second time into protected prayer and asked them if they would allow their story to be told. They could tell us yes or no. And they do, but as they do, they often give us an update on what they have experienced since the first time we met and spoke. Often, I hear my prayer partners say with surprise, "Oh!' or" I see," or simply, "Wow!" The one we've helped explains something that inspires a new thought about what the experience of the afterlife can be.

I feel an etymology coming on.

Anyone who's been around me for more than a few minutes knows I love words and their origins. I love the website, OnlineEtymologyDictionary.com. It's like one of those genealogy sites except for words instead of people. You just type in a word and in a matter of seconds you get its family tree. You learn its origin, component parts and how those letters and sounds came to express a particular idea.

Now, permit me to explain the word "explain." I knew that "ex" means "out of" or "out from," and "plain" suggests flat land. And that's where the word explain comes from. Think of topography that blocks one's view. A dense forest, mountains, or places prone to fog come to mind. Coming out of such places one might see plainly. One might even see a plain.

I live in Arizona, in a city ringed by mountains on three sides. I could drive about 15 minutes west of my home on a winding road that goes through the mountains to an overlook. The mountains stop and a broad plain is visible for miles and miles. It feels like you can see forever.

When someone explains a thing to us, they help us to see it clearly, plainly, perhaps for the first time. We might find ourselves saying, "Oh! Now I see!"

The stories we have chosen for this book are ones my prayer partners and I thought gave us new visions, new perspectives. I'm not writing a doctrinal book. Neither am I trying to insist, "This is the way things are!" I'm simply sharing experiences of persons we've met in doing this ministry. In each story I'll try to call out a few elements that made us say, "Oh! Now I see!"

At the start of each chapter, I've noted a Challenge, a Value and Three Explanations I think are represented in the story. Maybe as you read you will have some insight of your own. The universe is so vast. These afterlife glimpses we've been a part of are not the last word on anything. They don't exhaustively define or explain anything. But they are beautiful.

I hope you enjoy the stories of these awesome people, all of whom have overcome awful trauma. They've all been healing. They've grown into deeper truth. They've expanded. And they've gone on to new adventures. They have their own ways of telling their stories, as we all do. I hope you find their stories a blessing in your own life.

Godbless,

Father Nathan Castle, OP
December 2023

Joyful Friar Podcast   **Afterlife, Interrupted 1**   **Afterlife, Interrupted 2**

Prologue

I have been a campus minister working with young adults for most of my career. Because of that I've presided over an unusually large number of weddings. I've stood close enough to nervous brides and grooms to whisper the words of the marriage vows they then repeat after me.

Because of the afterlife work my prayer partners and I do I'm often asked about specifics of what I believe. The word believe comes from the word beloved. I believe in God, my Beloved One, and the many smaller beloveds God has created out of love.

In the chapters of this book, you'll meet many people I've come to love. They've explained themselves so well that they might answer for you questions you haven't even asked. I believe you will enjoy getting to know them.

First there is Omi. If there is anything normal about living in a war zone, 10-year-old Omi was enjoying a normal day at school. Soldiers not much older than he burst into his classroom abducting all the boys and forcing them to become child soldiers. He lived among so many flying bullets that the one that killed him didn't come as much of a surprise. It was a pleasant surprise when Nadi, whom we met in Book Two, came to help fellow Iraqi, Omi, make an afterlife passage.

The next three stories all involve college life.

Estella was a professor in Peru. She was furious that she died quarreling over a parking space. A surprising afterlife visiting lecturer helped her see things in a new light.

Lupe had excelled academically all her life and was accepted into a prestigious advanced degree program. Sadly, she succumbed to the temptation to falsify some research findings. As that was being discovered she saw no way forward except ending her life, at least the part of it that she was able to end. You'll see her learn a new way of being and of thinking about herself.

And then we'll meet Dr. Lawrence. He showed us his debilitating end-of-life decline. As his body failed him, he felt like a caged bird. He told us that upon his death he took the cage with him. He had lessons to learn about his new body, and he had plenty of good teachers.

In the next three chapters you'll meet Ellen, Iron Mike and Sylvia. They all suffered a trauma that didn't kill them, at least not on the outside. But they each moved through what remained of their Earthly lives in solitude and deep sorrow.

Ellen survived being raped in her own home. She decided to keep that assault a secret. It changed everything. Her life became dark. In her afterlife she got the help she hadn't been ready to receive earlier. Her mother came for her. She told Ellen, "I've come to help you turn your light back on."

Iron Mike was a minor league baseball player. His game-winning home run struck and killed a child. He never forgave himself. He wanted to crawl in a hole and die. He became a coal miner by day and climbed into a bottle by night. Here and hereafter he pushed away everyone who tried to help him. Finally, a little boy who had died playing baseball said, "Mister, after I died, I was mad too. But then I changed my mind." Eventually so did Iron Mike.

Sylvia was a young wife and mother of a child who was not yet two years old when her husband and child were killed in an automobile accident. It was all too much to bear. When she got a terminal cancer diagnosis while still a young woman, she saw it as her golden ticket. She had to learn to reengage with her own life. When she did, her family was there to greet her. I think you'll enjoy hearing how they navigated picking up where they left off.

Next, you'll meet Samuel the Clothier. He had a gift for helping men look their best. He was given an extraordinary afterlife opportunity to see himself look his best. If you have any difficulty understanding yourself to be well-made, you'll want to get to know Samuel.

Ritah with an H struggled mightily with addictions. She endured many failed rehab attempts. Her family tried their best to love her. After her death by overdose she entered afterlife rehab. The people helping her were well equipped, patient, and wise. This time it worked. Ritah healed. Then her sister took her for a wild ride.

And speaking of wild, meet Not-So-Simple Simon. What's it like to have a consciousness embodied on the autism spectrum when you die? What happens next? Simon got to practice at things he would have never wanted to experience before. All these stories are extraordinary, but Simon's is next-level.

The last three stories involve Catholic people helped by the communion of saints.

Rudolfo was only doing what was right, but it cost him his life. He took the side of vulnerable women against their oppressors. They shot and killed him. He compared his death to the carnival game Whack-a-Mole. "They whacked me, but I popped back up!" he laughed. The family of martyrs enveloped him with their love. His is a powerful story.

Tony saw humor in the moments before his impending death. He had only praise for the work of his guardian, whom he called Tinkerbell. Tony was part of a raucous Italian family whom he loved and who drove him crazy. He said they all bore some version of the name Anthony. When they came to welcome him home, he called them "The Floating Anthonys." They told him this good news, "We're not allowed to annoy each other for all eternity."

Finally meet Abraham and his family who both died in and survived the Rwandan genocide. He called forgiving his family's killers "a stubborn stain" that he is still working on. They received the extraordinary support of Saint Charles Lwanga. Mary the Mother of Jesus arrived to help too, under the title of Our Lady of Rwanda. They had all saved the scraps of things to turn them into more useful and beautiful things.

I hope you'll enjoy the people whom you meet here. I believe you will. I'm grateful for your interest in this work. And I ask God's blessing upon you as you share in the stories of *Afterlife, Interrupted, Book Three: Please Let Me Explain.*

Protective Prayer and Permission-Seeking

Editor's note: This text was included in Book Two. It bears repeating in Book Three because of its importance to the work Father Nathan and his prayer partners perform.

As a child I was **taught** that God made everyone good. God created no evil thing and no evil person. **Human** and angelic persons are good, but some are currently behaving badly. Some do so consistently and habitually. We must be careful around such persons while loving them as God does. Think of trying to raise happy, trusting children who must also be taught about "stranger danger."

In the spiritual world I presume goodness, but I don't do so naively. Not every spirit has good intentions toward me or those who assist me. That's why we begin each of the sessions you'll read here with protective prayer.

As a Catholic Christian I begin a prayer in the name of the Father, the Son and the Holy Spirit crossing myself on the forehead, heart and shoulders. I trace the cross of Jesus the dead-and-risen Christ over my body. I believe Jesus the Christ loved us to death and beyond it into eternal life. The work my prayer partners and I do is done in His name and in the Power of His Holy Spirit. We want to move only within the Spirit's intention.

In the Body of Christ are all who have accepted his love. I pray within the Body of Christ, inviting the presence and support of some of its specific members. When moving into the work we do, I think of us as being shielded in light, surrounded by loving helpers.

I always ask the presence and support of my friend Saint Michael the Archangel. He is the patron of police who serve and protect us. I always include Holy Mary. She is powerfully loving.

I am a member of the Dominican family; I always invite Saint Dominic to be with us. Here are some of the others I often invite to surround us:

- St. Mary Magdalen, who accompanied Jesus to the cross, the empty tomb and brought the good news of his resurrection to his followers.
- My own guardian angel, Philip James of the line of Michael. He never leaves my side.
- St. Rose of Lima, who has shown herself to be especially interested in this work.
- St. Francis of Assisi, known for his compassion for the poor and suffering.
- St. Maximillian Kolbe, the World War II martyr, who traded places with a condemned man.
- I often include St. Andrew and St. Paul who have helped me a lot over the years.
- I ask for the Holy Ones in my family line and in the family line of any we will serve in that day's session.

Our liturgical calendar is populated with many saints; I often ask the presence of the saint whose feast is celebrated that day.

On November 1 and 2 we honor All Saints and All Souls. It's our way of saying, "We don't always know exactly who our unseen helpers are, but we're grateful for your love for us." I often ask for and acknowledge the lesser-known ones beloved of God who might, for reasons of their own, want to join in that day's work.

We don't go on and on. We simply compose ourselves and invite loving, powerful protective presence. I ask the Holy Spirit for gifts of gracious speech, gracious listening, and gracious direction for the flow of our conversation. By the time our prayer is complete, I feel like I'm on the inside of a holy huddle. Then it's time to get to work.

In the construction of this book, we've made an editorial decision to describe this process up front. For the sake of brevity, we will not include the entire prayer each time we gather, though those prayers are in the original recordings and transcriptions. We will remind you that we have said our prayers before each session. We never move into the spiritual realm unprepared and unprotected.

In the stories which follow the sequence is essentially the same. I first learn of the person or persons needing help by being contacted in a dream. Upon awakening, I write the dream down in a journal I keep on the nightstand. I promise in prayer to be back in touch as soon as possible. That can be several weeks later, depending on my workload at the time. Remember, I have other responsibilities, as we all do.

After assisting in a crossing, I edit the recorded transcription and add the story to my files. I want to leave an organized record of these experiences for any who might want to know about them in the future.

But I also have felt urged to write and speak about some of these stories publicly, as I am doing here. These stories are highly personal, but must they be kept private? I wouldn't know unless I asked. And so, I ask. That's simply being respectful of another's privacy. I record those sessions too for my private use. Occasionally someone will choose an assumed name, usually out of concern for loved ones still here. Sometimes identifying details are left out on purpose.

In those permission-seeking sessions we try to keep it short. I'm not chatting up the dead for my own amusement. I have a job to do and am intent on doing it. The tender details of the stories of those we help are endearing; sometimes we become friends in the course of this work. Often enough, the yes or no question, "May we share your story publicly?" gives rise to an update on current events in the lives of those we've helped. We include them in this book, because they give such rich insight into some of the possibilities that may await us later.

Sometimes they let us know they're looking in on us and are aware of us and our world. I call out to them in prayer as a group; consequently, many have befriended each other. And several have made it clear they want to help with this book project. So, in addition to all those angel and saint friends we invite in prayer, I've begun asking for "the book people" to gather round and help the next person complete their crossing. That has a nice feel to it: first being helped, then helping. It feels like completing the circle.

SECTION ONE

Chapter One

Omi, Child Soldier:
The Friend You Hadn't Met Until Now

Challenge: Stolen Childhood
Value: Courage to Do What is Right

Three Explanations:
Ability to Choose to Recraft Ones Childhood
Promotion to Levels of Truth
Wisdom of Helping Those Who Hurt You

Sometimes my night visitors take me to far-flung parts of the world. In Book Two I shared the story of Nadi, an Iraqi businessman killed by a child in a wartime massacre. This is the story of Omi, a reluctant child soldier who would not pull the trigger.

||||||||||||||||||||||||||||||||||||||||||||||||||||||||||||||||||||||||||||||||||||||||||||||||||||||||||||||||||||||||||||||||||

Nathan: I am Nathan. Today is March 20, 2021. I am in Tucson on a Zoom call with Lisa in Phoenix. Today, we're going to be assisting a person who brought a story in a dream during the night of February 13, 2021. Here's that dream as I received it and wrote it in my dream journal.

I was a child soldier with what seemed like four rifles. I was pointing them out of a slit of a window at a woman opposite me. I could have easily killed her. She looked my way, but she didn't look like an enemy soldier. She just looked like a school-teacher or a businesswoman. She told me to put the gun down and I obeyed her. I awoke.

(There was a pause.)

We've said our protective prayers, then read the dream a second time. Lisa and I are inviting the child soldier in this story, and that child's guardian, who might be able to speak briefly and give us some clarity about who we're assisting and how we might help.

(A guardian emerged quickly.)

Guardian Najif: I'm going to use the name Najif, N-A-J-I-F. The one whom I guarded lived in a place of violence where people tried to go about their lives as though normal. One of those things was schooling of children. He was enrolled in a school. He was about 10 years of age. Militia members took over the school and forcibly inducted young boys into their fighting. The school closed, and the boys were made to live in a camp where they were instructed about guns and very little else, only how to point and shoot on command. I accompanied him, naturally, because I was his guard, but it was a circumstance that had violence on all sides. I did the best I could to keep him safe.

Lisa: Sure. A very harsh life for someone so young.

Guardian Najif: It was heartbreaking. The ones who were his captors and who became his leaders were not very much older than he. The process was just reproducing itself. They had come through something very much like what they were putting him through. It had something of the character of hazing of young men, making others suffer what they've suffered to belong to the group. I don't think that's always males, but I think they are more inclined to do that than females are.

He's been given all the resources he needs. He died as a young person. His life went from having the stability of loving parents in an ordered home to this chaotic madness of violence. He never gave himself fully to it, but he was not able to escape it.

I've said enough; he's listening. And as you know, he wouldn't be here today were he not deemed ready to do the passage that you assist with.

He goes by Omi, O-M-I.

Lisa: Hi Omi.

(Omi moves in.)

Omi: I'm not much older than 10, but they wanted me to be 20. They had already taken the men of that age who would have been more proper soldiers. They thought they were entitled to force the rest of us to behave like adult soldiers. They mocked us for behaving like children. Even though we were children, they shamed us for it. We were to become men just because they demanded it. They were giving us the power of life and death over other people. They wanted us to believe that this was our transition to manhood. Being a little boy in a school was for sissies. Being a man with a gun meant you could demand authority and respect or at least you could threaten: "You do what I say, or I'll shoot you."

Lisa: I'm so sorry you experienced that harshness. I'm glad you get to choose your age now and live in a different way.

Omi: Well, it's been some years in time since my dying, but I'm reluctant to age too quickly because I thought that my childhood was snatched from me. I'm not moving past it too quickly.

Lisa: I understand. That makes good sense.

Omi: They've told me that, if I complete the passage that you will help with today, I can choose to be in a peaceful place for 10-year-olds. I can circle back and move through events and experiences appropriate to that age that I was denied because of where I was and what was happening around me.

I think that's what I'm most inclined to do because I was enjoying my life. I had a good family and friends. I enjoyed going to school and learning. I admired my teachers. They seemed like people I might like to become. In the dream I showed [Father Nathan], they were trying to get me to identify whomever they thought ought to be killed as my enemy.

The moment I chose to show in a dream wasn't the moment I died. But it was a moment that I thought exemplified what my life was like. I was forced to point a gun out a small window. I could be seen from it. I was pointing a gun at a woman. She saw me pointing it at her and she spoke like a teacher, "You put that thing down this minute. This is not who you are." And I obeyed.

My oppressors punished me for not shooting her, for being a baby. They tried to shame me that I was no man. I was denied food and given all the worst jobs because I had disgraced myself.

Lisa: That's a terrible thing to have to go through. The fact that **you did not shoot** showed great courage.

Omi: Well, there was only a brief time of paying the penalty **of** being denied food and being shamed because not long after, I was killed.

The helpers who have instructed me afterwards told me, "You **can** tell your story in the way you want to tell it. Part of what happened to you was others came in and took away your voice and took away your power. We're **not** going to do that. We're **not** going to tell you how you must do this because there are different ways." So I said, "Well, I remember that one day. It wasn't very long before I died anyway, but when I thought about it, I was sort of proud of myself. I didn't have very much authority about anything, but I did **have** the authority not to pull the trigger."

Lisa: Absolutely.

Omi: And I didn't pull the trigger. I didn't kill a woman who didn't **deserve** to be shot. She recognized I was just a boy, so she spoke to me with authority and **reason** and said, "Put that down." And I did because it was right.

The details of my death have been dealt with by others and **don't** need to be the topic of this conversation. I found dying to be surprisingly easy. A bullet hit me in a place that caused my body to die quickly. I was not unduly terrorized.

Lisa: I'm glad to know you didn't suffer long.

Omi: No. And the helpers were rather clever about it. They had **organized** for my arrival something like the school that I had been taken from. I had **some** companions in the classroom who were, if you will, my kind. They spoke the language that I spoke and were from the land that I was from, Iraq.

But there were others who were from other places. We could talk to each other without a language boundary. Some of them were wearing dress I had never seen before or perhaps hairstyles or something about their appearance suggested that they're from a different time or place. Everybody had stories to tell, but they were all childhood stories. I learned later that some of them had since grown, but were purposefully coming back in this guise, not as a trick but a service. They were coming back in this way and being authentically who they were at a younger time in their life saying, "I'm intentionally coming to be with you in this version of me because I would like to be your friend. I would like to know you."

As I grew, they made me know that it's a little different than it was upon the Earth; once you leave behind an age, you're never that age again. Here that's often but not always true. If there's a wholesome purpose for reconstituting yourself as the young person you were, you don't do that with the loss of wisdom. You don't forget the intervening time. You may go back to that 10-year-old you, but you do so with the grace and wisdom you've acquired. I learned that my guardian stayed on the job. Sometimes he would be with me at what might feel like the end of the day. There was still something of a cycle, even though it's not exactly sunrise and sunset.

There would be something that felt like the end of the day where one looked back upon events. He would say, "That person whom you had a nice talk with today, this is the kind that they are. They lived in this time, and they've come back to help you learn. This is a possible ability for you in the future should you ever think you would like to go back. You're not the only child soldier who died. Should you choose that path all the lessons you would need would be given you."

Lisa: What a beautiful gift!

Omi: Life is good even if you have a really hard time of it, as I did near the end. I have some interest in helping the ones that were my captors because, as I mentioned earlier, many of them were not much older than I was. It's just that they somehow took to that way of life and embraced it. They simply assessed that this is the new reality, and to succeed in it, they must become good at using weapons. They must be good at commanding. They must be harsh with anyone who looks soft or unwilling to shoot as ordered.

Maybe I'll go back and help with some of that. But that's for another day. They've coached me that after my movement today, it might be best if I were a 10-year-old in a classroom again in a peaceful place where nobody could disrupt things. They said, "It can be resumed. It needn't be a copy of what was before, but it could have all the elements that made it so pleasant for you and more."

Lisa: That's lovely. I imagine you're going to experience great joy there.

Omi: There's a man emerging. Just a minute.

(Omi slides aside. The man emerges.)

Man: Hello, Lisa?

Lisa: Hello? With whom am I speaking?

Nadi: I'm Nadi. I was in his recent book. My chapter title is, "Nadi, A Massacre and a Parade of Floats." That's how mine played out. I was helped by his friend, Michael, and his wife, Linda.

Lisa: I see. Well, I'm so glad to meet you.

Nadi: I'm happy to help. I wish this help weren't needed, but if you recall I was shot and killed by a child, a little girl with a gun to her head.

Lisa: Yes.

Nadi: My death was not so far back in time. My own children and my wife are alive on the Earth. I have what I am told is an appropriate attachment. I have been both available to new things and my heart still has attachments to loved ones that are still here. My homeland, one would like to think, is getting more peaceful with each passing day. It's still a precarious place. There are still explosions that happen and people who still harbor grievances that they believe entitle them to commit violent acts. Nevertheless, life goes on and it does for this young person who it sounds like has wisely decided that there were lessons to be learned at the age of 10 that ought not be rushed by.

Lisa: Yes, he does sound very wise. And what an incredible thing for you to be able to help him today. You both lived amidst such violence. I don't even know what that would be like. I can't imagine that.

Nadi: I don't want you to. At least we're beyond it. There's no more such activity here on this plane. We're happy to welcome him from one to the next. I've had another promotion since the one that is recorded in his book.

Lisa: Oh, yes?

Nadi: There was another such crossing from place to place. I've only done two, but whatever fear there might've been about leaving the accustomed place to go to the new unknown is unnecessary. Fear of that kind, even the fear of dying, is understandable. But on the other hand, it would be nice if it were minimized because the same One who has loved you into existence, who's loving you all the time now is going to love you in other ways. There is a grand circle where what we thought we left behind isn't as past and absent as we might've thought.

Lisa: Okay. Thank you for those words of wisdom. I think they're going to help others.

Nadi: Oh, I hope so. Who knows if this becomes part of a book or some other thing. He [Father Nathan] uses other communication forums besides books where he might use these stories to inspire, heal or give people a fresh thought. But for now, our work is to get young Omi moved from place to place, which he is ready to do now. So off we go. Thank you.

(Omi and Nadi depart.)

Nathan: Glory be to the Father, to the Son and to the Holy Spirit as it was in the beginning, is now, and will be forever. Amen.

Lisa: Amen. Omi seems very wise for such a young boy.

Nathan: He didn't say it plainly, but he's not 10 anymore. He's moved past it. But he's unwilling to completely give up on being 10 because it was taken from him.

Lisa: Yes. Did he say how much time has passed?

Nathan: No, he didn't quantify it. He just said some time has passed. He said he'd had some growth since his death.

Lisa: Okay. We take so much for granted living in a place where there is not that wide-scale violence. To have to go through that, to have any person go through that is horrific.

Nathan: Yes, I hope our land will stay peaceful. I've had some misgivings about all our political foment, anger and divisiveness, these militias and so many guns. I hope that we get to live lives of peace and security without wondering who's on the other side of the mountain or coming down the road.

Lisa: I hope so, too.

––

To fully enjoy this story, you may want to find Book Two and read about Nadi's passage. He's such a fine gentleman. I love it when one of our "alumni" returns to help someone else. Throughout our conversations Omi returns to his decision to experience fully the childhood that was stolen from him. He's gained wisdom along the way. He speaks with a wisdom-beyond-his-years because he is beyond his years! I've met others in this process who suffered some childhood trauma who've spent part of their afterlife in a sort of "do-over." I remember helping a woman who'd been sexually abused as a four-year-old who wanted to know what it would have been like to have had a healthy, happy childhood. If you've endured a difficult childhood and carried its scars into adulthood, can you imagine having the opportunity to change your past? I've seen it done. In fact, that hopeful message is a large part of why I'm including Omi's story in this book. As always, we first ask permission to do so.

||||||||||||||||||||||||||||||||||||||||||||||||||||||||||||||||||||||||||||||||||||||||||||||||||||||||||||||||||||||||||||||||||||||||||||||||||||||||||||||||||||||||||

Nathan: I am Nathan. Today is July 24th, 2023. I am in Laguna Beach, California on a Zoom call with Michael and Linda in Pennsylvania, and Lisa in Phoenix. We are together to seek permission from Omi, who was a child forced into soldiering at a young age, and our old friend Nadi, whose crossing we participated in, and who came to assist Omi, his fellow Iraqi. That's our purpose today.

We've just completed our prayers of protection, inviting the presence of the angels and saints. I'm going to be still for a moment and ask for angelic help if that's needed or for Omi or Nadi to speak through.

(There was a pause.)

We are going to get Nadi first.

(Nadi emerges.)

Nadi: This young man is deferential to his elders. He was ripped away from a family that was trying to raise him to be a gentleman, but of course, there was nothing gentle about his life thereafter. He has been quite clear that he wants to be in charge of his development. He was enjoying being 10 years old as best he could in a country at war. But there came a day when his classroom was invaded, and he and others were taken away.

Michael: It's good to be with you again, Nadi.

Nadi: And with you. I believe you will get the permission you're seeking. You have it from me. But I'm junior partner to this session because this really is Omi's story. I was his assistant at the end.

I know the benefit of allowing one's story to be told in these formats because I've witnessed it. That will be for another day, but I've been approached by people who I did not know in life who came to me and said, "Oh, you are that Nadi!" The story that all of you helped make available has found its way into different hearts.

That was the reason for saying yes to it at all. And for Father Nathan's writing it and your assisting him as you do so faithfully. It's especially important because violence upon the Earth just never seems to stop.

There's always the next person who is ripped away from their life. Those who are left endure the carnage and the deep grief of losing someone to violence, often during war.

I might come on the line again. We never know how these conversations will flow. I think you know already that I made one more level of crossing like the one that you assisted with.

Michael: That's right.

Nadi: I came to the level that I was at with your help. It turned out I didn't need what it could provide for very long before they said the same thing. "You are a man in motion; you are going places!" They were appealing to the businessman in me who would've loved living in a peaceful land where I could have taken my entrepreneurial and business-oriented skills and created things that would've benefited others and my family. I'm getting to do something like that now.

At this next level where I am now many opportunities are opening for me. I'm doing something like networking, looking for potential partners, people with similar interests. Here one doesn't have to worry about the business ethics of a partner. You don't have to size up whether this person is a cheat <laugh>! You don't have to think about somebody being a dishonest business partner.

Lisa: If you have any wisdom about bringing peace in place of wars, we'd be very open to hearing that from you or Omi.

Nadi: Well, we'll see how that goes. I can at least give hope to people that there is a time and a place where war is no more and where people live in peace. They still must choose it. That's part of what the levels are about. People must live in the truth and truth and truth and truth and truth. <laugh> I think that's a most important element. I know only what I know and don't know what I don't know…but it seems to me this advancing in afterlife realms has everything to do with truth.

Linda: Nadi, I think you mentioned before that your family is still alive here.

Nadi: Yes. As time goes on that changes, but I had a clan. Many remain here on the Earth.

Linda: I'm sure you were attached to them. I was hoping you could speak a little bit about that.

Nadi: Things are better for them now than they once were. They couldn't have been much worse than the day that I left! As you know, your own country's soldiers are not there any longer, at least not in the visible public way they were before. There are probably clandestine operatives. That's the way they do those things. But it's not as though there are patrols and sentries on every corner. Things aren't blowing up to the degree that they did during my final days there. Thanks be to God for that.

I know a little bit of Christian prayer especially the one you call The Lord's Prayer. It seems like regardless of what kind of Christian you might be, everybody prays that prayer, or some translation of it. You ask that "thy kingdom come; thy will be done on Earth as it is in heaven."

Linda: Right.

Nadi: It seems that Christian peoples of all different sorts have in their imagination based on that prayer, the idea that there is a place where there is peace and no violence. You pray for its boundaries to expand somehow, or for the one to become more like the other.

Linda: Right.

Nadi: That isn't my tradition, but of course we had our own prayers for peace. I think every world religion does. We can continue to hope that those prayers have some effect.

I came on first today because Omi preferred that. I think you'll find that he has a blend of two things going at once. He wanted to start again at age 10 because he felt like his life was taken from him without his permission. He wanted to see what it would be like to grow in a way that unfolds naturally.

He really loved his teachers. If you remember his story in the dream that he presented, he was pointing a weapon at a woman, perhaps a teacher, who spoke to him authoritatively, while facing the point of a gun, and said, "Put that down." He wanted to be around more such people. He wanted to be taught by people who had that calling and that gift. Even though I wasn't formally an educator, in this little context, he's saying, "You're the elder; you're the teacher. So, you go first."

You have my permission to use my part of this story. I'll slide aside as the angels often do, and not go very far. But you'll next hear from Omi.

(Nadi slides aside. Omi emerges.)

Omi: And this is Omi. I am feeling like I have been called to the front of the classroom. I liked it when I was called on. I liked it when I would be singled out, even if I wasn't confident I had the right answer. I liked those moments. That's what this feels like. I'm being called on and adult people who are good want to hear what I have to say. The thing that you want to hear honors my freedom, because I don't have to say what I think you want to hear. I can say whatever I want, and you will respect it.

My answer is yes. I'm honored that you would want my story in a book. I know I am the only child soldier he has dealt with out of more than 500 of these stories.

Your country hasn't had war fought on its soil in a very long time. The problem of children being stolen and forced into soldiering at a young age could be something you pay little attention to. It's something that happens in chaotic places far away.

I'm grateful that you're even thinking of taking my story and placing it alongside other stories of car crashes or other kinds of swift deaths. Yes, it's true that I died suddenly and violently. Although I think I even said in the earlier conversation that I walked amid flying bullets for so long that my death was not a surprise. It was more of an inevitability.

Using that word might be a tip off that I'm not exactly 10 anymore. And, of course, I didn't speak English, but as you know, that doesn't affect this process. I simply form thoughts.

I was abducted way too early to have given much thought to what I would be when I grew up. But I did at least observe that even in wartime there were people who had chosen occupations and were trying to go about them in the chaos of war. There were still bakers and police and teachers. There were people who reported the news.

I've become a communicator, a storyteller, because of your helping me. This would only elevate that if my story goes beyond being a functional one of getting me from place to place.

Now I'm circling back and commenting upon it, updating, and possibly having things to say about it that would be explanatory. He [Father Nathan] thinks my story could explain something. I wonder, what do you think it would be? What do you think my story could explain?

Lisa: I think it took courage to not shoot. And I was particularly struck by your desire to help those who hurt you.

Omi: Thank you. If you remember, the people who took me away and coerced me to become a soldier were only a few years older than I was.

Lisa: Yes.

Omi: Father Nathan is translating in his mind. You know, international schooling systems have different ways of talking about grade levels. In your academic system, a 10-year-old would have been maybe fourth grade?

Lisa: Correct.

Omi: The people who were over me coercing me into shooting might have been in the tenth grade. No one would have mistaken them in another time and place for an adult. They were…what's the word…adolescent.

Lisa: Yes.

Omi: I had been told at home by my grandfather, "Remember, you're living in a country at war. It won't always be this way. One day it will turn again."

He said there will be a time when persons who are 15 won't try to behave like they're twice that old. They'll live more peaceful lives that won't demand of them that they be so hard of heart.

I remembered that when they were being hardhearted toward me. They were always mocking that if you cried, it was because you were a baby. Well, no, we were crying because we were frustrated, angry, lonely, and ill-fed. There were all kind of sorrows that could cause a person to cry. Even while they were cruel, I could see that they were victims of war just as I was. Everyone I ever knew was. It didn't matter what you might have done to accelerate it and make it worse. No one of us chose this setting.

I hope that I can remind people that we're all one, even when we don't think we are. Everyone has a story, and oppressors often have been oppressed. Being oppressed can create darkness inside if you allow hate in your heart. But choosing to exclude hatred from your heart is something even a child can do.

Michael: Omi, you said to Lisa that we're all in this together. To me, that's such a transcendent thought to have where you are now. That there's a commonality between religions, a commonality among all souls to evolve. There's a quote I love that's attributed to spiritual teacher Ram Dass, "We're all just walking each other home."

Omi: Yes. And maybe that moved me in the direction of talking a little bit about what I've done since being walked home. Mr. Nadi helped with that, as did Lisa and Father Nathan.

And you, of course, had helped Mr. Nadi do that in his own earlier moment.

I want to try to explain things. The way I've chosen to do things was my option. Others who went through a similar story wouldn't have necessarily chosen afterwards what I've done.

I stubbornly wanted to go back to my life before it was interrupted, which is a word that he uses in his book titles. That was my choice. I didn't have to do that, but I was stubborn about it. I was given a happy life that was taken from me, and I wanted it back.

I just wanted my life back. That might be a hopeful thing for people to hear. If you really have a wholesome desire to have back what once was and it's in right order, and the helpers around you say it's okay, you can have that. It's important to get this consult; otherwise, you can just spin off in your own anger, your own insistence on getting your way. Anger will only hold you down.

I chose to go back to being age 10, but I didn't remain that age for long. I think it was a little accelerated; time doesn't operate here quite as it does where you remain. You can speed things up and make it go faster.

They said I have about me a sense of progress. I'm trying to find a right word that doesn't sound like vanity, but…excellence. If I'd had the opportunity to have an uninterrupted academic life as a child and then perhaps into college, I think I would've tried to do my best. They said, "That's a truth about you. You don't need to go slowly. Here you can move quickly without the loss of anything important."

Lisa: That's wonderful!

Omi: I hope I explained that well enough. Here they have given me some roles within something like a classroom where I am helping ones coming up behind me. There are times when I'm a mentor or coach. I'm still young enough not to have completely launched. I'm not like the recent college graduate who has just gotten their first full-time job.

I like contributing in this way, but I don't think I would want to be a counselor because I lived through so much trauma in my life. I don't know that I have the stamina to walk everybody else through their trauma. But I think I can assist as a skilled listener and helper.

We can do that with each other without needing it to be a career. What interests me is: can we help people recognize true and false? Can we help them recognize tempting ideas that incline societies towards violence, coercion, and domination, and call out the falseness of it before it grows? I don't know what occupation that would be, but it would involve helping people keep from believing lies. They keep believing the lie that we're all separate from one another and must step over each other or on each other to ascend. We don't.

Michael: Based upon your experiences where you are, what is the one message you would like to give readers?

Omi: It's not an original thought, but it's this: I'm the friend you haven't met yet.
Or whom you are now meeting.

Michael: How nice is that?

Omi: I do believe we can all be a universal friend. I think Allah, God, Jesus, and any other name that one might give to the Highest One or Ones, is Friend. I don't know your scriptures, but he [Father Nathan] does, and I'm sharing his mind. He is thinking of John's gospel, toward the end where Jesus knows he will soon die violently. He tells them, "You have called me teacher, and that's true enough. You've also called me Lord, and that's fine too. But I really love it when you call me friend."

Michael: Beautiful!

Omi: It's in your Holy Book. There's a great goodness in being a friend. It can be even better to be friends with someone who thought they could only hate you because that's what they were told, "You must hate that kind because they are that despised kind."
I think Mr. Nadi, when he first spoke using this voice, said something like, "I can hardly believe I'm talking through an American, a Christian, and a priest!"

Michael: Right. <laugh>

Omi: These are categories he thought he would never have anything to do with. And then there was a loving collaboration. It's intimate, coming inside his mind and borrowing his voice.
How did I just put it? I'm the friend you haven't met yet, or maybe are now just meeting. Let's just stop at that. Anything I might try to add won't really contribute much more.
I will leave you now because it's time. I now know how to move about and come back here.

Michael: Yes.

Omi: I have been in school because I like school. One of the things that I have learned in this school is how to move between levels and realms. I can now come and be with you with very little effort. If you ever choose to call on me by name or even if, in the future, you call for "the book people" and I have become one of them, know that I would be in the crowd.

(Omi departs.)

Nathan: This is **Nathan**. Glory to the Father, to the Son, and to the Holy Spirit, as it was in the beginning, is now, and will be forever. Amen.

Omi explained well how he could see himself in the young men who were his captors. Had they grown up in a peaceful time and place they might have been good companions. He had no room in his heart for hatred. They didn't really get to know him. Perhaps when they do, they'll discover…the friend they hadn't met until now.

Chapter Two

Estella and Our Lady of Wisdom

Challenge: Assertiveness That Became Aggression
Value: Humility

Three Explanations:
Growing Up in Cultural Crosscurrents
Being a Teacher with a Learner's Heart
Ease of Relating with a Luminary

When we last spoke with Estella, she was trying to be brief. She said, "Later let's pull up a cloud," reminding us that when we're all together in the afterlife we can visit for as long as we like. Once you've met Estella, I think you'll want more of her company.

We'll learn from her that she grew up at a time of great cultural change, especially around the question of women's roles. She felt she had to assert herself in a man's world. But she also wanted to be a gentle woman. There can be a fine line between assertiveness and aggression. She crossed that line on the day of her death. But of course, that wasn't the end of her story.

||||||||||||||||||||||||||||||||||||||||||||||||||||||||||||||||||||||||||||||||||||||||||||||||||||||||||||||||||||||||||||||||||||||||||||

Nathan: I'm Nathan. I'm in Tucson on a Zoom call with Michael in Pennsylvania. Today is June 30, 2020. We're about to deal with a story brought in a dream on May 25, 2020. We've said our protective prayers, asking for the presence and support of the saints and angels. Here's the dream as recorded it in my journal:

I was near a university where parking space was scarce. Two women were trying to wedge cars into adjacent parking spaces on the edge of a cliff. One got out of her car to assess the situation, then got back in her car. The other car inched closer to the edge, then went over it, pulling the other with it. Later, I was with a man who'd witnessed it. He wanted to talk about it while walking through heavy traffic in a way that seemed unsafe. I awoke.

I'm going to be still for a moment, then invite the person or persons who brought this story, or a guardian who could shed light on whom we are to help.

There's already some agitation in this one. I could feel it as soon as I started reading it. This one involved a change in scene near the end. Someone witnessed this, so it would be helpful if a guardian spoke first, if that's possible.

(The guardian emerges.)

Guardian Pedro: You will want to know my name. I go by Pedro.

Michael: Welcome.

Guardian Pedro: He [Father Nathan] was wondering if he is in a Latin country, with mountains. He has memories of his own, of being in San Diego near the campus of the University of California, San Diego, which is in a high place where there are bluffs. But he was thinking, parking lots in that place wouldn't be so precarious. If they were on a height, there would be barriers or cement structures to keep this kind of accident from happening. He's correct, in that this occurred in a South American location. Some of this could be stereotypical, but in this event, whether that's true or not, these women were aggressive toward each other and given to angry speech.

I think on Earth, some places are known for more aggressive driving than other places are. Everywhere they have signage and rules, but in some places, the rules are observed in different ways. Here, there was more of a blatant competition for limited space. That was happening that day. These women did not know each other but confronted each other over being able to park a car. One of them was in my care. Both died that day. They died angry, and then had more reason to be angry afterwards, because their deaths had been over a parking space. You can imagine how that might cause a person to be what he calls "stuck." They might say, "You mean, after all I ever accomplished, I died falling off a cliff while fighting over a parking space!"

The one that you're helping today is not part of a group. She is an individual. I think that's helpful. And then the piece of it at the end about a man who observed it may pertain or may not. As you move through this, perhaps that piece comes into your plane, and perhaps it doesn't. But there was also a person traumatized by seeing this happen in front of him and feeling the need to talk about it. That may have happened in another plane. It might not involve you.

With that, have you any questions for me before I step to the side?

Michael: That's fine, Pedro. Thank you.

Guardian Pedro: God bless you for the good work you do.

(Guardian Pedro steps aside.)

Woman: My first language is Spanish, but I will speak in English.

Michael: Do you feel comfortable telling us your first name?

Woman: Estella.

Estella: That name means "a star." Sometimes, I was... In English, you would call it a "shooting star," which is not a star at all. It's a meteorite. It's something that flashes across the sky in a ball of fire. The fire is caused by friction. Even as a child, I was this force that could be described as friction and heat. I had a temper. I landed in a time and place where conditions were right for that to be supported or encouraged in a way that it wouldn't have been earlier.

I was in Peru, and my family had some means. Access to formal education was there early in my life. Some of what was happening around us was some of the breaking-down of patriarchy. People were coming to awareness of *machismo*, and some of the ways that women asserted authority, given structures that often wanted to exclude them, or relegate them to domestic life alone. And so, Iron Butterfly-kind of women learned that if there's a sphere of influence in which they can assert themselves, well, they will do it with an iron fist.

Growing up, I was not allowed to dress as I pleased, or to go where I pleased, because I was a girl. Any boy my age would have had much more freedom than I did. So, I was pushing against these things early on. I was attracted to... I don't even like the phrase, but the women's liberation movement, feminism, and how it played out in the culture. I was being raised in crosscurrents of learning about gender roles in other cultures and in historic times, matriarchies, just learning about the fact that things don't have to be the way they are. We create culture, and we don't need to simply be its victims or its accomplices when it's destructive.

I had a certain attitude of not allowing myself to be pushed around by anyone. I felt compelled to assert my influence, even my right to a parking spot.

It's just ridiculous that my end came as it did: falling off a cliff in a tangle with a person who I was angry with at the time, cars crashing because two people felt the need to fight over something as petty as a parking space. I was resentful that I didn't have my own parking space to begin with, and thought that, had I been male, I wouldn't have had to leave the house early each morning hoping to find a spot to park. There were others who outranked me, who didn't have to have this daily competition for a place to park a car.

Ours was an old city, laid out long before there were cars and the need for spaces to park them. There were plenty of informal parking places that were not laid out with barriers or protections against the kind of thing that happened. But it happened so fast! I was angry before, during, and after it happened. There was the opportunity for me, as I couldn't live in my body anymore, to go with a program right away. I rejected it. I rejected help. I was just in no mood in the moment to take direction from anyone who felt like an authority or a superior.

Michael: Estella, may ask if your anger was directed primarily towards the other woman, or anger at yourself for allowing yourself to be upset over the parking issue?

Estella: Both were true. If I had to quantify them... I did some social scientific work. I tried to put numerical values to these kinds of things. In social scientific research, you try to not only identify a deeply held emotion, but you assess the strength of it, in quantifiable terms.

I was angrier at her in the first instant than I was at myself, because I believed that had she not fought me, we would both still be alive. But you can't stay that way for very long and claim to be intelligent without recognizing your own foolishness.

At first, I was angriest at the woman who I felt caused my death. As I had the opportunity to calm down, I had to say to myself, "You were an equal participant in that silly encounter." Neither of us intended the outcome. Perhaps you've had to do this in your life sometimes, Michael. I don't know. You seem a very calm person, but if you ever are enraged, there's a process of having to calm oneself down and maybe allow someone you trust to speak truth to you or question your own formulations of things.

|||||||||||||||||||||||||||||||||||||||||||||||||||||||||||||||||||||||||||||||||||||||||||||||||||||||||||||||||||||||||||||||||||||||||||||||||||||||||||

Estella's virtuous humility is in plain view here. She can critique her own self talk and call it out as foolishness. We can watch her grow right in front of us.

|||||||||||||||||||||||||||||||||||||||||||||||||||||||||||||||||||||||||||||||||||||||||||||||||||||||||||||||||||||||||||||||||||||||||||||||||||||||||||

Michael: Have you had an opportunity to work with this other lady on the same level or realm where you are now?

Estella: No, not yet. That's an agenda item for a later time. I'm already not as angry about that sequence of events as I was at the time. On my end, I would need less processing of that, somehow, than I would have immediately afterwards. I was Catholic, and I knew about the idea of purgatory. I was taught that it was mostly about serving a prison sentence, a certain amount of time you had to sit still. I thought of it a little bit like the way that children might have to have a time-out, where they take their tantrum to their own room, and come out when they're ready to play nice.

For me, it's been a little like that. I needed time to let some of my rage pass over, almost like a thunderstorm that plays itself out. There's a certain volume of tears, or rain, that needs to fall, and then there's a calm after the storm. I've had sufficient time for the emotional storm to calm down, and then to be able to engage my own intellect a little bit more, to say, "All right..."

Michael: Was Pedro working with you during this time-out, to help expedite it?

Estella: He and others. Even that was a crosscurrent. I did believe in God, although I was taught by a patriarchy, and taught to call God "Father." Some of that I pushed against, but I didn't reject the idea of a Creator. I just don't know how anyone could, especially when you look around at everything that is. Did it all just spring into existence out of nothing, with no plan? That never made sense to me. I was a little bit of a student of comparative religion and of indigenous religion. The idea of there being other kinds of creatures that were the spiritual kind made sense to me because there was so much biodiversity and complexity in the world that I could see. Why wouldn't that be true? Would there only be one kind of thing, a god, and that's it?

So angels made sense to me. And while I had paid no attention beyond that, and I never spoke to him, other than in childhood... I think I was taught a prayer to the guardian angel, maybe around the time of my First Communion, but that was not a practice of mine. But then, he knew me, and he knew my history. I'm saying "he," even though angels don't have gender, but he presented as more masculine than feminine, even though I was often the first to reject those metaphors.

He transported me, got me from that accident scene and out of it, to a place of safety. Then he sat with me as a family member might. So, on the one hand, his first job was more like that of a paramedic. The second role that he took on was more of a family member who stayed by the bedside of someone in and out of sleep. He would provide information or reminders. There were other people who were helping me talk through this. Sometimes I would latch onto a passionate idea and begin to express it, and he would say, "Yes, *mija*, but do you remember this?" And because he had always been with me, he could supply data points that I couldn't argue with, always gently, but I admired him because he was wise and true. He could stop me in my tracks when I began to veer into polemics, and say, "Yes, part of what you say is true, but do you remember this?"

Had I lived longer, maybe I would have been a calmer woman, but I think I was still... I mentioned a shooting star at the beginning of this. I was still ascending, and my ascent was important to me. I needed to make my way in the world, and I needed to assert myself. I even needed to do so in a dispute about a parking space.

Michael: Because you are assertive, was it your decision, for the realm in which you are, to move to another level, or was that a decision made by Pedro?

Estella: Oh, they're very careful with me to, at every turn, make it clear that I am in charge. I know I have overdone that, and that there's room for weakness and receptivity and not knowing. But they have never said to me, "You must do this because it's time, or someone said so." No, they've left me utterly free to really acknowledge the truth that the services of the environment that I've been in are almost exhausted. It's just time to move on to the next place.

Most of what I've done here is about me, my thoughts, passions, objections, and my need to be right. They've said, "Had you lived longer, you might have found there was a mellower version of yourself that you would enjoy. And you might encounter her. It doesn't mean you can't be many things. You are multifaceted; all of us are. There are parts of your full being that you developed well for specific reasons. There are other parts that are yet undeveloped, which we invite you to explore now. Would you like to do that?"

Michael: You mentioned your agenda. As you move toward another agenda, how do you see that differing from where you are now?

Estella: I would rephrase. I'd rather talk about similarity. I wanted to be of service, and I wanted to be an agent of change, so that there was fairness. I objected to the stacked deck, giving someone advantages based on gender or skin color or economics, sexual orientation or who you knew, who your family was. I wanted there to be more fairness. I've found that in this realm where I am, that's a commonly held value. There isn't a domination system at work. Nobody has the upper hand here. No one relishes their power over others. I'm enjoying that very much.

Michael: I assume, that, to make this next step, that you've already been in discussions with Pedro and others about someone coming forth who will assist you with this next step?

Estella: Yes. And for that, I need a moment to go deeper with him as you, I think, understand.

(There was a pause.)

Estella: I don't know if it would surprise you, but it would be Mary, the Mother of Jesus, who is also Mary, the Mother of God.

In the early centuries of the church, there was an argument about whether anybody could be called Mother of God, because God always was, and had no beginning. How could anybody be the mother of one who didn't have a beginning? She showed up for me as something of a visiting lecturer, because I would respect that. I liked seeing a woman at the front of the room, teaching me.

||||||||||||||||||||||||||||||||||||||||||||||||||||||||||||||||||||||||||||||||||||||||||||||||||||||||||||||||||||||||||||||||||||||||||||||||||||||||||||||||||||

There's an inherent humility involved in taking a class or attending a lecture. You might be quite learned, but learned people got that way by allowing themselves to be taught. Lifelong learners know that. Apparently, afterlife-long learners do too. Estella has a learner's heart.

||||||||||||||||||||||||||||||||||||||||||||||||||||||||||||||||||||||||||||||||||||||||||||||||||||||||||||||||||||||||||||||||||||||||||||||||||||||||||||||||||||

Michael: So, you've already been working with her?

Estella: I didn't understand at first glance that it was she. She spoke about, if it were in Eastern culture, it might have been yin and yang, of action and passivity, of power and weakness, and how everything belongs. They don't need to be in conflict. The water and the land don't have to fight. Sometimes they do, when the waves crash upon the shore, but other times, one lies gently against the next.

So, I got to know her as something of a visiting professor and learned that her wisdom is quite broad. Even though, in this lifetime she wasn't schooled, she was more learned than many people knew. She was literate, which was notable. People assume that any woman in first-century Palestine was unlearned, but that was not always true. What people could do in their own households differed.

Nevertheless, she told me that a moment might come when I might want to go for a walk with her. And I said, "Well, that sounds delightful." When I met her, I was in a group of people, and she was teaching all of us. I never wanted to be one who rushes the stage at an end of a presentation and tries to clamor. It's funny, because after having described myself earlier as someone who's sort of pushy, in an academic context, I didn't want to behave that way.

Michael: Are you at a point now where Our Lady has said, "Estella, do you want to go for a walk with me?"

Estella: Yes, she told me that the invitation was open-ended, and I would know when the moment was right. And the moment is now.

Michael: That's great. Is she in your vicinity now, or do you need to call her forward?

Estella: I've asked about that, and I've been told, "Well, you probably knew the answer to this already, but she's never far away, because nothing is." Everything is nearby, and distance is an illusion. And so, she's near.

Michael: I have talked to Our Lady through Father Nathan previously, and it was one of the most wonderful experiences of my life. I was hoping she was in your vicinity now to step forth and say, "Hello, Michael."

Estella: Oh, would you like a word? Well, that will be up to her. Let me stop for a moment.

(There was a brief pause.)

Michael: Oh, God!

(Here's Mary!)

Mary: Well, of course, dear Michael. Here we are again! The work that you do and the work that I do, sometimes they converge. We're just trying to help. You have a phrase, "walking each other home." Isn't that a phrase dear to you?

Michael: Yes! *(Michael is the hospice field.)*

Mary: Yes. In eternity, how does one ever get all the way home, whatever that means? There's some sense of a finish line, a destination. And of course, that has its place. Just like waking and sleeping do, resting in peace. Yes, but that's so that you can rise and greet the new moment with energy.

Anyway, today, we walk her home, but always there's a next thing to be done, a next person to be helped, a next joy to be experienced, a next tragedy to be moved through. You know, I have so many titles: Mother of Sorrows, or the Pietà. Especially for women, womanity and femininity were very important to her. They still are. So much of the world's suffering is borne by women, and not always shared as deeply with men. This has not changed very much over the centuries. Women disproportionately bear the brunt of tragedy and trying to hold a family together.

So there's no shortage of people to walk home, or to struggle with. Some find me a solace, a place of comfort and strength that they can go to when they're sad. His own father, Father Nathan's father, used me as his prayer place of last resort. He felt he could deal with most things with God the Father, and with Jesus, and the saints and so on, but I was the last resort in his life. Sometimes people do that with me. I'm somehow their last hope.

Anyway, Estella had an affinity for me from very young that never completely went away, even though the way she might think of me was challenged, pushed, and grew. She was a learned person living in a university world, and so lectures were common to her. Part of what was put before her was, "Would you like to attend a lecture?" She liked that. When I was brought in as the visiting lecturer, I wasn't introduced with a title that she recognized right away. But she found my message and my way of presenting myself attractive. I think you heard her say that even though she was a competitive person, she didn't want to compete for my attention.

But then she was told, "Well, you needn't do that. If you would like an appointment with her, she has office hours. You can meet her one-on-one should you like." She chose that. That's when I was able to say, "Well, I'm the person whom you've known all along. I would be honored to take a walk with you when the moment comes, to complete the transition that was not completed earlier." She came to understand that her abrupt death was just too overwhelming. There was too much anger, too many things happening at once. She needed the leisure to kind of dissemble some of it and put it back together in ways that made more sense. I said to her, "When you've finished that task, you'll know, and you'll know it's time to invite me."

Michael: Of course, I could sit here all day and just revel in your energy, but I understand that that's not my role right now. I would normally, at this point, wish you and Estella a wonderful journey and ask God to bless both of you. But asking God to bless you almost sounds like an oxymoron. Would you please bless me and bless Father Nathan as you leave?

Mary: What is a blessing, what's a grace, except a loving energy moving between persons? Because one wants it to move to the other, it's not about who has the most, or who is the brightest star in the sky, or any such thing. It's just love moving between persons. Offering me a blessing is an exchange of love. And I would receive it.

Michael: Thank you so much. That's such a beautiful love. I will treasure that insight.

Mary: It's one you had already, isn't it?

Michael: Yes.

Mary: We'll be on our way. Estella no longer needs to be a shooting star. She can glide. If you watch the starry sky, the stars have their own kind of graceful dance. They don't have to shoot off in a violent way.

Michael: God bless you, Estella, and Our Lady.

Mary: All right, she doesn't feel the need to come back into the voice. She has said all she needs to say, so I will say goodbye for the two of us. God bless you.

Michael: Thank you.

(Mary and Estella leave to begin their walk.)

Nathan: Glory be to the Father, to the Son, to the Holy Spirit, as it was in the beginning, is now, and will be forever. Amen.

Michael: Amen.

Nathan: All right. You have any reflections for the transcription?

Michael: I hope you didn't mind me jumping in there. It was such an emotionally moving moment. I always hope Our Lady is in the vicinity and willing to come through. That she did it again has my heart overflowing.

Nathan: Well, she did because you invited her. I'm glad you did, because we got some more insight into how she came as a visiting lecturer. When you study the history of Mary of Nazareth and all her different titles, one is Our Lady of Wisdom.

The Christian tradition presents Jesus as the first fruits, not as the one and only Christ, but as the one who begins the category. We all live in the Christ. We take our place in Christ's consciousness. She's the same way. Even though a lot of Catholic piety... maybe not just Catholic piety, but in the Orthodox Churches, at least those two parts of the larger Christian world, sometimes she's exalted to the skies in a way that would make you think, "How in the world can I ask a blessing upon you? Because you are full of grace, how could you be any more full than full?"

Michael: Yes.

Nathan: Yes, but on the other hand, she's a model for what we are. She's not set apart from us as some unattainable ideal.

||||||||||||||||||||||||||||||||||||||||||||||||||||||||||||||||||||||||||||||||||||||||||||||||||||||||||||||||||||||||||||||||||||||||||||||||

My prayer partner Michael and Estella both display a lovely ease of relating with a luminary. I'm calling Mother Mary that on purpose. We are all energetic beings of light, but she's among the brightest. I think of her light as more lunar than solar. It's unsafe to stare at the sun. But we can gaze at the moon for as long as we like.

||||||||||||||||||||||||||||||||||||||||||||||||||||||||||||||||||||||||||||||||||||||||||||||||||||||||||||||||||||||||||||||||||||||||||||||||

Nathan: I'm Nathan. Today is June 8th, 2023. I'm in Tucson on a Zoom call with Michael, who is in Pennsylvania. Today we're asking permission to use a story brought by Estella, a professor in South America. We're considering using her story in an upcoming book because we think it explains things so well.

We've said our protective prayers, inviting the presence and support of the angels and saints. We're hoping to talk to Estella, her guardian, or perhaps Mother Mary, who in that story was referred to as Our Lady of Wisdom.

||||||||||||||||||||||||||||||||||||||||||||||||||||||||||||||||||||||||||||||||||||||||||||||||||||||||||||||||||||||||||||||||||||||||||||||||

Nathan: So, Estella, Estella's guardian, Holy Mary, Holy Spirit: that's our request. I'm going to sit still for a moment and invite presence.

(There was a brief pause. Estella emerges.)

Estella: This is Estella. I was trying to yield the stage to either my guardian or to Dr. Mary, but both took a step back so that I might be at the front. Both are like that.

I'm honored that you are considering me for inclusion in this new book. I'm flattered that you thought well of my language describing what happened to me initially. I described parts of my upbringing. I described the event that caused my death and the death of another woman. I described psychological processes that, for a Catholic reader or listener, would describe my purgatory. I think I even mentioned that I had been trained in that thinking. But I was directed to think of purgatory as punitive, the serving of a sentence that one deserved because of bad behavior. As it turned out for me it was really consequences of thought patterns and actions. And, as with anyone else, there are parts of my wholeness, my fullness, that went undeveloped because I didn't give them time and attention.

Michael: I asked you originally whether you had an opportunity to meet the other woman, and you said no, but it was on your agenda. Have you met her yet?

Estella: Not yet. It's still an active part of my agenda. I've done what I can on my end. I would offer an apology when the time is right. It was not necessary to quarrel over a parking space to the point of causing each of our deaths. That's just ridiculous. But once it's done, it's done. Any emotion one brings to it that moves away from truth, I'm just not interested in.

Michael: Alright.

Estella: The whole of my surroundings here are always about the unfolding of a deeper truth, greater clarity, and deeper peace. But not always peace, because there's also a kind of rush, like adrenaline, that one might have before giving a talk. You're not necessarily feeling peaceful as you stride to the podium. There can be an energy that is motivating. Maybe you're at peace by the end of a talk, but <laugh> as you begin it, if you're really challenging yourself, you're taking a risk.

Michael: I understand completely. I used to teach public speaking at a university.

Estella: All right. Well, I loved challenges. That's part of why I chose the academic life. I expected to be a lifelong learner. Here, I am continuing to learn, and my choices aren't as limited as they used to be.

It used to be that I had to devote my time and energy to something in my academic sphere, but now I'm around people who have a love for things that I didn't care for, and it costs me nothing to be with them and see them enjoy the thing they enjoy.

Anyway, I'm going on. You asked me a simple question. So, the answer to the yes-or-no question, "May you use my story?" is "yes."

Michael: Okay. Thank you very much.

Estella: There's a little bit of embarrassment over having been so vain. I could say stupid, but I think it's too harsh. But it was certainly unwise to take that track. I had a feeling that I needed to force my way into circumstances to progress somehow. There was a time and place for that. It was not the time and place to fight over a parking space in a dangerous spot above a cliff.

So maybe I can be a model. I think this has come up before in some of your other stories. I think of the lady Wilhelmina. [ed. note: Wilhelmina's story appears in Book Two.] I think she agreed to be a negative example, "Don't do what I did." I don't mind my story being one of caution. Maybe my story speaks to very driven persons who have a story that moved them in that direction. Perhaps they developed a habit that served them well professionally or in one aspect of their life, but not another, and then couldn't turn it off.

I could be the patron saint of [Very Driven Persons] if that's a thing. Not that I've ascended to that level of wholeness [of a saint]. I've met many of the ones who have those titles. I called her Dr. Mary. She is wise. In the way that she manifested in my story, she was not introduced by name. She just emerged as a person who was competent to speak at the front of the room. And she spoke. There is no hubris in her. I'm at least on that trail. I can't say that there's no hubris in me, because it wouldn't be completely true.

I was aware of my accomplishments and, at times, made others aware of them just in case they underestimated me. But here, one of the realities all around us is that we're all well-esteemed. We don't have to earn the esteem of another. Although when we put forth effort that bears good fruit and we improve in some way, that's noted. But we're loved before, during, and after that process.

Michael: Right.

Estella: That doesn't always come across in classrooms and in grading.

Michael: I think it's a beautiful insight and apropos to all you are about. Thank you.

Estella: Well, I still have the heart of a teacher; that hasn't gone away. I was delighted to learn early on that my career hadn't ended with my death because I really valued it. I was still a young woman. I was still ascending somehow and broadening my gifts and perhaps the reach of who I might impact. Here they've shown me how to look at the whole body of my work until the time I died. And not just my work product, but my personhood and my interior life. They've helped me sort which parts should be carried forward and which parts should just be acknowledged and thanked as part of my past, then allowed to go sit down.

Michael: Do you still think of yourself as the "Iron Butterfly" as you referred to yourself previously?

Estella: It works. There was an aspect of me who needed to be hardened. It wasn't always a good fit for me because sometimes it came off as too harsh, too abrupt, or vain. You would've thought that would be a great fit for me, given my upbringing and my chafing against all the strictures placed upon a girl and young woman. But like many, I also didn't want to sacrifice having a gentle heart. There were times when I did that, that I can now look back on and say, "I don't really need to forgive my former self. I just acknowledge who she was and who she was trying to become." But there's also a present version of me who doesn't need to go to any excesses to live happily and continue to grow.

Michael: I understand. Thank you.

Estella: Let's leave it there. I've said enough. There will be a day when you and I or Father Nathan…if you want to, you can pull up a cloud! That's the way I used to think of it. Then we can talk for as long as we like, but that's not today.

Michael: God bless you, Estella. It was wonderful talking to you.

Estella: All right. We'll meet again.
Dr. Mary is stepping out from the wings and applauding the way that someone might when they're the master of ceremonies or something. But she doesn't feel the need to come to mic. She's just leading a little applause.

(They depart.)

Nathan: This is Nathan. Glory be to the Father, to the Son, and to the Holy Spirit, as it was in the beginning, is now, and will be forever. Amen.

When Estella introduced herself to us, she reminded us that her name means star. She was still ascending when she died and felt she must be a shooting star. In the end, Doctor Mary had this to say, "Estella no longer has to be a shooting star. She can glide. If you watch the starry sky, the stars have their own kind of graceful dance. They don't have to shoot off in a violent way."

Estella, thanks for sharing your story to teach us that important lesson.

Chapter Three

Lupe, College Suicide,
Angel Shelley, and Jane Stanford

Challenge: Academic Dishonesty
Value: Humility and Teachability

Three Explanations:
Pressure to be Excellent
Movement into Light
The Cosmic Do-Over

In choosing stories for this book, I wanted individuals who explained themselves particularly well. I wanted to share stories that could enlighten us.

I'd like you to meet Lupe. I wish I had known her during my career as a campus minister. Maybe I could have helped her then. I'm grateful that she's given me the opportunity to do so here.

As you'll hear, Lupe gave in to the temptation of academic dishonesty, and it had disastrous effects. In an afterlife she never expected to inhabit, she had good teachers. She humbled herself. She learned. Here is her story.

‖‖

Nathan: I am Nathan. Today is June 8, 2023. I'm in Tucson on a Zoom call with Michael in Pennsylvania. We've said our protective prayers inviting the presence and help of the angels and saints. We're about to help someone who brought a story during the night of April 10, 2023. Here's that story as I received it and wrote it in my journal:

A young woman had turned down Stanford University to enroll elsewhere. She was caught up in some intrigue about the funding of a project. She had lied about her involvement and was being called on it. At night at the entrance of an academic building she was secretly overhearing a conversation that exposed her lie. A man suddenly appeared a short distance away with what appeared to be two large candlesticks. This alarmed her. I awoke.

(There was a long pause.)

This is still Nathan. We've sat in stillness and read the story a second time. We've asked for the help of a guardian, the person in the story, or one of the holy ones to get things started for us today.

The guardian is about to emerge. This guardian is going to go by Shelley.

(Angel Shelley emerges.)

Angel Shelley: And this is she. I'm choosing this name for a couple of reasons. He [Father Nathan] is thinking of seashells. When they are growing, they're at the service of the form of life that inhabits them. Mostly they are calcium. They create a safe home for the occupant, the clam or the other kinds of animals that can live in a shell. When people collect them it's because of their beauty even after they've served their principal purpose. If they're left alone, they get tossed about in the waves and they turn back into sand. They return to where they came from.

But there's also a thing called a "shell game." It is practiced deceit on the part of someone trying to mislead others for their own gain.

I think the classic version of it involves some object, a coin, or a ball underneath a shell. The person who's skilled at doing this, does sleight-of-hand to make others lose track of under which of the three shells is the object.

The one whom I loved and guarded, and whom I love still, went down that path unnecessarily. She was academically skilled. In the way that she told her story, she accessed Father Nathan's Stanford memory bank, establishing herself as someone who turned down Stanford. That already tells you that she was very bright and sought-after.

When he served at Stanford, he used to take part in a thing they called "Admit Weekend." He had the experience at Stanford of being valued and devalued in the university's life. He was reminded at certain times while working there that he was adjunct and not a Stanford employee.

This Admit Weekend was mostly for the young ones, the undergraduates. University officials crowed each year comparing themselves with Harvard about what percentage of their applicants they refused!

Michael: Yes?

Angel Shelley: It was usually about 96 percent.

Michael: That's sounds right.

Angel Shelley: But annually, on this Admit Weekend, even he was fully included. Everyone worked to put the university's best foot forward, and to receive as many of the admits as possible.

For some their Catholic faith was important. And so, he and his team would be drawn into the recruitment of those the university wanted to receive. This one told her story by saying she turned it down.

Stanford has a majority of graduate and doctoral students. There aren't very many universities that have more of those than the undergraduates. He had to adapt to that campus by reallocating funding and staffing to reflect that. He put resources into helping people like the one who is the subject of our attention today.

Unfortunately, many found it stressful having to compete with so many others at such a high level. It's a subject that's very dear to him. He breaks down words as you know. He liked to parse the word "competitive." *Com-petere* means "to strive with." It does not mean to vanquish, conquer, or subjugate. It just means to strive with.

When his students would tell him how competitive it was in a tone that suggested that that was a bad thing, he reminded them, "You chose to come here. You wanted to be in the company of the best and brightest, and you are one of those. So, calm down. You're where you belong."

He often told them they didn't need to do the other thing, which he called *rivalry*. That means to observe others drinking out of your river as though an entire river needs to flow down your throat. That includes the idea that you would somehow be diminished by someone else's having a drink.

The one I guarded often saw others as rivals and felt that she needed to do things that were dishonest to gain advantage. It is not out of order for me to discuss this with you here. She did something dishonest to advance her progress in a way of rivalry. That brought about darker things. That's what she'll be working with today.

Michael: Okay.

Angel Shelley: As you know, she wouldn't be here were she not **deemed** ready to advance. She's done plenty of work involving coming to truth and is ready for a passage that you'll facilitate. I'm grateful for your work and the methodical character of it. We were able to choose this because your methods are so clear and consistent that we didn't feel that we were taking some large risk in opting for you.

Michael: We're here to serve.

Angel Shelley: All right. I'll slide to the side, and in a moment, you'll hear her use of the voice. So, goodbye for now.

(Angel Shelley slides aside.)

Nathan: This is Nathan. I'm getting the impression that she is Hispanic, Latina. Her name makes that evident. Her name is Lupe.

Michael: Welcome, Lupe.

(Lupe emerges.)

Lupe: And here I am. Thank you for being available to me.

Michael: I always like to say we're all just walking each other home.

Lupe: Well, I went home earlier than I would ever have thought, as a young woman. I was named Lupe for Our Lady of Guadalupe. I didn't like the name. For one thing, there were times when I wanted to pass as more white than brown because I thought it would help me somehow. And the word sounds like "loopy" which is a synonym of airheaded or flighty. And it was a dead giveaway that I was Hispanic, which wasn't always advantageous in some of the circles I moved in.

It depended. The union that produced me was both Hispanic and Caucasian. In my appearance, I looked whiter than some others. I'm only bringing this up because it was a feature. I had this idea that to be in elite academic circles, there was a backlash against this movement in recent decades of trying to get more minority persons in the upper echelon schools. Just looking Hispanic could make one wonder, "Do other people think I'm only here because of affirmative action, and that I took the place of somebody more deserving?"

Michael: What was your relationship with your parents?

Lupe: They never married. My birth father was originally not on the scene. My mother went to the trouble of seeing that he made financial payments, but it was my mother and her mother who raised me. I eventually met my father, but it was not a warmhearted relationship.

My mother got pregnant while she was a college student and had to make the decision to bring me to term and give birth to me. It did cost her some academic progress. She managed to receive a degree and work professionally. But there was some objective truth to the fact that the reason that she didn't progress more in her career, was because of the time spent caring for me.

Michael: I understand.

Lupe: I was working toward a PhD and had a lot of progress toward it. But the research that I was conducting under supervision needed funding. It involved laboratory work. I falsified some academic credentials. That kind of research money is attracted by previous success. You create exploratory models, you hypothesize, you create an idea that this could be that. You can create conditions that prove it. But you don't know at the outset if the experiment you're creating will produce the outcome you're hoping it will. That's especially true about causation. You assert that this causes that. Now, can you prove it?

Michael: Right.

Lupe: Some PhD candidates have years of work involved in a process that produces an undesired result. You can spend years only to find out that the thing you thought might be causal is not.

Now, if this were a beauty pageant, there would be some round of applause for being Miss Congeniality or First-Runner-Up, but it's not at all the same as winning. As a researcher, you have advanced the growth of knowledge by at least disproving that this caused that.

But that's not going to win you widespread acclaim.

I wanted widespread acclaim. I told a story that wasn't true about some earlier work I had done to win the esteem of people who had the ability to fund my next work. I told a lie. I injected a lie into the body of human knowledge. I wasn't the first to invent this way of behaving. It's despised in academia that anybody would mislead every other researcher in your field and claim as true something that you know is false. But I had done that, and my lie got discovered. It was a matter of how high this knowledge would go. How would this be told or disseminated? Who would find out? And so, my whole standing as a student and as an aspiring professional in my field was at risk.

To describe the events that caused the end of my life. I need to pause and go deeper.

Michael: Okay.

(There was a pause.)

Lupe: In the dream I showed him, I was on the outside of an academic building, listening, and overhearing a conversation inside of it. That is dream symbology.

I was on the campus, but outside of the building. That was a way of saying that I was here, but not truly in my life. I was in a false version of it.

There was truth being spoken inside the building, but I was outside the building.

Michael: I understand.

Lupe: In the dream, someone approached bearing something that looked like candlesticks. Very often in academic iconography, or heraldry, universities have crests and shields with some Latin word in them. Often there's a flame, light, lamp, or the sun. Light appears because the mission of this organization is to bring the world the light of understanding through some new discovery. In the dream, there was someone coming toward me with light, but it would be light that shone upon my attempts at deceit.

I had some options. One of them was to stamp out this discovery before it could spread. Another one would have been just to let things play out, be discovered, be called to account, and lose my position. Another was to turn out the light; just end it. And that was my route.

Michael: Oh.

Lupe: When I thought of what my life would be after having been widely viewed as a dishonest aspiring scientist, I just didn't see a path forward in my chosen career. If I had this on my resume as a young person, nobody's going to confer a doctorate upon a student who cheated in their research. So that would go away. I would probably have been able to find some job in industry after a time because it wasn't that I didn't have skills. I certainly did. But would anyone hire me if I presented myself truthfully? Would they take on the risk? Could I be trusted after having shown myself to be so devious?

That would've been a comedown even if I did secure a decent job. And then what about my private life and personal relations? I had been celebrated for most of my life, for being so smart and being the local girl done good. I was the one who, despite all odds, arrived at such an esteemed level. Now all of that would go away. Then there were the most immediate concerns about losing university housing and losing my reason to wake up in the morning. The work that I was doing was trying to establish a truth. It's just that I had done it with deceit.

The suicide of college students, especially at the most competitive schools, happens almost annually, sometimes several times a year. He [Father Nathan] is familiar with that. The most common way college students take their lives is with sedatives. It's just not that hard to swallow a bottle of pills of some kind and not wake up. That was my exit. I didn't make a big theatrical display of it. I didn't leave a note. I just turned out the lights. I thought the way to do that was by waiting until it was nighttime. I thought that when it was time to go to sleep, I'd just ingest enough sleeping pills to see that I didn't wake up.

However, I woke up.

Michael: Yes.

Lupe: I don't need to go on at length about it. You probably already understand that when people end their lives as I did, they are still surrounded by a supportive team. The one who called herself Shelley, described her reason for taking that name. The last months of my life did feel like a shell game because I lived for several months under the weight of knowing that I had been discovered. But if I continued to shuffle things around like a shell game, I might buy myself some time. I could hope that maybe the research that I was currently working on would be a fantastic success. And people would say, "Well, she made this earlier error, but look at the work she's just done!" I could hope for that for a while. But it did begin to feel like the walls were closing in. Time was running out. The damning conversation that I overheard involved going to university authorities to expose my deceit. So, I did swallow pills, only to awaken here in the care of mostly professionals and then a few paraprofessionals.

There were other students who had taken the same route but were further along in their recovery from taking their lives.

Michael: I understand.

Lupe: They could speak with credibility and compassion. I think the most important thing that they did was enable me to imagine positive futures again.

Michael: That's so important.

Lupe: I had spent much of my life doing that. I had plenty of encouragement from school counselors and people saying, "Well, you really shouldn't settle for this because you're capable of that." And for a large part of my life, that was true. There were people saying, "You need to think bigger because you're capable of bigger."

Here they did that too, but it had a different character. The idea of needing to climb up a ladder and shove others out of the way in the process just went away. They began to show me that egoistic vanity just doesn't have a place here. "If you want more of what already ruined you, you may have it. But why would you want it? And now that you know that you can live in at least a little of the light, why wouldn't you more want more of that? Why wouldn't you want to develop your true gifts?"

Now I'm on the cusp of making a move. I'm told that this move doesn't displace anyone else. I've not earned my slot in medical school at the expense of somebody else because there were only so many slots. The advancement that I'm about to make today doesn't come at the expense of anyone else. Somehow, I augment, or... I don't use this kind of language normally... bring a blessing to the next level.

Michael: What occurs to me, Lupe, is Shelley starting out the conversation, talking about seashells. Oysters live in shells. If there's a piece of sand that gets in there as an irritant, the oyster covers it over and over again, until the spec of sand becomes a beautiful, valuable pearl. That's where I see you now as this beautiful pearl moving forward.

Lupe: Well, thank you. That's an image I can ponder, the creation of a pearl. I'll take that thought with me, but for right now, it's time to move. And so, that's where you come in.

Michael: Will you be asking anybody to assist you with moving forward?

Lupe: I opted not to choose in part because of a rightly understood sense of unworthiness. Not groveling; we've had to do some work on this. A part of the truth that I carry forward is I didn't earn advancement. And so, I don't want to choose somebody as much as be received by the right person. I have encountered only right persons ever since I arrived here. Whoever the right person is, I'm confident they will emerge and help move me from one place to the next without me needing to feel like I deserved it or earned it.

Let me be still for a moment and see how this journey proceeds.

(There was a brief pause.)

Afterlife *Interrupted*: Book Three

Lupe: We're near the end of this session. I think she wants you to know that she's not going to speak. She's someone, he [Father Nathan] has had a fondness for: Jane Stanford. Of Stanford University. I didn't go to that school, but I'm being told that she and her husband lost their only child at the age of 16.

He had already been accepted at Harvard but died before going there. She helped design the university that's named for their son. She wanted it to be co-educational, but it was she who limited how many women could attend because she didn't want it to be perceived as a women's college. Most of the women's colleges had lower standards. She felt it was important to make sure that the reputation of the university was high and that any women who did get admitted to it were the most exceptional ones.

Michael: Right.

Lupe: She was a woman of her time and felt that was the best route to go. She also used to entertain lots of students in her home on campus, but she had some activities that were just for the women. She was around plenty of women who felt more pressured than their male counterparts to produce. It was so uncommon for women to go to university, especially to go to one so well regarded.

She's adamant that she doesn't want to talk because she feels like there's nothing she needs to say. Actions speak louder than words and her action is simply to invite movement.

Michael: Well, as you probably know, Lupe, Jane has interacted with Father many times previously. She is an outstanding model or mentor for you. I'm very confident you'll have a wonderful experience with her.

Lupe: She's been gone a long time and she's learned a lot on this side. She's letting me know that there were certainties that she had about life that she had to surrender later, some of them later in life before her death, and then others afterwards. She'd be happy to not only transport me from place to place but be a part of my team going forward. So, with that, all we're doing is going for a walk.

Michael: You have a beautiful journey.

Lupe: Well, you have that phrase about "walking each other home." It's home very broadly understood. It doesn't have to be some homestead that has been in your family for generations and will be for many more. It's more of a being at home wherever one is.

Michael: Absolutely correct.

Lupe: Well then, off we go.

Michael: God bless you.

(They depart.)

Nathan: This is Nathan. Glory be to the Father, to the Son, and to the Holy Spirit, as it was in the beginning, is now, and will be forever. Amen.

||||||||||||||||||||||||||||||||||||||||||||||||||||||||||||||||||||||||||||||||||||||||||||||||||||||||||||||||||||||||||||||||||||||||

In the conversation that follows, we asked Lupe's permission to include her story here. She describes her transformation in a few words:

In my own immaturity, I just thought I would be the exception to the rule. "I will only contribute things that make me shine." Well, part of what I've been learning here is that I and everybody else shines all the time anyway.

Jesus once said, "I am the light of the world." I believe any movement toward truth is a movement toward light. Lupe didn't need to work so that others could see her shine. She was shining already. And so is everybody else.

||||||||||||||||||||||||||||||||||||||||||||||||||||||||||||||||||||||||||||||||||||||||||||||||||||||||||||||||||||||||||||||||||||||||

Nathan: I am Nathan. Today is August 7, 2023. I'm on a Zoom call. I'm in Tucson; I'm with Michael and Linda who are in Pennsylvania. Today we're gathering to call upon Lupe the college student whom we assisted recently. We want to ask Lupe if she would allow her story to be used in an un upcoming book. We thought her story had powerful, explanatory detail. That's what we're hoping to have as a theme of the new book.

We're going to be still and say our protective prayers; then we'll invite Lupe to be with us.

(We invited many of our angel and saint friends. Michael added…)

Michael: How about Our Lady Guadalupe?

Nathan: Our Lady Guadalupe, pray for us.

I'm going to be still. I have spoken to Lupe in prayer just within the last hour to give her a heads-up that we were going to be inviting her into this session. Now I'm asking her to come forward and speak through if she would like to do so.

(There was a brief pause. Lupe emerges.)

Lupe: This is Lupe. It's so good to be back with you; it's a nice surprise. It wasn't that very long ago that we were together when you helped me make a movement to a next level.

I understand that the purpose of this gathering is to ask if I would allow my story to be told publicly in a book. A short time ago, he was at prayer with me. One of the aspects of doing doctoral research was always to get a verified, which means true, result that would be turned into an academic paper and then published.

Michael: Right.

Lupe: Results were published for the benefit of anyone capable of or interested in reading them. This was especially true for researchers in the same field or an allied field where, if one told the truth, one just made everybody else smarter if they took the time to read what you had contributed. The problem for me was, I knowingly contributed to the ongoing body of scientific research, less than true and sometimes blatantly untrue data. I explained the why of that, the pressures to excel and especially, to have a result that positively proved the thesis that I put forth because it just was nowhere near as fun to have posited a particular causality only to find that my research failed to bear that out.

There's an irony in that. I was the one who brought up Stanford. I was within him when I did that. It lit up all his Stanford memories. He hasn't been there for years, but Stanford was recently in the news because its president was found to have supervised a lab so poorly that bad results were moving into print because of poor oversight.

Michael: Right.

Lupe: It has cost the president his job. So, this very topic that might seem arcane and something that people have never even thought about, has recently been in the news.

Michael: Correct.

Lupe: First of all, I'm honored to be considered for inclusion in his book and membership into something of a fraternity/sorority of others who've been selected for this project. He put it to me and said, "If you say 'yes' your name will be in print <laugh>! It might not be for the research that you put so much work into, but you still might be able to right a wrong and put back into the stream of human knowledge something true that comes from your story." He doesn't want to persuade me. He only wants me to tell the truth and say yes or no to what I'm being asked.

Michael: Yes.

Lupe: It's a great fit for where I have been recently and where I'm headed with your help and the help of the team that prepared me to be with you. You would not know of me at all had I not appeared in a dream that he wrote down and then brought to you. But to even have the opportunity to appear in his dream only happened because a team of people supporting me thought it was appropriate and timely. They felt it seemed good for my progress.

I had been pursuing excellence, but I ruined that by being dishonest.

Michael: I see.

Lupe: With others' help and with yours, I was able to allow confrontation. I was able to allow the truth to be spoken to me and simply own up to it as truth. Almost instantly it felt like…He has an image that I think is biblical. I think it was St. Paul who had scales fall from his eyes. He was a young man who was a student of Judaism, I think, and was trying to kill early followers of Jesus. He was blinded and then at some point had scales fall from his eyes. Do you know that story?

Michael: I do.

Lupe: Well, something like scales or a heavy film fell from my eyes. There was some heaviness that just left me. Suddenly I had energy that I'd forgotten I'd ever had. It was refreshing because I had once been a very highly energized, happy, eager student and researcher.

I had paid too much attention to what others thought of me, probably my whole life. It was a joy and relief just knowing that I was given an opportunity to take the entire thing as a lesson. It was the way I should have treated the data to begin with.

Part of what I've been learning here is that I and everybody else shines all the time anyway.

If we could quit paying attention to what somebody else said or thinks, we all are magnificent way beyond merely good. We don't have to reach for anything else, just be who we are.

I don't know this **quote**, but in his Dominican order there is a woman named Catherine of Siena. She's a doctor of the church. She's been given an honorary PhD that the church can confer on people. One of her quotes is, I'm paraphrasing, "If you will simply be fully what you are, you will set the world on fire!"

I think I'm going to make her acquaintance and try to see what we might ignite.

Michael: Lupe, that's a wonderful message. You can be just who you are and be honest in all that you are doing, understanding that it's a reflection of divinity. And that's all that's important.

Lupe: Had I lived longer, I might have matured beyond the behavior that I exhibited or the thought patterns that provoked it. But I might be able to say in a directed way to younger people who might feel like they need to constantly strive to be more and more impressive, that maybe they can listen to my story, and it will hit them at the right moment in the right way. Maybe they can simply calm down. For people who work in research maybe they can be at peace. It's quite common for theses to be disproven. Sign your name to it and go on to the next thing.

Do that with the awareness that you did contribute to scientific knowledge. You did so with a negative result rather than a positive one. But the truth is the truth.

With that, I think I will simply circle back around to the fact that this conversation was to answer a yes or no question: would I allow my story to be used in a book? Yes. I am thrilled to allow it.

Linda: Lupe, by agreeing to be in Father's book you're going to reach many people with your message.

Michael: God bless you, Lupe.

Lupe: God bless you, too.

(Lupe departs.)

Nathan: Glory be to the Father, to the Son, and to the Holy Spirit, as it was in the beginning, is now and will be forever. Amen.

Michael and Linda: Amen.

I firmly believe in what I call the cosmic do-over. As a child I took years of piano lessons. Sometimes my mom would come into the living room and sit on the couch while I played. She wasn't expecting concert hall excellence. She loved listening to me learn.

Sometimes I'd be playing a piece of music well and then come to a difficult part that I messed up. In her loving presence I didn't mind just saying, "I want to start over."

Lupe did that on a cosmic scale don't you think? She learned from her very big mistake and then moved on. She's willing to have her story be instructive to persons coming up behind her. She feels light and free. She has a bright future ahead.

We're honored to have you as a part of our team, Lupe. The best is yet to come.

Chapter Four

Dr. Lawrence, Long Illness, Mary, Angel Abel, and the Parents

Challenge: Decline in Body and Imagination
Value: Memory of Success

Three Explanations:
Bringing Along the Cage
Interior Clutter and Overwhelm
Becoming the New You
     Practicing Becoming Younger
     Parents' New Faces

Most of the people my prayer partners and I are asked to help died suddenly and violently. But not Doctor Lawrence. He got so used to being in ill health that he could imagine nothing else.

This dream and subsequent prayer session came at a time in my life when I was feeling overwhelmed. Sometimes I bite off more than I can chew. I had a lot on my mind; my consciousness was cluttered. Watch how that gets handled!

||||||||||||||||||||||||||||||||||||||||||||||||||||||||||||||||||||||||||||||||||||||||||||||||||||||||||||||||||||||||||||||||

Nathan: I'm Nathan. Today is February 10, 2023. I'm on a Zoom call in Tucson with

Karen, who's in Southern California. Today we'll be assisting someone who brought a story in a dream during the night of January 7, 2023. Here is that story as I received it and wrote it in my dream journal.

I was an old man in a bed in my home. Someone, a nice lady, was shampooing my hair in my bed. Then I had to walk past a lot of clutter to get to the bathroom, to rinse off the shampoo. I awoke.

We pray in the name of the Father, the Son, and the Holy Spirit. We call on Michael the Archangel with gratitude for all that you do for us. We call on our own guardians. We invite the presence of Holy Mary and Joseph, Saints Dominic and Francis, St. Rose, and St. Mary Magdalene, Padre Pio, and St. Benedict, the members of our family lines who are in the light, and any who have been through this process before, who might like to participate today. Do you have some you'd like to include?

Karen: St. John of the Cross.

Nathan: St. Maximilian and Pope St. John Paul. We ask, Holy Spirit, for gracious assistance in listening, discernment and speaking. Help us to be in the flow of your highest hopes for the time that we spend together today with the person whom we'll be assisting. We ask this through Christ our Lord. Amen.

Karen: Amen.

Nathan: I'm going to be still, ask for help, and see what comes.
The first voice is going to be Mother Mary.

(Mary emerges.)

Mary: I've been present to all the conversation that you've been having about Father Nathan being over busy. I wonder, have you ever seen me depicted with a broom in my hand?

Karen: I don't think so.

Mary: Probably not. But I was a wife, mother, and housekeeper. Hardly a day went by when there wasn't the need to sweep and tidy. I'm doing a little of that inside Father Nathan because as you just **heard**, he feels like there's rather a lot of clutter around him. It makes him feel hemmed in. **And** so, when he was doing a little bit of deep breathing just a moment ago, I was trying to **help** him push aside things to make space to do today's work.

Karen: Thank you.

Mary: You might **think** of the time centuries ago as a simpler time? You might think of your modern, complex world having multitasking and heavy agendas. It's true that our lives were organized differently, but there were certainly plenty of times when we felt like there was more to do than **there** were hours in the day. It's not an unfamiliar emotion. But for the task at hand, I'm **trying to** just clear a path. It doesn't all need to be put away this minute, but there does need **to be** enough space to do the task at hand.

Karen: We **appreciate** you.

Mary: Yes, I know. **We're** grateful for this work. We're aware of his workload. He's also aware that if he just **continues** to walk in faith, there'll be more and more help provided along the way.

 With that, I'm **sliding** aside. I think the guardian is ready to assist.

(Mary slides aside. Angel Abel emerges.)

Angel Abel: I'm **a guard**ian; I'm going to be known as Abel today, partly because we want to assure him [Father Nathan] that he is able.

 On whatever **realm and** whatever kind of being we are it's not an unfamiliar feeling to have a sense of **reaching** one's capacity or pushing against it. Sometimes that can be frantic, unhelpful, and counter-productive. Other times, it is something like the natural process of expansion. Father **Nathan** talks sometimes about the universe expanding and that when we're universal, we **expand** also. Sometimes when we expand, we pop. Jesus spoke of a seed needing to break **open** so that it can bear 30-, 60-, 100-fold. It might just be that he is at a moment of that kind **of** breaking open, and that it's momentary.

Karen: That makes sense.

Angel Abel: We **have work** to do today with the one who presented as an old man in what was apparently a sick bed. There's really no need for me to add detail. It is a simple story, and he is well-spoken. **He was** well-educated. Part of his struggle was that he had such a life of competence that when an infirmity affected him, as it did, even something like washing his own hair began to be something beyond his strength. So, I'll slide aside and allow the one whom we're helping today, whom I love, tell his story.

(Angel Abel slides aside.)

Nathan: This is Nathan. This man's name is Lawrence.

(Dr. Lawrence emerges.)

Dr. Lawrence: And this is he. That's my surname. I've never spoken using another person's voice before, so I'm adjusting a bit.

Professionally I was Dr. Lawrence or Professor Lawrence. My helper, who today is using the name Abel, mentioned that I had a dominant cluster of emotion and thought around competence.

I was the child of well-educated parents who filled my childhood with competence-gaining activities. Not just the schooling that any child of that time and place would have had, but extra everything. It was so much a part of the air I breathed that I didn't feel like it was overdone. It was just how we did things. Most of the day was spent on the main schooling that other children did. But then after that, there were music lessons or extra tutoring, or museum tours. We hardly ever did anything that wasn't helping me gain more knowledge and skill. My parents tried to have other children unsuccessfully. I think, had they been successful at having other children, maybe the energy that they poured into me might have been diffused among several children. But as it turned out, they had several miscarriages before my successful birth. They had reason to believe they might not have other children after me, and that's how things played out. But they really did lavish upon me all this attention to see that I was more and more skilled and competent at a great many things.

I think they wanted me to be a renaissance man. They wanted me to know lots of things about lots of things.

My parents weren't religious people, but they were interested in many of the philosophical questions that are at the root of a lot of religious practice. You know, how did we get here? How did this place get here? Why are we here? What's our destiny? Those kinds of questions. I was introduced to them more through philosophy and maybe comparative religion. Although spiritual practice, something like prayer or communion with a larger spirit or personal God was something I tried to supplement throughout my life, I was never really part of a worshiping body, but I tried to understand people who were.

Karen: I see.

Dr. Lawrence: I didn't speak the language of a particular faith group, but I knew enough about them through study that I could feel like we were somehow sharing the same questions. I'm being verbose.

I lived long enough that my body began to fail me. My ordered world began to be disorderly because I didn't have sufficient strength to keep up with it. When I was more vital, I would've received the day's mail and gone through it. I had a file for everything and lived a very ordered existence. In my professional life as a professor, I not only kept up with my own responsibilities, but research, and the guidance of graduate students. I had many compartments where I knew very well how to keep everything in order. But there began to be a time when that had to be set aside. I didn't retire into leisure. I retired into ill health.

Karen: And you probably needed help then.

Dr. Lawrence: Eventually. I had a fall and a broken hip, which moved me from a certain level of independence to heavy dependence all at once.

Karen: That's really hard.

Dr. Lawrence: Well, it was. They did say I needed surgery, that the rehab period would be a certain number of weeks, and that I would be able to gain back skills. But that was all optimistic. As it turned out, my body didn't respond well to the surgery.

I did the rehabbing, but it was really the first time in my life where I trailed behind the curve. I was accustomed to excelling at things. But this time, I did not. My body was failing. And sleep was a problem. There were awful long nights of pain and the inability to sleep, disinterest in food, people having to care for me.

I showed him in the dream a scene: who gets a shampoo while they're in a bed? Even washing my hair was something that had to be done for me. I suppose they could have just trundled me into a shower and sat me on a stool and done that. In fact, there were times when they did that. But they were trying to also help me regain some independence. "We're going to shampoo your hair over here, and then you're going to walk across the room to the shower." I don't know why they did that, but that's what they did. It just was a memory, a vignette that symbolized a whole lot of what my life was about: ridiculousness.

It made me feel angry. Sometimes it was angry with people trying to be as positive as they could be, but in ways that just seemed a little too chirpy, too cheerful, you know?

Karen: Right. You didn't have any family, professor?

Dr. Lawrence: Well, I did. But I didn't want close family members having to do the tasks that a healthcare worker did for me. I had good insurance and the means to hire for that work.

Part of the family script reads, "That's not the way we do things. We don't turn each other into healthcare workers. We hire out that task and give support in other ways."

Karen: Understood.

Dr. Lawrence: I did show him that I had to walk past clutter, which bothered me a great deal because I had always been very orderly. But then I didn't have the capacity or the energy to keep my quarters ordered the way I would've liked. Then there were all these extra things that needed to be brought in, most of which reminded me of how decrepit I was: a potty chair next to the bed. And all these hospital things: a cup with a straw, because you can't sit up enough to drink out of a cup. You must drink from a straw. There were lots of cluttery reminders that I was a patient who would probably never be anything but that.

Karen: It's all necessary, but it's all a hit to the ego, isn't it?

Dr. Lawrence: Yes. When I did sleep, I got tired of waking up to the knowledge that now that I'm awake, I'm awake in a circumstance that feels entrapped and unpleasant. I had to put forth the effort not to snap at people who were doing their jobs and trying to serve me. I think they began to understand that the very worst thing they could do around me was to be chirpy, saying, "Ooh, look at this pudding! Open up so you can have some more pudding!"

That kind of thing drove me crazy. I didn't want to be spoken to as a child, because even when I was a child, I wasn't spoken to that way.

I did not take my life, although that idea was attractive to me.

I was never able to push through to do any interesting reading. I couldn't get my imagination to land on anything interesting. My imagination, my consciousness had nothing to occupy it other than ill health, incapacity, and pain. I just felt so caged.

Karen: Was it a long period of time that you felt that way?

Dr. Lawrence: It felt like it went on and on forever. Unfortunately, when I did pass, I didn't get blessed relief. I wasn't a bird who flew from its cage. I kind of took the cage with me.

I had gotten so used to being in that decrepit state that it overrode my earlier way of being.

I died while asleep and awoke in a place not unlike what I had just left. It took some time to understand that I had died, because it didn't seem much different from what I had left behind. Later, I learned that the ones who were helping me after my death could only work with what I gave them to work with.

I wasn't receptive to happy or pleasant things. My life had become so unpleasant that I just lost hope. I didn't have a vivid sense of an afterlife, even though I know that was a part of the ideation of lots of religious people and maybe even some who weren't religious.

Did you hear how he explained himself. Not only did his failing body decline, but so did his imagination. Immediately after his death, without actively choosing it, this poor caged professor-bird told us, "I kind of took the cage with me."

Dr. Lawrence: They had to continue to work with me, using what I gave them, which was a rather low level of dissatisfaction. Hopelessness is probably too strong, but joylessness, certainly.

And so, I pretty much created an afterlife nursing home. I kind of transferred the whole thing to the next plane. You know that I'm with you today because they deemed me ready to leave this behind and move on to a new thing. So there has been progress. It's just that it was necessarily slow because of what I brought to the project.

Karen: Do you remember a point where things turned for you, where you either took the help that was being offered, or you wanted more help from them?

Dr. Lawrence: Yes. It had to do with my hip, which was the instigating event. The broken hip and the surgery that followed was the big turning point. Things afterward went downhill for me.

My helpers said, "You once thought there were different possible outcomes. You were told that more than once. It's just that you got an unwanted outcome. But it wasn't the only possible outcome, and now there's the opportunity here for a different outcome." They helped me understand that I wasn't in the same material form that I had been earlier, although it was analogous to it, and that there were possibilities here that were not available previously. And that here all the remedies worked.

Here, everything succeeds. Everything works as it ought. They began saying to me, "Do you remember all that physical therapy you did after your surgery that never improved your condition? Well, here you can put in that work, but you'll see progress and growth."

And so, I did very similar therapy to what I had done earlier, except I did begin to gain strength. I regained mobility. After a time, I could go outdoors, for example. I could be in the sunshine. I could hear bird song. I could play with a cat, though I still was this old man who was recovering from an illness.

Then they began to say, "We would like to reintroduce you to some of the intellectual life that you enjoyed before your body failed." And then there began to be people who would've been my intellectual peers who began to visit and who demonstrated possibilities. One of them, for example, transmuted in front of me. He came in as a rather old man, and said, "Pay close attention. Watch me." And he turned about 40 years younger in front of me. He said, "The kind of bodies you and I have now can do this. They don't have to continue to age."

Karen: Beautiful.

Dr. Lawrence: He challenged me and said, "When you did think of a heaven or a pleasant afterlife, aren't you aware that most people thought of it as a place where they would not be sick or decrepit?"

I said, "Of course. I never heard anyone talk of a heaven with wheelchairs and sick beds. <laugh> And potty chairs!"

He said, "Well, your body can do this too. It's just, you haven't allowed it yet or tried it yet. He helped me practice. He said, "Let's pick an age. What age was a happy age for you?" I chose around 35, when I had finished my PhD and was starting my career. He said, "Let's practice forming your intention to make yourself be that now. And so, almost like a miracle, I turned from being an old, ill man to a healthy 35-year-old.

Karen: It was that easy?

Dr. Lawrence: It only lasted for a brief time, and then it seemed to fade. He said, "That's all right. You see, you can do it. If you will sign up for the course, you'll be shown how to leave behind the version of yourself that you've gotten used to being and become full-time this other way." I thought, "Well, sign me up! Absolutely."

Isn't that beautiful? His afterlife helpers knew he'd been successful in academic pursuits. They suggested he take a class in becoming young and healthy.

|||

Karen: Right!

Dr. Lawrence: I absolutely want that. Then some of the crankiness and despairing began to go away because the circumstance went away. The frustration of ill health and sadness wasn't so present when I was in the younger version of myself.

Karen: And you got to practice being younger!

Dr. Lawrence: Well, I think sometimes that's necessary because a person can't imagine themselves being different; you help them to reimagine their life. Except I didn't need that so much because I could change my circumstance. I didn't need to do a lot of emotional work, because if I could just stay in the younger state for a time, I could see that I was automatically happy.

There began to be some regimen of being younger again. It was almost like they used a stopwatch. "Let's see…last time we did it you lasted in the young state for this amount of time. Let's see if we can stretch that out and do it a little bit more the next time."

Karen: I bet you loved the challenge.

Dr. Lawrence: Well, I liked the release of pain. Then they put it to me in terms of gaining another degree.

I had succeeded at being in degree programs, moving through them, and seeing the sequence of things that needed to be done in a certain order. All of that was familiar. They just said, "Here's how we think this will move for you; here's the plan." And they had me agree to it.

I no longer felt helpless. I still had something like sleeping and rising. I wasn't alert all the time, but I would rest and rise. When I rose, it was time to do today's work. They mixed it up. Sometimes it would be artistic. "Now we're going to enjoy some classical music and we're going to talk about that." Or it might be some simple gardening project. We were learning about the physics of the world that I was in that was different from the physics of the world that you're in currently. It's not all about gravity or states of matter. They began to give me little teases about things that I might study about the world that had opened to me by dying.

Karen: It's so interesting. You got to work on things of mind and body.

Dr. Lawrence: Yes. And spirit. Then I began to enjoy visits from people I hadn't seen in a very long time. But they weren't coming to see a sick man. They were coming to see a person who was getting better every day. That made a great deal of difference.

I made enough progress that one of my helpers suggested, "We think that soon you'll be ready to leave this level or realm, to walk out the door under your own power as your young self." I might bound into the joyous afterlife that perhaps authentically spiritual people anticipate or participate in. Many of them, perhaps you included, think of what will happen after you die as something to be anticipated with joy. I really didn't have that. I was willing to intellectually allow for continued living, but it didn't enter my imagination that it would be joyful.

Karen: No?

Dr. Lawrence: Except here, there began to be people who were encouraging me to do more than have another spoonful of pudding. They helped me be more positive, encouraging me to anticipate joys I hadn't yet known.

I think I'm talking too much. I think it's time to move.

Karen: I'm interested in and fascinated by your story. Our next move is for you to decide who you'd like to have help you move to the next level. Have you thought about it?

Dr. Lawrence: Well, I'd been told to anticipate the question. But before I go, I know that you record these conversations and they become written transcripts. Remember, I kept files and records of everything, and I was meticulous about it. I would like it to be known should this ever become public to anyone that my story sounds laborious and sad. It is not. True, it's not very joyful in the beginning. If it were put to music, it would not begin as a jaunty little tune.

Karen: There might be a little cello.

Dr. Lawrence: A cello, okay. But it's beautiful. It moves through a kind of fugue. If it were colors, it would be grays and dark hues. But there's a dawning about it. And so, whether you think in terms of light or sound, it's positive.

Karen: Wonderful.

Dr. Lawrence: It **might** sadden people to think, "Oh, my loved one died in a sick bed. I hope they don't have an experience like this man is talking about." Well, I would say to any such person, "Calm **down**. It's not your business anyway. Everybody has their own journey to make, their process."

When people grieve a loved one, part of their grief can be wondering where or what the circumstance of their loved one is. Sometimes they bring to that idea extra sadness or extra anxiety, presuming what they don't know to be true, that their loved one is probably unhappy, or unhelped. I don't want to be a part of that at all. There was never a moment where there weren't supportive people around me helping me get better all the time.

Karen: I think you've been clear about that. Thank you.

Dr. Lawrence: Right. Well, that's enough of that. So let me be still and see how this does move.

(There was a pause.)

Dr. Lawrence: Do you know those novelty glasses that have a big nose, a mustache, and horn-rimmed glasses? My parents are here with those on. <laugh>

Karen: Is that how you remember them?

Dr. Lawrence: <laugh> No, but remember, I'm using this man's, [Father Nathan's] voice and can access his memories. He's recalling when he was called upon, because he's in the ministry, to perform the funeral for his own father. He had to speak publicly in front of his father's casket with his family in the front row. His father was notorious for never wanting to show emotion in public. He would wear dark glasses to a funeral.

Father Nathan was at his parents' home after his father's death, when his sisters arrived at the door wearing these silly-looking glasses. They didn't do grief. They didn't want to create another cycle of crying every time the door opened to a new person. So, they came wearing those glasses. That's a part of his story.

Karen: No more sadness?

Dr. Lawrence: My parents never owned these novelty glasses, nor was there very much room for anything so frivolous in their rather buttoned-down lives. They're just showing up to me in a visual that informs me that, "We're not as stodgy and such sticks-in-the mud as you might remember us to be. We are what we've always been, but there's a level of silliness, foolishness, or fun that we will introduce you to."

They're showing me that there's fun to be had and, "We can take part in it a bit and help get you started. You're on your way to something fun."

Karen: Well, how lovely!

Dr. Lawrence: They loved me very much. And again, because they only had me and no other children, I was the recipient of their extraordinary attention. They are just here to say, "We've been waiting for a long while to be with you again." And that day has arrived!

It's a happy ending. So, again if we set this to music, it does need something lilting and sweet at the end of it. If it were light, it needs to be…well, the colors here are beyond anything that I can describe. I think lots of people who have passed or have these Near-Death Experiences talk about the spectrum of color being way beyond what eyeballs were able to take in.

Anyway, it's time for me to go.

Karen: Great to meet you, Dr. Lawrence.

Dr. Lawrence: Yes, off I go. Thank you.

(They depart.)

Nathan: This is Nathan. Glory be to the Father, to the Son, and to the Holy Spirit, as it was in the beginning, is now, and will be forever. Amen.

Do you have anything for the recording?

Karen: Oh, my goodness. It was just fascinating, wonderful, inspiring, sad, happy. And so different than many we've helped before. We haven't had someone who took their current life into the afterlife like this.

Nathan: Especially so much illness.

Karen: And things didn't immediately get better in his afterlife.

Nathan: Right. He wouldn't leave until he made this point: "Don't let this sadden you. I never was unsupported. I always had what I needed. So don't let my experience sadden you."

He tried to say it was beautiful. Even if the music was in a minor key and if the colors were muted at first, it was still beauty.

Karen: Beautiful. I loved it. Thank you.

Nathan: Good work. Thanks again for your help.

||||||||||||||||||||||||||||||||||||||||||||||||||||||||||||||||||||||||||||||||||||||||||||||||||||||||||||||||||||||||||||||||||||||||||||||||||||||||

I loved how Dr. Lawrence's "buttoned-down" parents showed up displaying a playful side they rarely if ever showed. He knew in an instant that they were inviting him to something joyful.

||||||||||||||||||||||||||||||||||||||||||||||||||||||||||||||||||||||||||||||||||||||||||||||||||||||||||||||||||||||||||||||||||||||||||||||||||||||||

Nathan: I'm Nathan. Today is July 22, 2023. I'm in Laguna Beach on a Zoom call with Karen, who is also in Southern California, and Dave in Buffalo.

||||||||||||||||||||||||||||||||||||||||||||||||||||||||||||||||||||||||||||||||||||||||||||||||||||||||||||||||||||||||||||||||||||||||||||||||||||||||

We just did a reading of Dr. Lawrence's crossing story to refresh our memories. We're quite confident that his story would be a very good addition to the book if Dr. Lawrence chooses to give us permission to use it.

We've said our protective prayers earlier. I'm going to be still for just a moment. The earlier story included Mother Mary, the guardian Angel Abel, and Dr. Lawrence; all three of them were part of the initial conversation. So, any of them are welcome to speak. I'll be still and make my voice available.

(There was a momentary pause.)

This is Nathan. The first voice is going to be Mother Mary.

(Mary emerges.)

Mary: And good morning to you.

Karen: Good morning. Good to be with you again.

Mary: You're grouping stories in this book according to the idea of explaining how things might operate in the world after one dies.

I'd like to explain how I was helping in your earlier meeting with Dr. Lawrence. I asked you, Karen, if you'd ever seen me depicted with a broom, and you said you had not. I was quite confident that would be your answer because *I've* never seen me depicted with a broom.

At the beginning of the first conversation with Dr. Lawrence, Father Nathan had an unusual amount of distraction and something like overwhelm. He is a person who, for much of his adult life at least, has chosen to have many projects going at once.

He's managed to live a balanced life doing that. In his campus ministry years, even though he was quite busy, he wanted to be sure that he wasn't modeling for young people a frenetic pace of life. He didn't want them to have the impression that to be a follower of Jesus, you must exhaust yourself day in and day out. Balance was always something that was important to him. It's just that at the time that we did this crossing, he was feeling too many things coming at once.

In this session he arrived at your appointed time with less composure than was normal for him. In the story, Dr. Lawrence mentioned several times that those whom you try to help always work with what we give them. You're a counselor. You know very well that you might like to do things for a person who is in pain, but you must respect the parameters or limits that they give you.

On this day, Father Nathan was interiorly distracted. We just needed him to have more interior calm. So, at the beginning, I moved inside him because I was invited in prayer, but I didn't just sit there. Once I was invited in, I began to try to tidy his interior space so that he could focus and not be distracted by other things around him. He does something like that with simple meditative practices. He's conscious that he's got many things on his mind, but he tries to be still and breathe for several minutes or do something contemplative to help his mind focus on what's most important. I thought he needed a bit of help with that this time.

Karen: Well, you've been super helpful.

Mary: I think he has always looked to me for that. You might know because you've worked with him before, that he felt like he was so well mothered by his own mother that he didn't always use that category with me as the primary one. I might be Mother Mary, and he hasn't any problem with that idea, but it doesn't have as large a place in his heart as Mentor Mary. He trusts me to be a competent coach in ways that he would like to grow in.

He's had such good relations, love, and respect for colleagues, including the two of you, that it's not demeaning to me to be thought of as colleague with him. Nor is it arrogant on his part. It just feels **natural** that we co-operate, we work together. I was happy to help his consciousness be clearer.

I'll move aside and be actively helping. I don't think the guardian, Abel, feels the need to speak. I think you'll get Dr. Lawrence right away.

Karen: Wonderful. Thank you.

(Mary slides aside. Dr. Lawrence emerges.)

Dr. Lawrence: And right away is right. This is Dr. Lawrence. I was on the scene because Father Nathan spoke to me in prayer earlier telling me that he was pivoting, shifting in the direction of using my story rather than another one that you might have engaged in today. Karen, you recommended my story to him.

Karen: I did.

Dr. Lawrence: Do you know why?

Karen: Your story was very compelling to me because of how hard things were at the end of your life here. I'll never forget how you said that you were a bird in a cage, and you took the cage with you. I wanted to understand that, and you explained it so well. I was just so fond of you, and I am excited to hear how things have been going for you since.

Dr. Lawrence: Well, there's almost nothing left of those nursing home surroundings. I went in the direction of the person who showed me how his body could turn young and who recommended a class I could take to learn how to do that. I think I told you that they were using something like a stopwatch to see how long I could sustain it and get stronger at doing that. That seemed to be the most important thing I could do, because when I sustained that, I was pain free and no longer so crushingly dependent upon other people to do things for me because of my disability.

Karen: You needed the help, but then you just practiced and practiced. It sounds like you've healed.

Dr. Lawrence: I had been through laborious therapies, which were so ineffective. This was not difficult to sustain because the improvement was so evident. I was engaged in getting used to being in a body that was youngish, healthy, and happy. Then I could be available to do lots of other things I really wanted to do.

Karen: Yeah. Then your friends came and helped you.

Dr. Lawrence: They did. You know, there's a phrase, "When you've got your health, you've got just about everything." That's what I was doing. I was regaining a sense of being in a healthy body. One thing I would like to emphatically say to people is, "Don't you dare listen to my story and think, 'Oh, my mother died in a nursing home. She probably is like that poor man.'"

DON'T DO THAT! <laugh>

One of the things that Father Nathan thinks is most important is joyful hope. He thinks that in every moment of your life that's not pleasant, the moment will turn. I didn't appreciate that enough.

I think Martin Luther King used the image of an arc bending toward justice. Do you remember that? I believe that the universe bends towards joy for everyone because of the way it's constructed.

Joyful hope is more than a kind of mental temperament. It's not just one temperament among options. It really is the truth. Allow room for joyful hope to grow. It's more than, "I hope I win the lottery," or, in my case, "I hope this surgery goes the right way." Well, it didn't. But then, in the next moment, you can say, "Well, I'm going to be joyfully hopeful today while some chirpy nurse makes me eat pudding, <laugh>. I'm going to be grateful. Whatever I must endure, I'm going to have joyful hope about it." I think if I had done that, I might not have brought my cage with me.

Karen: I love your story because, although the healing was not successful here, and then looked a little shaky right after you died, the healing continued. Your story inspires joyful hope.

Dr. Lawrence: Thank you. I loved that my parents appeared wearing those goofy glasses, something I never in my life thought I would ever see. That was of course, borrowed from his family's experience. But it really was an effective way for my parents to show, "Look, there's fun that you didn't anticipate. And even we can do a little bit of it."

Karen: So, Dr. Lawrence, it sounds like you're giving us permission to use your story.

Dr. Lawrence: Thank you for making that explicit. Yes. I am giving you permission and I'm honored that you would even ask. You know, I chose a career in academia because I wanted to have an impact on young lives early enough that I might affect a positive outcome for the long term.

That's what I did. When you include this story in a book, you don't know who will ever read it.

Death and the pondering of what happens next is topical across the age spectrum. Telling stories like mine, you don't know who it will help. You could make a big impact. So, this feels consistent with the way I lived my life. If you think my story has educational merit, then use it.

Karen: Thank you. We really do believe that it will impact many people.

Dr. Lawrence: All right. Well, let's stop there. That sounds like the ending of a chapter to me.

|||

It does to me too, Dr. Lawrence. Thanks again for sharing your story. We can all learn a lot from you.

Chapter Five

Ellen, Who Survived Rape, St. Cecilia, and Ellen's Mom

Challenge: Assault, Violation
Value: Appreciation of Beauty

Three Explanations:
Dimming One's Light
Turning the Light Back On
Straightening What's Crooked

Ellen is a beautiful person. I think you're going to love her.

She had married her childhood sweetheart, and they raised their children to productive young adulthood. Then she learned of her husband's infidelity. After that came divorce. She wasn't interested in dating again, but she invited a gentleman acquaintance to her home for dinner. He was not a gentle man. He raped her. She told no one.

The light went out of her, dimming more and more until her death. She received some afterlife help. That's where this part of her story begins.

||||||||||||||||||||||||||||||||||||||||||||||||||||||||||||||||||||||||||||||||||||||||||||||||||||||||||||||||||||||||||||||||||||||||||||||||||||||||||||||

Nathan: I'm Nathan. Today is December 18, 2021. I am in Tucson on a Zoom call with Karen in Southern California. We're about to help someone who brought a dream story during the night of December 1, 2021. We've spent time in protective prayer surrounding ourselves with the love and support of the angels and saints. We're now ready to help the person who brought the following story:

"I saw the face of a well-dressed, possibly wealthy woman, who appeared to be in her late 40s or early 50s. Her eyes were closed, and she was screaming. She was being raped. I awoke."

Nathan: That's all there was to this dream story. There's very little detail. I don't know if she died in this event. Sometimes we deal with someone who had a trauma that they survived, but it so colored the rest of their life here that they kind of died inside and are dealing with that in the afterlife.

I'm going to pause the recording so that we can go into a little quieter, deeper prayer. I'll ask the assistance of a guardian to flesh out the story for any detail that might help us do our work today.

(There was a pause.)

We paused the recording for a time. We're going to continue to be still for just a moment as we invite the guardian of the person who was in the story or anyone else who might give us some detail that would help us do this work today.

There is a female presence. Her name is Cecilia. She might be human. She might be St. Cecilia.

(St. Cecilia emerges.)

St. Cecilia: And I am she. He's allowing me to borrow his voice this morning to assist in this lovely, simple work.

I think you very often engage an angelic person in this work, and I am not that. I was and am human. I am the one who is known as St. Cecilia, the patron of music. I was martyred. That much is clear in all the stories about me. I belong to the genre of story which far too many women share, of men deciding that they know what's best for us and whom we ought to marry. Many cultures have insisted that young women marry someone unknown to them, often for financial reasons or something having to do with clans and tribes. Sometimes political alliances were forged by making a woman marry a man who would not be her choice. I was in a situation like that, to which I objected. That brought about torture, which included physical disgraces.

So I have something of the personal resumé that might assist in the passage of a woman who was sexually assaulted.

We can all survive **any** manner of things. So today, it's not just me. Some of these works that he [Father Nathan] has done when it comes time for people to make the crossing part, they might see something like a wedge, where someone is at the front and behind them people fan out in a group going back into infinity, getting larger and larger. Today, I'm rather like that. I stand at the front of a much larger field of women and men who share the sad experience of being assaulted by another, but who also can testify to the resilience built into us. We need not simply be on the receiving end of someone else's violence or anger but can regain ourselves if we feel that something was stolen from us, including our soul.

The woman you'll be helping today has been listening in on this and has been cooperative, especially of late, in letting some things fall away that are beneath her and attached to her, but not of her. So, I will speak no further, slide to the side, and invite your work to proceed.

(St. Cecilia departs. Ellen emerges.)

Nathan: This is going to be Ellen.

Ellen: I'm Ellen. I'm adjusting to borrowing this voice. They gave me a few choices to consider when making this passage today. They said this one might be helpful because it involves overlap, moving into another, out of love, to communicate. I hadn't thought of it that much. As you know, I was raped. A man opted to crash into me uninvited and penetrate me without my permission in a way that harmed me and left me, I would earlier have said, permanently scarred.

My experience crowded out just about every other experience or way of thinking about myself as a human being. It changed everything in an instant. I didn't die that day, at least not physically; I felt a soul-death, after which I lived like a zombie or something. After my rape, I quit immersing myself in anyone or anything. I built up rigid barriers to try to be an isolated thing, which could not be entered.

Karen: It is not an uncommon reaction to want to protect yourself from further harm. Do you want to tell us anything about your life before this heartbreaking event took place?

Ellen: In the story he wrote down, it was very brief because that's the way I told it. He saw the face of a well-dressed, possibly wealthy woman, who appeared to be in her late 40s or early 50s. That was me. Wealthy people don't normally refer to themselves as wealthy. I was wealthy, although I never said that to myself.

I'm going to go a bit deeper, since we've already come this far, and give you only a sketch of what occurred. I've told the story enough times that it's not terrifying any longer. But give me a moment to gather up that story.

I was recently divorced after a 30-year marriage. We had raised two children to young adulthood, including college, and had seen them into the world. When the children were away and only returned for visits, especially at holiday times, we knew it was time for us to do a midlife review and decide what we wanted next. What would be our next chapter? We were only beginning that process. That's when I learned he was having an affair.

Karen: Did he finally tell you, or did you just find out?

Ellen: It was within our circle of friends. We belonged to a country club with many people our age. His paramour was someone known to me, someone in our circle. People's secrets aren't always quite as secret as they might hope. There began to be murmurings of this possibility. I chose to ask plainly, "I'm hearing rumors. Is it so?" To his credit, he admitted the affair.

I had all the emotions: heartbreak, disappointment, and curiosity. I thought I knew him so well, and here was a part of him I'd never imagined.

Karen: Some people compartmentalize well. Maybe he was good at that.

Ellen: Well, she wasn't even younger. Sometimes it's the secretary or some young thing who turns a man's head in a midlife crisis. The woman he became involved with was my own age and was like me, sort of the same moment in life and much of the same circle of friends. "Why this? It looks so much like what you have in me. Why would you do that?"

He didn't have a very good explanation. All he could do was stammer.

The thing I didn't anticipate was we did divorce. It broke up two households and left two sets of young adult children disillusioned. There was dividing up house and goods and who gets what. Initially, I hadn't any plans to move anywhere or be anything other than what I already was.

I got the house, but it was just me and the dog, rambling about. I was mostly the overseer of an estate, taking care of the garden. There was always something broken. My husband used to handle most of these things. Then it all fell to me.

Karen: I've worked with people who have gone through exactly what you went through. It's just heartbreaking. The betrayal feeling is so high. How did you manage that and move along?

Ellen: I just tried to force myself out of bed in the morning. I did get a counselor. I had different ones, including a financial counselor. Your financial planning must be redone because everything has changed. My former husband dealt fairly with me, although any divorce deals a financial hit to each person.

But I had no financial worries. It was clear to me that living in such a large home that was designed for a growing family no longer made sense. I would be better off to invent a new lifestyle. Then there was the issue of who gets custody of the friends. We mostly ran in a circle of married couples. Occasionally, there would be a divorce. But the group was able to absorb the occasional breakup and welcome new people.

What I didn't appreciate fully until it was my circumstance was the degree to which the innocent spouse, if you will, the cheated upon one, becomes this awkward fifth wheel. People had gotten so accustomed to engaging me as half of a couple, they didn't quite know what to do with me as a unit. And then there can be some cattiness about women not wanting a divorced or unmarried woman near their husband.

Karen: That happens.

Ellen: Everything had collapsed. I didn't think of myself as someone who was going to date and look to remarry. The last thing that I was interested in was anything sexual with somebody that I didn't know very well. I had been faithful to one husband for decades, and I didn't think of myself as some cougar who wanted to put herself out, make myself available for that. But now I'm getting to the more difficult part. I did accept a date with a man who was divorced and who had been a part of our circle.

I thought he was safe company and arranged something that I thought was safe. I invited him to dinner in my home. It seemed to me somehow safer because I'd never felt unsafe there, rather than getting dressed up and going out on something that was quite obviously a date, like dinner and a movie, getting dressed up and being brought to a nice restaurant and having the chair held for me and so on. I didn't want to be so much someone's date as someone who could prepare a nice meal and enjoy a glass of wine, the fireplace.

Karen: You did what was comfortable for you.

Ellen: Yes, I wasn't thinking of myself as dating. I was just...

Karen: Having a friend over.

Ellen: Yes, having a gentleman over for dinner. I just wanted to invite a bit of companionship and make a tentative step out from the isolation that I had been in into something else. I just didn't have any idea that he was going to look upon...

(There was a pause and a welling up of emotion)

I'm trying to honor his [Father Nathan's] desire that no one cause him to cry. The simple fact was [my attacker] looked upon most of the evening as prelude. His interests were carnal and mine were not. He made an advance that I tried to gracefully deflect with a giggle and a turn of the head and some attempt to…

Karen: Get the message across?

Ellen: Yes, and to suggest I was flattered by the interest, but no, thank you.
That turned, almost instantly, to aggression. Without getting any more graphic than necessary, not even a bedroom, just the couch and the floor of my living room in this violent assault. I would never, ever have thought this man capable of what he did to me, or that it would even be pleasurable to him. There was nothing tender or loving in what he did. It was just horrid.

Karen: It's almost never about sex.

Ellen: Well, it became this awful thing. And then, as he prepared to leave, he made a threat that if I thought I was ruined by a divorce, "Just watch your step. Because if you ever speak of this, you'll have hell to pay."

Karen: He threatened you.

Ellen: He didn't specify what the other awful things he might do, but I received the message.

Karen: Were you frightened?

Ellen: I didn't speak of it. It's hard to say was I frightened. I was frightened during the assault. I'm struggling with using the word "decided," because I don't know that I ever gave myself the option of a decision, like deciding to go to the police or telling anyone. I don't think I so much decided, as I defaulted into silence.
I opted not to speak of it. I cleaned myself up that evening and went to sleep in my own bed. I made sure the windows and doors were locked. I had a new security system installed. That looked like a rational thing for a divorced woman living alone to do. So, I shielded myself in ways that looked socially appropriate without people knowing that I was shutting down in lots of different ways. But that was gradual.

Karen: What he **did to** you was horrible. I'm so sorry.

Ellen: It changed **everything** about me. My children noticed, but they just thought it was a consequence of the divorce. They didn't know of the assault. They kept trying to tell me how attractive I was and how any number of men would love to be with me. I tried to steer them away from telling me how I ought to behave. And then I would get sharp with them if they persisted.

"Leave me alone. It's my life. You go live yours." When they had their children, I could engage my grandchildren a little, but my home had become a crime scene. I didn't want them staying overnight with me. I was much more of a remote grandmother. I was a gift giver, and we could do things on my terms. We could go to the zoo. We could do events in the daytime, but no sleepovers. Even though I had plenty of room in the house for them to stay, my rule was when you come to visit, I pay for the hotel. I'll arrange the dinner, but I wanted very controlled circumstances. Everything was on my terms and don't ask me to do anything that I haven't suggested on my own.

Karen: That's how you kept yourself safe. After a while, what did your life look like?

Ellen: There was polite interest on the part of my children and of my little grandchildren. There was polite interest from a few people who didn't give up easily. I did work out a few areas of my life where I continued trying to appear as normal as before. I did sometimes have sort of girl dates with other divorced or widowed women. I once did a cruise with some girlfriends, hoping that that might be a new thing in a life that had very little new in it. But I found them quarrelsome and petty. It's not easy to travel with people with whom you haven't traveled before.

I had always been a reader and encouraged my children to read. I steered clear of anything that had a rape in it. I didn't want bodice-ripping romance novels or even some legitimate theater or movies that might involve some sort of sexual content that was not completely consensual or was conflicted in some way. I wanted nothing to do with any of that. I was selective about any entertainment. I'd never been a church woman, so that really wasn't an outlet.

Eventually, I began to have the ailments that come with advancing age. I had the means to relocate to a nice place that could accommodate my physical issues. Such places are disproportionately female, and so there were plenty of other women that I could have meals with.

Karen: Did you have a peaceful passing after that?

Ellen: Well, it was cancer, so there were symptoms, diagnoses, tests, and treatments. Much of this was...

Karen: Pain?

Ellen: Well, pain and bustle, the calendar filling up with doctor appointments, visits to specialists, and complicated bills. My children began to be dutiful and wanted to take over. My brother, too. Sometimes his best intentions were unwelcome. Even if I didn't say so, I think I communicated it well enough.

Yes, there was pain, but the other part of it was I had gotten used to wanting to be left alone. Cancer becomes a common project somehow. Now your body's illness becomes the concern of the masses. Everybody has something to say about your body, your treatment. It begins to feel like not your own anymore which, of course, triggered me because my body had been treated like I was not in it.

I don't think my death was peaceful, but it was orderly. My husband had provided well for the two of us, even in our split. Money wasn't an object. I could always afford whatever was needed.

Karen: What's it been like since you passed? What's it been like in the afterlife?

Ellen: My passage itself had a trajectory that was predictable in the last couple of months. There began to be conversations with oncologists and others who said, "You're now in this phase of your illness, and the time is short. Get your affairs in order." They were already in the best order that I knew how to get them in. So, it was really like the approach of anything that is predictable. Summer or winter's coming or it's swimsuit season, so you need to lose weight. The stores always were selling something that was for the coming season.

The coming season began to be my death. I had to have higher doses of pain medications that made me sleepier. My awake time was less, and I couldn't suddenly open my heart and profusely do storytelling to my children and grandchildren. I wasn't going to do that, anyway.

When I did leave the body, I did what was familiar to me, which was to try to stay as isolated as the next life permitted. Although there was a companion who did not speak at the beginning of this, a guardian angel who made herself available. I did need a little bit of explaining, like, "What kind of guardian angel allows their person to be raped?"

She explained, "Well, you raised children. You know that even if you want to, you can't follow them about and protect them from every bad thing. I did all that was permitted to try to protect, defend, and help you regather." I had to acknowledge my part in it, that whatever receptivity another **might** have brought to that, I didn't have to give. I didn't even know I had a guardian angel. Whatever that could have been didn't develop until after my death.

Karen: You probably worked on your trauma with that guardian angel, which brings you to us today, huh?

Ellen: Yes. Even **though** I had counseling about the divorce and a lot of things afterwards, I never spoke the **worst** part to a counselor or a therapist.

Karen: No? That **happens.** I'm sorry.

Ellen: I could **dance** around it. I could talk about a lot of things. If the therapist got too close to the point, I **would** move to another therapist.

Karen: It probably left you depressed and irritable though, which is kind of what happens.

Ellen: And tired. I wondered, "What's my body like at this age or this age and this age? Is it because of physical **things** or am I bringing emotional things to this and making it harder?"

Karen: Right.

Ellen: "Am I more **tired** because my body is aged or is it because I'm mentally unwell or not tending to things as I ought?"

Karen: It's exhausting, holding secrets. It just is.

Ellen: Yes.

Ellen: I believe I'm **going** on too long. I think I should wrap it up.

Karen: Well, have **you** thought about who you might want to help you make your next move?

Ellen: It's my **mother.** She died also with cancer, ovarian, as a youngish woman when I was just married. I **longed** to have her guidance as I moved through different stages of my married life. She was **not** around for the birth of my children and to see them grow up. I missed not being **able to** share photos with her.

I wasn't a person **who** prayed. Neither was she. So, after she died, I just thought that was the end of that. There's nothing left but memories and photos. But then afterwards...

She's visited, and she's explained to me that there's something of levels here. She's allowed to visit at my level, and I will be allowed to visit at a next level after today. She said, "When that day arrives, remember I'm available to come and be with you, which is all that you wanted for so long. You wanted me to come and be with you. So, when it's time, remember to ask for me."

Karen: I'm so excited for you. I know you and she will have a really good time together.

Ellen: Something is shifting right now, so I'm to be still and allow it to present itself, I think.

(There was a brief pause.)

I'm seeing my mother in a sunrise on a horizon. She is backlit. In photography, you want to make sure that you don't have a backlit subject because you can't see their face, there's so much light coming from behind them. But somehow the light's coming out of her. It's not hitting her. It's emerging from her. There's light behind her and light within her. She's radiant. I think she's showing me that that's my future.

Karen: Wonderful!

Ellen: My light went out some time ago. The next part of it will be working on turning the lights back on without focusing on the darkness that happened to me.

I guess there's some work around that, where progress can be made without somehow triggering things that might send me running to hide again.

So, she's here. We don't need to do anything except allow her to come nearer. The rest of it will be ours, and your work will be complete.

Karen: We wish you well, Ellen. I'll keep you in my thoughts.

(Ellen and her mother depart.)

Nathan: And they've made their way. This is Nathan. Glory be to the Father, to the Son, and to the Holy Spirit, as it was in the beginning, is now, and will be forever. Amen.

Well, that one was one of the more emotional that I've been involved in. As you saw, she was trying to contain it and work within the parameters that I'm comfortable with.

It felt like she hasn't **told** that story very many times. She was sort of at the low end of the threshold of being **capable** of doing this today, but she was pushing herself to. Somehow somebody got **through to** her and said, "You don't need to wait any longer. You've waited so long already. You're **capable** of this. If you'd like, we'll help you. Ready, set, go."

Karen: She did a **good** job, but you could tell it was still fresh.

||||||||||||||||||||||||||||||||||||||||||||||||||||||||||||||||||||||||||||||||||||||||||||||||||||||||||||||||||||||||

Ellen's mom came **to help** turn her light back on. Even a dim light can be beautiful. Night and day both belong.

||||||||||||||||||||||||||||||||||||||||||||||||||||||||||||||||||||||||||||||||||||||||||||||||||||||||||||||||||||||||

Nathan: I'm Nathan. Today is July 8, 2023. I'm in Laguna Beach with my dogfriend, Toto. I'm on a Zoom call **with** Karen, who's in Southern California. We've already said our protective prayers with **the angels and** saints. I'm going to invite Ellen to speak if she would like.

(Ellen emerges.)

Ellen: And this is she. You know enough about my story. I wish I could have edited out an evening that changed my life remarkably, but that wasn't happening. Although this afterlife way resembles that. It **doesn't** allow obliteration of unhappy experiences, but it does allow one to edit one's **response** at the very least. I'm grateful for that cosmic second chance.

Karen: Well, we **want** to thank you for coming back and spending some time with us. We're so moved by **your** story.

Ellen: I've had so **much** coaching help since my passing that I can see where my initial conversation with **you** could have a helpful or healing impact. I'm not the first of those you've helped in this **way**, who responded to a painful challenge with a kind of shutting down that in the end **was** costly. Nor is that an uncommon way for people to move through painful life stories **and** issues. If you share my story in a book, maybe there will be someone who sees themself in my story. Maybe they'll reconsider and not wait as long as I did for things to turn.

Karen: Is that you **giving us** permission?

Ellen: That's me giving you permission. That's exactly right.

Ellen: I had a network of people who loved me, who because of my response [to the assault], were denied my full presence and being. I began to put people at a distance. Sometimes I would be brittle or short with people if they pushed against that. Some could see that I wasn't happy and that I was making choices that didn't seem to promote happiness, freedom, or anything good. But I kept choosing it. You know, when you do that long enough and you push people away and tell them to mind their own business, after a while they do. Eventually you create a lonelier version of yourself than is good.

Karen: Yeah. People do go away, don't they?

Ellen: Some do. And then others stay around at a lower level of engagement because they understand that is all you will tolerate. That's what I did to family members and a few friends who continued to try to engage me. Some could remember the more vital me that was fun to be around and hoped that she might return. They kept trying. But others didn't.

Karen: Sure. So, Ellen, St. Cecilia came when we were last with you. And so did your mom. Are they still around you? Do you hang out with them at all? Or do you have different companions?

Ellen: Let me pause a moment and go deeper.

(There was a brief pause.)

Ellen: Well, Cecilia was helpful in that she was someone who had known violation, but who was better known for the creation of beauty. I don't think of myself as having been extraordinarily creative, but I had the means and the leisure to have a well-ordered home with nice things. I did pay attention to the beauty of my own surroundings. I kept things clean and neat; that mattered to me. If there were some framed art on the wall that was a little crooked, I immediately went to it to straighten it. I liked order and line, color, and texture.

Cecilia's gifts were more musical, but we shared an appreciation of beauty. Some of that had drained out of me. I began to not get joy from my surroundings. Instead of feeling good that I straightened the picture because it now looks better, I would do it out of annoyance. "I need for things to be orderly and you're disorderly, and so you better straighten up!" I'd take an attitude to things around me that they needed to be just so, because I felt so unhappy inside.

Karen: Sure.

Ellen: I projected some of that onto ridiculous things.

I remember wanting to laugh out loud at Ellen's description of two approaches to straightening a crooked picture. Of course, she was using my voice at the time so I couldn't laugh out loud.

I was once an art student. I often want to make things more attractive or orderly. It's true you can do that to create beauty that you and others enjoy. Or you can just be a jerk. You can straighten a picture and be annoyed that it needed straightening. I thought that was insightful of Ellen.

Karen: Yes. We talked a little bit about the irritability. Has that gone away?

Ellen: I wish it had gone away earlier, but it's gone now. They have allowed me in a program where I can sit in on conversations and hear people from all different places and times talk about how hard their lives were. They do this on the way to healing; they're not just whining or commiserating. I've been allowed to listen to people talk about sorrows and struggles deeper than my own. That helped create some sense of solidarity.

Part of me wished I could have taken an eraser or scissors to my story and get rid of the worst part. They've shown me how to help it find a place, a context. "This is part of my story, and it needn't be jettisoned, ignored, or worked around in unhelpful ways." For so long I tried to pretend it never happened or not speak of it.

Karen: You must work at it. Huh?

Ellen: You must work at it, and you might have to try several times. Anyway, there's still more work to be done. I know that I'm not there yet, and I know that I don't necessarily have to be. There's no rush. Some people choose to do that on the way to their healing. They say, "This awfulness that became part of my story is like that. It's a dark chapter that gives texture and richness to a redemption story." In your Christian story, Good Friday becomes Easter morning. That's a theme that Father Nathan returns to a lot.

Karen: That's true.

Ellen: I think this is going to be a part of my ongoing story for quite a long while, maybe always, I don't know. But I'm not unhappy and I'm not hiding. I'm grateful that I've had help here on this side. It's a little like dawning.

One thing I enjoyed, even after I ended up in the house alone, was my garden. I often didn't sleep well. I would be awake before the sun rose, but I could make the coffee. Even when the weather was a little too cool, I would bundle up and sit outside with a cup of coffee just to enjoy watching the light emerge.

Karen: Well, the light and dark theme was important when I first met you. I remember when your mom came to get you, you described her as backlit, and emitting light.

Ellen: Yes. And it was beautiful.

Karen: She said she was coming to turn the light back on inside you.

Ellen: Yes. She came to turn my light on.

Karen: That meant a lot to me, just to hear her say that to you.

Ellen: Yes. That was lovely. Since she came for me, I've enjoyed getting to know her as a human being who got here before I did, and who had the role of mothering me. Those are still roles, but they're sort of accidents of time and space. We've gotten to know each other beyond mother/daughter, as two co-equal persons with overlapping stories. That's been a nice discovery.

Karen: I bet. Well, I want to thank you for giving your permission.

Ellen: And thank you. I'm happy for both of you that you've been drawn into this work because you're good at it. You're receptive to new things. That was my big issue. I wasn't receptive to anything new. I just stopped everything. Now I'm not doing that.

The openness that you and others have shown in helping Father Nathan is a pebble in a pond. It's radiating out; it finds a place in hearts, here, there, and elsewhere. I'm happy to be part of it.

Karen: Thank you so much. I will be praying for you.

Ellen: Well, and I for you. I'm learning more about prayer. For me, prayer felt like talking to the wall. But I've learned; I've watched how loving energy moves from person to person. I can see it in different ways now than I could have earlier. My mother and I have talked about it some, because neither of us were conventional prayers. But we were loving, compassionate people. I've learned that prayer is love formulated, thought, or expressed, and then sent. I always did that. I just didn't call it prayer.

Anyway, this time I'm going. I hope that you enjoy whatever you do next.

Karen: Thank you so much, Ellen. God bless you. Bye-bye.

(Ellen departs.)

Nathan: This is Nathan. Glory be to the Father, to the Son, and to the Holy Spirit as it was in the beginning, is now, and will be forever. Amen.

Karen: Amen.

Nathan: I can tell you have a fondness for her.

Karen: I do. I like her order.

Nathan: I like that too. I liked the way she just explained how you can take two different attitudes towards straightening a crooked picture. You can either desire beauty or you can be angry at disorder <laugh>.

Karen: Yes. That was perfectly said, wasn't it?

|||||||||||||||||||||||||||||||||||||||||||||||||||||||||||||||||||||||||||||||||||||||||||||||||||||||||||||||||||||||||||||||||||||||||||||||||||

Thanks again for sharing you story, Ellen. All of it. I'm sure someone is going to see themself in it. Maybe someone they trust will help them turn their light back on.

Chapter Six

Iron Mike, Back in the Game

Challenge: Inability to Forgive Himself
Value: Memory of Advancement

Three Explanations:
Stubborn Attraction to Darkness
Effective Childlike Simplicity
Truthfulness at Last

I wasn't born on home plate in a baseball stadium, but I may as well have been. I received my love of baseball from my mother.

Growing up in New Orleans in the 1920s and '30s she remembered going to Pelican Park to cheer for her team. In 1945 she became engaged to my father, Max. He was a sailor based out of Philadelphia, so for a time she lived with a family there and became a fan of the National League's Philadelphia Phillies.

Through the 1950s and early '60s my parents had us five kids. In April of 1962 our family welcomed a new member, a major league baseball team in nearby Houston. At first, they were called the Colt 45s, then three years later, the Astros.

They played 162 games a year. We listened to all of them on the radio. When their games were televised, which wasn't very often, mealtimes shifted, or we ate in front of the TV.

My dad wasn't a big fan of baseball, but he was a huge fan of my mom. He knew taking her to a game filled her with joy. That wasn't easy to do with four or five kids and a two-hour drive one-way. But sometimes he'd finish a job moving a ship, and instead of enjoying a relaxing evening at home, he'd phone to say, "Mama, let's go to the ball game!" Quickly we'd all take baths, dress in Sunday clothes, and pile into our station wagon. We wouldn't get back until one in the morning. It was like we had gone to visit family.

Once we were all grown and out of the house, we all knew better than to call to talk to Mom during the ballgame. I might be watching or listening to the game in whatever faraway place I lived, but she would get the signal of it five seconds before I did. We'd be in the middle of a conversation when she'd shout out, "He shouldn't have swung at that!" or "Run, run, run... Ohhhh!"

My parents' later years weren't so golden. Dad got Parkinson's Disease. It was a 10-year slide into dementia. She watched him all day to keep him safe, but he'd tire and go to bed early. Mom's widowed best friend, Doris, would come over after dinner and they'd watch the Astros together.

When Mom died, many family members and friends attended her memorial service sporting Astros jerseys. It was a fitting tribute.

Mom didn't just love the team, she loved some of the players. Hall-of-Famer Craig Biggio was her favorite. He is a Catholic and a family man. She liked that. I hope she gets to meet him someday.

But in the meanwhile, she's gotten to meet baseball great, Iron Mike. He didn't get to play in the major leagues, but he was a baseball guy through and through. I got to know Iron Mike as one of my night visitors. He told a story in my dream that was thrilling: a bottom-of-the ninth three-run home run to win the game. But the joy was short lived. The ball that left the field flew into the stands and struck a baby. The baby died. Iron Mike died inside.

I don't get home to Texas very often, but I had come back to be a part of a little reunion of some of the members of my graduating class of 1974. Ours was a small Catholic high school. Our athletic teams were almost always underdogs to the larger schools we played against. After a day of reunion activities, I was relaxing with old friends Jeanne Marie and her high school sweetheart-turned husband, James. It was baseball playoff time when I asked if they would be my prayer partners to help a person who had a baseball-related story to tell. They hadn't done that before, but they were game. Here's how that session went.

Nathan: I am Nathan. I am in Crystal Beach, Texas, with James and Jeanne Marie. Today is October 3, 2021. We're about to help a person who brought a story in a dream on September 17, 2021. We have just said our protective prayers, inviting the angels and saints to surround us, protect us and assist us. I'm about to read the story of the dream as I received it and wrote it in my journal on September 17. Here's that story:

Someone hit a game ending home run. There was the beginning of a celebration, but what followed was confusion and uncertainty. I awoke.

(There was a pause.)

I've paused the recording so we could be still and go into deeper prayer. We've re-read the dream and have invited the person's guardian to assist.

I have a feeling of some gathering like that in the movie, "Field of Dreams." A bunch of baseball people have gathered for this one.

We are James and Jeanne Marie and Nathan, and we would like to help. Guardian, if you would like, would you come on the line first, and give us a little better sense of who we are to help and how we might do that?

(The Guardian moves in.)

James: Hello.

Guardian: Hello. You are Jimmy. Is that right?

James: Yes, I am.

Guardian: You were quite the stud ballplayer.

James: I used to think so <laugh>.

Guardian: He [Father Nathan] is participating in a bit of teasing. You two were having a cigar last night, and you went through year by year, how many games your teams won. 22 and 1, were you?

James: Yes, one year we were that good.

Guardian: Around me right now is the baseball world, because on this day, there are games going on in many cities, all of which directly impact who goes on in the playoffs.

He's been keeping track on his phone, which is also making a recording. The Astros are winning, and his mother is over my shoulder.

She doesn't want to talk, but it's baseball, and the Astros are in the playoffs. Then there was recently an important game that was held in Iowa. There's a movie called, "Field of

Dreams." It features the story of a father and son. The father has died, and it has a lot of the elements of what we're about here, crossing over, moving along, and getting over resentments and grudges.

Jeanne Marie: Yes, I know the movie.

Guardian: Well, there was recently the first-ever major league baseball game played on that field, in a cornfield in Iowa.

Many who loved baseball have a kind of mythic, mystical sense of it. There's a story here of triumph and tragedy. Somehow, it's attracted a crowd. Baseball does that. It draws a crowd. I'm hearing a tune inside him, "Buy me some peanuts and Cracker Jack." Today, would you just call me Cracker Jack?

Jeanne Marie: I like that. Hello, Cracker Jack.

Angel Cracker Jack: The one whom I guarded had a great love of this game. He [Father Nathan] is feeling a lot of emotions. Father Nathan has a rule about not crying when we do this work. We are adjusting our frequencies to both do what we need to do, and to be as observant of his ways as we can be.

The one I love is very dear to me, and we are excited that he will move along. It has something of the excitement of making the playoffs, going to that next level, where there's joy and excitement about reaching this moment. I'll be right over here to the side, praying and assisting.

(Angel Cracker Jack slides aside. Iron Mike emerges.)

Iron Mike: I'm here with you. My name is Iron Mike. I lived a long time ago. I know about this movie, "Field of Dreams." I played ball, semipro and minor leagues in the era where radio began to be part of the way that people took part, listening to the games. There were many long bus rides.

I need to go a little deeper. I got to this first level, but I think I need to go a little deeper.

(There was a brief pause.)

I hit a home run that won the game. It went down the left field line, and it went above the glove of the outfielder. I had hit it very hard, and at the plate, I thought, "This one could leave the yard." It did.

There were two men on base, and it was, I think they now call it a walk-off. Except it hit a child in the chest, a babe-in-arms, a small one. I was too far away to see that. It was a home game. The crowd was immediately excited because they just saw the game won. I was circling the bases and got all the way home. But then there was some weird commotion going on in the stands. Then people quit cheering, and everybody turned to look at the stands. There was rushing about, people in an agitated state. This child had stopped breathing.

You live in a different time with more advances in emergency care, but there wasn't much to be done. Whatever people attempted to do was ineffective. There was some running about to try to get to a car and get to a doctor or something, but the whole place had a pall over it. Then there was an announcement over the loudspeaker, "Ladies and gentlemen, this is what's just occurred," and, "Might we all stop and say a prayer?" The players from both dugouts came onto the field and said a prayer. The bat I'd just used was lying right there. The baby died.

The short story is, I wouldn't hear any consolation words. Nobody could tell me, "It wasn't your fault. It could have happened to anyone," or "Just get over it," or whatever. I was young, I was 24 years old. I had hopes that I was going to keep advancing and make it to the next level, and maybe one day be in the majors and stuff. It's like everything I aspired to do and to be ended on the spot. Just about everybody I knew was a teammate. When I walked away, I walked away from every friend, and I walked away from the thing that I most loved. I got mean. If anybody tried to be kind to me, I pushed them away. They got the message and stayed away.

I couldn't forgive myself. I was never happy. I couldn't be around any woman long enough to be good company. For a little while, I worked in a coal mine. It suited me because I felt like I could crawl into a hole and die. There was plenty of coal mining done where I was from in Pennsylvania. Then I just drank and didn't take care of my health. I figured coal mining's real dangerous, and you breathe unhealthy air. I would have never wanted to be a coal miner. You see those guys that do that for a living, and they all die when they're 50, if the mine doesn't blow up, or the tunnel doesn't collapse. They weren't very good about workplace safety rules.

I just took this job and got some little boarding house room, a flophouse place to sleep and eat. I'd do nothing but crawl in a hole, day after day. When I got out of it, I drank. Sometimes people call that "crawling into a bottle." I just wondered if there'd be release at the end of it when I died. If there was anything after, maybe it would be something happy. The thing was, I'd gotten so good at pushing people away, it was second nature.

When I did die, afterlife people started coming around. They sounded just like the ones I'd been pushing away ever since that moment. I didn't want them around. I didn't want their company. "Are you going to do the same thing everybody else did? You're going to tell me it wasn't my fault? You're going to tell me it was really bad luck?" I think that's why I'm conscious that in this moment, I'm an old timer in this process. He, [Father Nathan], I think, deals with lots of people that moved along much faster than I did. I just kind of kept digging that hole deeper. There was a way that it kind of came with me. I'm the one dug it, and I was the one that had to look at it and see that I dug it. I had to find a way out or take the hand of somebody that would lead me out.

I was just so out of the habit of being hopeful, that I didn't give them very much to work with. They tried different things. They tried athletes; they sent some athletes around. They sent some little kids that died playing baseball, who chased a ball into the street and got hit by a car, whatever. They tried lots of different things, every key at the lock, I think. Something must have worked, because here we are. There's something that's supposed to happen today that takes me from a kind of low level. I was used to thinking of levels in baseball.

They got me thinking: "You remember before that happened, you used to advance. Minor league baseball has lots of levels. As you improve, you move up. You advance. You just have to put your mind to it. And then you must be coachable. If you think you know it all already, you won't be a good teammate, and no coach is going to want to recommend you." You can't be a team player while you're all bound up in your own anger.

I began to just pay attention. It wasn't any one person, but it was a whole bunch of different ones. The little kids got to me, because one of them told me, "Well, Mister, I didn't know what to do after I died playing baseball, and I was mad, but then I changed my mind." Anyway, I'm to the point where there's kind of a crowd gathered today, because it's apparently a spectacle about to happen. They want to cheer for me. I'm not sure. I think I might be doing your job for you, but I'm at the moment when people get asked, "Who do you want to come for you?"

James: I would like Lou Gehrig to come for you.

(*The voice shifts. Nathan speaks for a moment.*)

Nathan: This is Nathan. You're right on the mark, Jimmy. He's already here.

Iron Mike: Well, you are good at this, because Lou Gehrig is already here. He's saying, "I'm the luckiest man alive."

James: He was in the middle of his career.

Iron Mike: He was.

James: He was tragically taken away from it like you were.

Iron Mike: Yes.

James: He accepted his fate and went home.

Iron Mike: I'm going to yield the microphone now.

(Iron Mike yields to Lou Gehrig.)

Lou Gehrig: I am the luckiest man alive. My name is Lou. Now I'm better known for a disease that's dreadful, that has my name on it. People wear my jersey when they get that dread disease. They walk around with my name on their back. The scientists keep working on a cure, or treatment, but the people that have it right now are mostly having long, slow exits.

I got concerned about this fellow, Mike. I don't have to go on about it. I just wanted to say "hi" because I'm here. They did say "You would be a really good fit for this man," because like you said, his life was interrupted. I guess that's a word that he [Father Nathan] uses in his books. We've got something for Iron Mike to do.

It's just this fellow needs to let some light in. He lived in the darkness a lot. Some of it he created; I think he told you he crawled in tunnels on purpose. He felt dark inside, and he felt better in the dark than he did in the light. But he's coming around. We're not throwing him a great big party, but there'll be something fun.

I went out onto the field and spoke into a microphone to a whole stadium full of folks. I think they even had motion picture cameras there, didn't they?

James: They sure did.

Lou Gehrig: He knows about that, and we're inviting him into that scene. I'm going to be still for just a second.

(There was a pause.)

Iron Mike: This is Iron Mike. There are ball boys, and all those summer girls. There's boys and girls that are dressed in children's baseball uniforms. They've been picked. I think they won a contest, or they somehow got chosen for this honor, like throwing out the first pitch.

They're happy and excited because they get to do this. I will ruin it for them if I don't let them walk me onto the field, because that's their job. There are children that are excited that they're going to take Iron Mike out to the place where Lou Gehrig is.

I don't remember putting it on, but somehow, I'm wearing the jersey I was wearing that day. Except it's glowing, and it's warm. I don't know why. I don't have to give much of a speech. I don't think that Lou Gehrig's was very long.

All I want to do is say, "I'm sorry for trying the patience of anybody who tried to help me. I know the truth: I didn't kill a child. I swung a bat and hit a home run, and it killed a child. They just think it's important that I tell the truth. I didn't mean to harm anybody. I want to thank everybody whose patience I tried that was trying to move me here. A lot of you are in the stands. That's just why I want to say thank you for putting up with such a hard case.

And I want to say one more thing: Play ball!

(Iron Mike and his entourage depart. Nathan speaks.)

Nathan: He's being escorted off the field by my Mom!

James: Oh great!

Nathan: She wants to say hi to both of you, because she remembers you.

James: Thank you.

Nathan: She doesn't want to talk; she is just walking him to the dugout.
All right. Our work is done. Glory be to the Father, to the Son, and to the Holy Spirit, as it was in the beginning, is now, and ever shall be, world without end. Amen.
You got any comments for the recording?

Jeanne Marie: It seemed like he lived a miserable life, and then afterwards, he wanted to stay in that misery.

Nathan: That happens.

James: He couldn't forgive himself, even though it wasn't his fault.

Nathan: He mentioned at the end, "I have to tell the truth." He had to say it out loud in front of other people. In his case, it was into a microphone in a stadium. "I know I didn't kill that child."

Jeanne Marie: He's from the 1930's or '40s. He kept to himself a long time after his death.

Nathan: Well, his afterlife was what he chose it to be. He just had to un-choose it to change it. And eventually he did. That was a short dream and a long story with a happily-ever-after ending.

‖‖

I wanted to share Iron Mike's story with you here, but I wouldn't do that without first asking his permission. It's his story after all. Recently I had the opportunity to reconnect with Jeanne Marie and James and our friend Iron Mike on a Zoom call. Here's how that went.

Nathan: I am Nathan. Today is July 18th, 2023. I'm in Laguna Beach, California with my best dog friend, Toto, in my lap. I'm on a Zoom call with James and Jeanne Marie, who helped do a crossing in person. We were together in Crystal Beach, Texas.

It was in October, not quite two years ago. It was right as the baseball playoffs were starting. In the first round it was a one-game sudden-death format. No one had been eliminated yet. So, there was exciting baseball in the air, and our Astros were part of it. That was all some of the context.

That day we did a crossing. We met this nice man, Iron Mike, who was a baseball player. An event in a baseball game sent his life spiraling down for quite a long time. Today we'll start with a prayer. We'll gather the angels and saints to stand guard over us; then we will invite Iron Mike to step up to the mic if he'd like to.

We pray in the name of the Father, the Son, and the Holy Spirit. In the Holy Spirit of the Risen Christ, within the body of Christ, we call on St. Michael the Archangel. Please come and stand guard over us and keep us safe from all who would distract or try to do us harm. We call on Holy Mary our mother, and St. Joseph. We invite St. Dominic and St. Francis, St. James, and St. Joan of Arc. We invite Paulus, Padre Pio, St. Benedict, St. Maximilian Kolbe, and St. Rosa of Lima. I'd like to invite the members of our family lines who are in the light, even ones who died before we were born. If you'd like to be with us, gather round.

In this story, there were what were referred to as "baseball people," people who just had a love of baseball. We also had grandstands that were full of people who had tried to help Iron Mike along the way. We had Lou Gehrig and my own mother, Miriam. All of you, we'd like to invite you to be present and take part in any way you'd like. Would you like to add to that prayer, guys?

James: Thanks. Saints Peter and Paul, and St. Terese, the Little Flower.

Nathan: We ask, Holy Spirit, for gracious listening, discernment, speech, and direction. Help us to be in the flow of your energetic grace. We pray that the time that we spend together will be in accord with your highest hopes for Iron Mike and for us. We ask all this through Christ our Lord. Amen.

James and Jeanne Marie: Amen.

Nathan: I'm going to pause the recording for just a minute while I'll be still and invite Iron Mike.

(There was a brief pause. Iron Mike emerges.)

Iron Mike: Hello. It's me again. You might be surprised. You only met me that one time, but you heard my story and how much I had chased people away before I died, and even after.

You might think from that, that I was no fun, kept to myself and hardly had anything to say. Well, I wasn't like that before the bad day and I'm not like that anymore. I started being more like my real self than that angry man who had crawled into a hole. So, it didn't take me much to be with you today. He [Father Nathan] did pray to me last night and told me to be ready. So, I was ready. And as soon as he said the word, here I am. Bam! Just like that.

James: Welcome back!

Iron Mike: We may as well go with "Iron Mike." You know, most baseball players had some sort of name they went by, and I'm happy to be Iron Mike. So, what do you want?

James: Well, the question that we have is Father Nathan is writing a book, and he would like your permission to use your story in it.

Iron Mike: You're asking me a yes or no question. And the answer is yes.

If I ever had gotten an award and had to give a speech to receive it, I probably wouldn't have known what to do, you know? And then in the thing that you helped with, there was the most famous baseball speech ever given. That was the context, a reference to poor sick Lou Gehrig, who didn't look poor or sick that day. He said he was the luckiest man alive.

But I did give a little speech that day when we were together. I talked a little bit mostly to apologize to all the people who I put through too much trouble to try to help me.

Now that I'm not pushing everybody away, it feels like I'm like a balloon that you keep blowing into. It expands and expands and expands, and it doesn't pop. It just keeps getting lighter. Anyway, I'm having lots of fun. Baseball was supposed to be fun to begin with, and it was most of the time until the bad day. So anyway, yes is the answer. Put my story in a book if you want.

James: Thank you for that.

Iron Mike: What do you think?

James: I think it'll be a great story and will influence a lot of people.

Jeanne Marie: For Americans, baseball players are heroes.

Iron Mike: Yeah.

Jeanne Marie: I hate that your life turned tragic. But now your life can be something glorious that other people look to for inspiration. In your defeat, maybe others can still look to you for inspiration about how to go on with life amidst tragedy.

Iron Mike: That'd be the hope. You know, they tried everything with me and nothing much worked. Eventually it did, but only after putting people through lots and lots of trouble. Maybe this book, if my story is in it, finds an audience or at least finds a place in somebody's heart and is the thing that does the trick.

One of the things that's been fun for me since I met with you people and did that crossing part, is getting to know his [Father Nathan's] mother. She walked me back to the dugout. Do you remember that?

James and Jeanne Marie: Yes.

Iron Mike: She kind of waved at you. She remembered you both.

Anyway, after that I think they knew that I had had too much loneliness and too much moping. Part of it is work, because some people did start getting to me, but it was always a kind of a labor to let them in and hope that I could change or that maybe I could be forgiven.

They wanted me to have some fun. And what do baseball guys do for fun? We play baseball!

Jeanne Marie: <laugh>. There you go!

Iron Mike: You know how at ballparks, sometimes they'd create some reason for fans to not just be in the stands. I think sometimes now they have a day where you can bring your dog to the park, or you can have your children run the bases or throw out the first pitch. Those things get people into the action somehow.

It's a little like that here except way more. I've been at some things where, oh my God, you never know who's going to show up because the invitation list is not restricted. It's anybody who cares.

So anyway, I've had baseball fun, and other kinds of fun too. And then there's Mr. Gehrig. I can't call him Lou. He hung with me for a while just to make sure I was okay. He said, "If you want me to introduce you around, I'd be happy to. If there are any baseball heroes you want to meet, I know most of them. I could introduce you around if you wanted that."

I've learned a little bit about coming back here to be with you. It's not something that everybody knows how to do right away. I knew how to do it when I was called by you folks, but they've said, "Would you like to go to a game now? Would you like to see some of the cool new stadiums?" So, I've done a little bit of that.

At some point I will visit the little child that died, and the parents. It hasn't happened yet, but my helpers said, "It's so close to happening that let's think of it as on the calendar, the way that you might have done that when you were living inside of time." They said, "You don't even need to anticipate that it will be some big tearful scene. Nobody's mad at you and everybody's whole. You had a sad life and they had sadness in their lives." So, one of these days, we'll see each other and that'll be a fine time. It just hasn't happened yet.

Jeanne Marie: Okay. You're not afraid about meeting this child?

Iron Mike: I would've been earlier. But not now. First, I had to lighten up, to move away from the idea that I had killed anybody.

Jeanne Marie: Okay, then you've come a long way.

Iron Mike: It was a long way that took too long to travel, but I got here. Everybody keeps living and nobody has to be defined by the way they died, or the emotions that surrounded it. Think of it as starting over or just moving on.

You know, ball players and other famous people will sometimes go to a hospital to visit sick children? They put me to work doing a little bit of that. Teams often had an advance man who somehow promoted them. Somebody would write a little script for the radio guy or for the newspaper that made your coming to town as the opponent interesting to people.

"You might not know this about the team that we're about to play, but here's something." They would pique peoples' interest. And now they do that for me.

I have something like a little advance team here that says, "If you haven't heard of Iron Mike, here's what you've missed!" Sometimes they arrange for me to be at some event. It's almost like they built a new supermarket and they cut a ribbon in front of it. <laugh>. They create some little excuse for people to be together, excited about something. Well, now I'm one of these guys that shows up to cut a ribbon! I'm some little local somebody who can lend some fun to something.

Jeanne Marie: Well, that won't be very far off the mark with you starring in Father Nathan's new book!

James: You also mentioned when you were crossing over that there were children around you couldn't disappoint.

Iron Mike: Oh, of course. Here there are kids who have died more recently. They have been through injuries or awful cancers that sometimes happen to little children. Sometimes I meet ones who have died of it. I do that because I can. I don't really look at it as payback anymore because that's not helpful for me.

They said, "You didn't have to pay back anybody to begin with. You thought you owed the world a debt you could never repay."

That's still part of my story. I had deep sadness around making a kid die. So now I help kids who are new arrivals. Some of them like baseball. I might not be able to fix all their troubles right this minute, but that doesn't mean I can't show up and try to help.

I knew how to do some things. I could juggle <laugh>. There could be a lot of time between innings or during rain delays. I could juggle baseballs. We always had bubble gum and I could blow big bubbles. Anyway, I like being around kids; I never had any of my own. So sometimes over here when there are kids that could use a little bit of cheering up, I help with that.

Nothing big. I'm just a man enjoying his life after a long time of not enjoying it.

I think I've finished what I've got to say, unless you have any other questions for me. I know this conversation might show up in the book, too.

Oh, he [Father Nathan] is wondering about his mother. He's pretty sure she won't talk because it's just not her way. But I'm going to be still for just a second, just in case she wants to.

(There was a brief pause.)

She doesn't want to talk. She's saying she's happy for the two of you. She knows that you're old enough now to retire if you want to, and that she hopes that you have fun doing whatever you want to do with this part of your life.

Nathan: This is Nathan talking now. That didn't turn out to be the most fun part for her and my dad because he got sick. She's not talking through my voice but she's talking next to me. She'll be at the game tonight. The Astros are playing the Rockies in Colorado. She remembers taking me to Denver when I was a novice. They drove me to Denver to drop me off there when I was first joining the Dominican Order. But that was before Denver had a baseball team.

She's going to the game tonight. If she wants to, she can be with Astro players who have already passed. She can be in something like luxury suites, a skybox <laugh>!

Jeanne Marie: She's a VIP!

Nathan: Exactly. She said it's great fun. There are lots of people who love baseball and love the Astros. So, I'll be listening tonight, and she'll be at the game. That's what she said.

All right, well I guess we're done. We got Iron Mike's permission. Thanks for your good help.

||||||||||||||||||||||||||||||||||||||||||||||||||||||||||||||||||||||||||||||||||||||||||||||||||||||||||||||||||||||||||||||||||||||||||||||||||||||||||||||||||||||||||||||||||||||||||

Some people stay sad for a long time. But eternity's a really long time.

Sometimes ballplayers get hurt. They go on what's called "the injured reserve list." They stay there until they're healthy again. Then, when they're ready, they get back in the game.

After the bad day, Iron Mike's thoughts went dark, and they stayed that way. And he was stubborn about it. Sometimes people will take a dark emotion and cling to it. Iron Mike deceived himself that this was the only way he could be: he could only live in the dark here and hereafter.

He told us that there wasn't any single word or deed that caused him to change his mind. But he did quote a little kid who died playing baseball, remember? "Well, Mister, I didn't know what to do after I died playing baseball, and I was mad, but then I changed my mind." That childlike simplicity was a way out of the darkness. Iron Mike would need to stop digging and simply change his mind.

Then he had to one more simple thing that had eluded him for so long: he had to tell the truth. He was escorted onto the field by little children and spoke that truth into a microphone.

Do you remember the last two words of the speech that set Iron Mike free? He shouted with joy, "Play ball!" He didn't run off the field that day. My Mom walked him back to the dugout.

Baseball is very proud of its traditions. A favorite one is the seventh inning stretch. At the end of the top half of the inning all the fans stand. They've been sitting for so long by now. Before the home team comes up to bat, they stand up and stretch. Together they sing, "Take me Out to the Ballgame."

Sometimes by then the home team is behind, maybe even hopelessly so. But the lyrics insist,

"For it's root, root, root for the home team. If they don't win, it's a shame. For it's one, two, three strikes you're out, at the old ballgame."

When your team is losing in the bottom of the ninth, fans can still hope for a come-from-behind win. A three-run walk-off home run would be just the ticket. That's what Iron Mike provided that day just before the tragic event that broke his heart.

But he made it clear to us that he now has a lot going on. He is living his own come-from-behind story. He's in the early innings of a new and happy life that includes helping little kids. And he's even become an afterlife tourist attraction! Imagine that!

Well, done, Iron Mike. You've done it. You're back in the game!

Chapter Seven

Sylvia, Who Was Grieving Her Husband and Daughter, and Angel Amalie

Challenge: Crushing Grief
Value: Humor

Three Explanations:
Truth as the Ticket to Higher Realms
"We can choose to have new past experiences."
Advice: Don't let the worst thing define you.

Sylvia's life went dark the day her husband and their only child were killed. She trudged through the rest of it, then got sick and died young. She describes all of it with poignant humor, first dark, and now, light.

||||||||||||||||||||||||||||||||||||||||||||||||||||||||||||||||||||||||||||||||||||||||||||||||||||||||||||||||||||||||||||||||||||||||||||

Nathan: I am Nathan. Today is December 7th, 2022. I am in Scottsdale, Arizona with Lisa. We're about to assist someone who brought a story during the night of October 27th, 2022. Here's that story as I received it and wrote it in my journal.

I awoke in the night in an unfamiliar house. I got up to use the bathroom. A Natalie Cole record was playing on a turntable. It was a sad song that never stopped. I wondered how it could keep going on and on. I heard a little girl crying, "Mama, mama." I awoke.

I'm pausing the recording to go into quiet prayer. We've already done our protective prayer, inviting the angels and saints to surround us. We'll be still and invite conversation with the person who brought this story and perhaps their guardian.

I think this angel is using the name Amalie. She presents as female. Her voice will be the next voice you hear.

(Angel Amalie emerges.)

Angel Amalie: And this is she. I'm taking a moment to conform my wavelength to his.

He is a little quiet, maybe a little more tired than normal. His energetic signature reflects that. I'm just conforming mine to his so that we can do this well.

It's so gracious of you to make yourself available for this work, both this part of it and the other things you do.

You know the people who come into this line all have a trauma story; all have healing to do. There are teams of us who have a role to play. You're part of that team. Today's work involves the crossing of one person, not a group.

As you know, we would not have been in this line were there not …what does he call it…a vetting process?

Lisa: Yes.

Angel Amalie: We are quite confident that the person at the center of this story is equipped to do the crossing, or the elevation, however you want to think of it…the movement that we hope will occur today.

Nathan: Her name is Sylvia.

Sylvia: I'm glad you're helping me because my life came to a tragic end. But they've been helping me put some of that to rest and contextualize it. Part of it has been the idea that "time heals all wounds." Even though we're not operating in clock time, still, there's sequence and there's some sense of distance from those events that enters in.

The help I've gotten has prepared me for this day. There'll be a movement from a therapeutic realm to a world beyond that. You're helping with that today.

Lisa: We're glad to help.

Sylvia: Thank you. I'm going to be still and settle in a bit with him.

He's wondering **how** these events flow together, waking from sleep, hearing Natalie Cole on a turntable, a sad song that repeated, and then the sound of a child's voice calling for its mama.

It's up to me to tell a coherent story that links these things.

I haven't done this before, linking my thoughts with another person's consciousness. It's interesting how it **works**. Well, I am the person who brought the story. I am the narrator, if you will, the person waking from sleep, just using the restroom in the night, hearing the song playing. The song is "Unforgettable." Do you know this song?

Lisa: I do.

Sylvia: "*How the thought of you does things to me. Never before has someone been more unforgettable…though near or far. That's what you are. The thought of you does things to me.*"

I had been married and had a young daughter. I'm one of those who are unusual in this modality of yours. I didn't die suddenly. This story is not about my sudden death. It's about the sudden death of my husband and daughter in the same event. A car crash.

We were only three. My husband and I had one daughter who was not yet two years old when they were in a fatal automobile accident. My life went from my marriage and raising a small child to having no one in the house but me. The silence of it was the hardest part, although, I don't know, there were so many hard parts. But the silence of it…going from a household that was bustling to only hearing the refrigerator go on and off, or the air, or the heat, or the little creaking sounds that buildings make. I felt like I was living in a haunted house.

It was my home. I didn't want to move out of it because it had memories. Other people said, "Maybe you should make a fresh start somewhere else." But I was in no position to walk away from the place where I had been so happy and brought a child home.

Of all the ways a person can grieve an event, I felt trapped. There's the idea that there's no place like home, or that one's home base or home turf is supposed to be the place of comfort. I felt I didn't have a good option. I was miserable in it and felt I would've been miserable leaving it. The scene I showed him in the dream was about waking up in the night. That was the worst because I knew that I wouldn't fall back to sleep easily. A 2 a.m. trip to the bathroom that might once have been momentary on the way back to sleep now became an ordeal. "Now I'm going to toss and turn and wake up tired." That's when I would hear the voice of my child in my head.

It wasn't really that the house was haunted. I didn't really hear an external voice crying out the way one might hear some ghost. It wasn't that. It was just my own imagination running away and causing me pain.

Lisa: I'm so sorry. That must have been devastating.

Sylvia: Well, it was. Naturally I wasn't the only person to grieve those losses. His parents were still living; they were elderly, but they were still living. We had a circle of extended family, friends, and coworkers. I did receive some great support.

I learned that being the survivor of an event like that, there could be extra isolation. People were so ill-at-ease around me because they didn't know what to say. They would keep their distance. Suddenly single people often find themselves excluded from couples' activities. I lost the capacity for socializing, like hosting a party or something.

My sad house no longer felt like a place to host a party. I wouldn't have wanted to accept an invitation from me. So, I went on for a few years, going through the motions of working so I had a reason to get out of bed. There was life insurance and a settlement because the accident had been caused by another driver. I could pay off the house. Had I wanted to be a lady of leisure, I could have been, but why would I want to do that? I'd have only more of my own somber company. So, I continued to go to work just so I would have a reason to get dressed in the morning.

Lisa: I understand.

Sylvia: I think the light went out of my eyes. At work I kept everything to business only. I did the obligatory Christmas party, but there was no after-work socializing with anyone. I grew lonelier and odder. I created a few little hobbies; I was doing things so that I would have something to say to other people if they dared inquire about what I was doing. "Why, I've taken up needlepoint!"

Why did I want to do that? I didn't really, but it was something that could keep my interest for a while. I felt if I was going to just be watching TV like an idiot, at least I was producing something while I was doing it. I wasn't much of a television watcher, but when there was no one else in the house and nowhere to go, I began to watch more television just because it was a diversion. I'd been a well-educated woman. Just the thought of sitting and watching TV hours on end, I just couldn't bring myself to do it. I thought maybe if I created something while I was doing it, I could legitimize it to myself that I at least produced this thing. I still had a few little gift-giving occasions, so I could say, "Look, it's my new hobby, and here's your thing, <laugh>, whatever it was. I shopped in these craft stores. They had different silly things. There'd be a pattern of a sailboat, and maybe I knew somebody that had a boat. So, I could do that for them. But I was really bored with my own existence.

Lisa: You were trying to do the very best you could to process extreme grief.

Sylvia: Yes. I just never opened myself to a future, which is part of what grief counseling tries to get you to do. Grief naturally takes you into your past, wishing for what you once had. There'd be longing for what you won't ever have. You won't see your daughter's wedding, or you won't have grandchildren.

The very idea of dating again was a non-starter. I wasn't in any condition to try. I couldn't even live in my own heart not to mention share it with anyone else.

The saddest turn of events was getting a diagnosis of uterine cancer and welcoming it. I just thought, "Is this my golden ticket?" Not very many people would look on that diagnosis with some sense of excitement or anticipation. Neither of those really fits; I wasn't excited, but I wasn't devastated, either. I didn't dare tell anybody, "Good news! I've got uterine cancer." But I thought, "Maybe I don't have to live a long life this way."

Lisa: I get it.

Sylvia: The sad song that wouldn't end was my life. <laugh> It was just such a bind, loving my husband and loving my daughter, and then having them both taken away in the same instant. And not wanting to forget them but wishing I could.

Lisa: It sounds like you did the best you could in an awful situation.

Sylvia: Well, it ended up that I did die, as everyone does. I was competently cared for. There were appropriate visits on the part of people who wished me well and wanted to be there for me.

It wasn't utterly lonely. Even in my marriage, I was kind of the driver of a lot of things. I was the organizer, the planner. When we were talking earlier about parties, that's part of what I did well. I figured things out in advance, and then took all the steps to make something look effortless.

I could approach serious illness in that way and make calculated decisions and plans for my care as I would need more of it. I could find competent people who could be durable power of attorney for healthcare and help with getting my bills paid and all those things. I found that easy to do.

The part that was more challenging than I thought was I had not really been a very religious person. I'd had some church life in my childhood that I didn't sustain. My husband really wasn't very interested in that either. We were young and healthy, and we still had our parents. We hadn't even been through any of that, you know? We hadn't lost a parent or a sibling. We hadn't had an up-close experience of death until the very bad day.

But I left the body and discovered, "Oh, my! Yes, there is still me. <laugh>. If there were a doubt before, there's not now, because I still exist."

At the end of my illness, sleep was attractive because my pain was increasing, and unconsciousness was one form of relief from it. But on the other hand, I was unsure about whether we do survive death or not. Do you know that creepy prayer, "If I should die before I wake <laugh>?"

Lisa: Right, right.

Sylvia: I didn't like the idea of dying in my sleep. People make that sound like it is the most peaceful way. But I was like, "If I'm going to die, I want to be alert to it." So, I didn't allow myself to be medicated into sleep. I tried to be as alert as I could. And then when I went out-of-body, it was quite lovely. The pain stopped.

Aesthetics were always important to me. Visuals, sounds, beauty: these were always important to me. And there was beauty right away. There was just the right amount of engagement including that of Amalie. She proved to me that we'd been in relationship for a long time, even though I wasn't aware she existed. It didn't take much. She could tell stories with details of things she couldn't possibly have known had she not been around me the whole time. Isn't that amazing?

Lisa: Yes. That's beautiful.

Sylvia: Well, it was nice because I'd gotten used to putting so little effort into relationships. I had just shut down. Then here comes this person who requires almost no energy from my end, who can engage my heart, make me laugh, make me wonder at things, help me see things from a different point of view and who had a knack for pulling me from a trough of sadness or aloofness.

She could cajole me into engaging with others. She'd bring people around and make me be in the presence of some new person. I would at least have to be polite. Before long, she was coaxing me into reengaging in my life. There was nothing automatic about catapulting out of the body and suddenly being on Cloud Nine or something. First, I needed to commit to my own being.

Lisa: I love how you described that. I love how you described the beauty. You saw beauty.

Sylvia: Yes. Part of it was the absence of conflict. There was no one arguing. There was no sense of undone business. That bothered me a lot. I had gotten sluggish in my work habits because I was so sad so much of the time. Sadness drains away a lot of energy. I would see things that I knew if I were my better self, I would've handled long ago. And yet there it sits undone.

That began to fall away. If I wanted to do a thing, I was on my way to doing it. And I thought, "I remember when I used to be like this."

Lisa: That is a thing of beauty.

Sylvia: Yeah. They were working with me. Not too long ago, I'm still conscious of the passage of time, they said to me, "We want to make you aware of something we think you already know. You're moving beyond what this level is constructed for."

I had needed something like therapy, the way one might receive help relearning to walk or something, or do self-care. They just made me acknowledge that I was capable of doing things that in the recent past I hadn't been able to do.

And that my progress was to be expected. Whatever the universe is, it was not built in such a way that one calamity would have an eternal opportunity to ruin everything.

Lisa: Isn't that a wonderful thing?

Sylvia: Yes. I knew people who had been much more successful in managing their grieving, perhaps even remarrying, or having other children. Some moved on in careers, relocated, and had new stories to tell. And they could laugh again, all of which I never did. So, it's not as though it was a brand-new concept that you really could reengage in a life that has hope and joy.

Those ideas began to enter in. They made me think about how nurses' stations have Santas or little Christmas trees. Those decorations are kind of creepy because they're in a place where everybody's sick <laugh>. Everybody wishes that they weren't here, but we're going to have this little Christmas tree here or that snowman over there.

Amalie has a sense of humor. She said, "If you'd like, we can keep you here on the ward and we can decorate with reindeer. We can watch the seasons pass and we can put up bunnies in springtime. But wouldn't you rather get out of here and go somewhere nicer? We don't need to launch you into something you'll find overwhelming. We know very well that you need to take things slowly, but that doesn't mean you have to be inert. You really can move."

I said, "Okay, then I defer to your wisdom. I will do the thing you propose that I do." Amalie took that as all the permission she needed to say, "I'm going to do the research for you, and I'll propose a plan."

I liked that, you know? I did that with financial advisors and later medical advisors. "Well, you seem competent, so go ahead. Make a plan." She came up with you people, and I'm so glad.

Lisa: Well, me too.

Sylvia: She promised it would not be difficult and it hasn't been. I think something is about to happen that brings this across a finish line of some kind.

Lisa: Yes. You're ready.

Sylvia: I think I'm to be still and anticipate somebody coming or something happening. I don't need to do anything except welcome it and agree to whatever it is.

(There was a brief pause.)

Sylvia: I'm thinking of signs that I've seen before that have different pictures, ones that change. The sign is a picture of something, but it changes and becomes a picture of something else. In the 1950s, it was neon motel signs that moved somehow, you know? Like a sign of a cowboy on a horse that rises and bucks and goes back down.

Lisa: Yes, I understand.

Sylvia: It's my husband and my daughter. I guess they feel like I'm ready for that. The first picture is what they might have looked like on their way out the door that last day. And then the next one is how they've aged. My two-year-old looks like a young lady and my husband looks like a handsome middle-aged man. And then I see them go back to younger times. They're kind of smiling like they're proud of themselves that they can do that. They can become whatever I need them to be.

I think they're trying to show me that if I prefer to start where we left off, we can do that. But I think the implication is, "Let's not stay they're too long <laugh>, because we're not that anymore, and you're not that anymore. Let's move on to the up-to-date version of all of us. We'll catch you up on the intervening time." But anyway, they're showing me that they can be whatever I need them to be. They're trying to do it in a lighthearted way that doesn't make me all weepy.

Lisa: And just the right way for you to receive them.

Sylvia: Yes. We're just going for a walk, that's all.

Lisa: I'm so happy for you!

Sylvia: Well, I am too and grateful to you. I will move along now.

Lisa: Bye.

(They depart.)

Nathan: Glory to the Father, to the Son, and the Holy Spirit, as it was in the beginning is now and will be forever. Amen.

Lisa: That was beautiful. I was hoping it would be her husband and her daughter. It was amazing how that turned out.

|||||||||||||||||||||||||||||||||||||||||||||||||||||||||||||||||||||||||||||||||||||||||||||||||||||||||||||||||||||||||||||||||||||||||||||||||||||||||||||||||||||||||||||||||||||||||||||||||||||||

To share Sylvia's story, we reached out to obtain her permission. Here's how that went.

Nathan: I am Nathan. Today is July 27th, 2023. I am in Laguna Beach, California with my dog friend Toto in my lap. I'm joined on a Zoom call with Lisa and her dog, Daisy. They're in Phoenix.

Today, we hope to talk with Sylvia. Sylvia lost her husband and young daughter in a car crash. A few years later Sylvia also died. Lisa and I assisted with her crossing some time ago. We thought her story could be beneficial to readers. We're getting permissions of people who would allow their stories to be used in an upcoming book. We'll be inviting Sylvia to be with us and to let us know if she would allow her story to be told.

We've said our protective prayers, asking for the presence and protection of the angels and saints. We'd like to speak with Sylvia or any of those who are assisting her.

(There was a brief pause. Sylvia emerges.)

Sylvia: This is Sylvia. This is the second time for me to be inside his imagination and to be with you, Lisa. Lovely to see you again.

Lisa: It is very lovely to be with you again, Sylvia.

Sylvia: You get to be with a more whole version of me than I was able to offer the last time we were together.

Lisa: You were still a delight to meet then.

Sylvia: Father Nathan loves words. He knows that Sylvia means "woods." Just now I showed him a picture of me kind of walking out of the woods. He was thinking of that Broadway show "Into the Woods." Do you know that show with all the nursery rhyme characters? The woods were this place of mystery, sometimes dark danger, and certainly of adventure. I showed him me coming into a bright clearing in the woods where we could talk.

Lisa: That's beautiful.

Sylvia: Even before meeting you when it was proposed to me by my guardian and other helpers that I get in your line to do the crossing that you facilitate, I already was very intrigued by it. And then subsequently, even though there were so many new things to learn about, I didn't want to pass that over as simply a past event. I wanted to delve into it some to ponder and study.

So, I've become something of a student and follower of your work. I have read the other books and have met some of the people who have been in them because they said yes to the question you're asking me today.

Many of them had happy things to say. Readers who had no previous practice of prayer involving people who had died but who were touched by a story did reach out in the ways that they knew how to. Some of your "book people" found themselves helping others across the divide.

I would be honored to be a part of any such thing if that's the way that it flows. Father Nathan reread my story yesterday. He made a list of those who've already "made the cut" to be included in his book, but felt it was short on women's stories. He went back into a message you'd sent recommending my story. He opened that file and reread it. I think the feeling he had right away was, "Yes, this one." It was something of no-brainer. It had elements that he felt would give a roundedness to the lineup of stories.

In recent years, he's been brought into the grieving process of people who found him through the internet. No one's grief needs to be compared with anyone else's but from a distance, someone like me, a young woman early in a marriage with a small child losing husband and child in an instant, that would bring out compassion in even the hardest of hearts.

Maybe that whole awful experience can be put to good use. Maybe people can see, "Well, here's how this one person made it through." I was humbled to hear that you both thought that my story was well told. I don't think of myself as a funny person, and I don't think Father Nathan thinks of himself that way either. But I think he appreciated that I had something of an odd take on my circumstance. Like going to the craft store and finding some little sailboat thing that needs to be filled in with yarn and given as a gift, just as an excuse for watching television; he just liked details like that, and he's a writer.

I've gone back into some of it too. There's a way in which we can relive just about anything we ever want to relive almost like rerunning the tape. I've revisited the conversation that we had together when I made this crossing that you helped with. I do think I expressed myself well; I don't think I would go back in and try to change anything.

Lisa: Yes, I think you're very eloquent. You come across that way. I do agree that I think your struggle with grief will assist others with theirs because you described it so truthfully, and honestly.

Sylvia: I disclosed that I wasn't really a religious person, but I did wonder about an afterlife. It made sense to me that there would be one. I had some hope that, upon my own death, there would be a reunion. It was such a shock seeing them off that day, not knowing I would never see them again. Of course, if you do believe that there is an afterlife and there is the opportunity for reunions, "never again" isn't the same thing as forever. So, I could be something of a spokesperson for non-religious persons. I can explain what opened up for me when my time came. I didn't have to show my religious ID at the gate <laugh>. I wasn't left outside or any such thing.

Lisa: Has your idea of faith changed?

Sylvia: Well, one thing was available to me before, but more now than ever. Whatever the Oneness is or who the One is, surrounds me. Which means I'm in that Presence always. It doesn't have to be thought of as a person on a throne or located in a place where you are not allowed, some holy-of-holies or height-of-heights.

Now that I've done a little upward movement, I guess you could call it, even that's sort of a metaphor…it's like falling in love. You know, as you move into a relationship, which in my case, became a marriage, that didn't happen in a day. It grew, expanded, and deepened. And of course, the very significant downside of that is if you marry a mortal or give birth to one, they can die and leave you heartbroken.

But hearts mend. Ours didn't need a lot of mending. We didn't have complicated interpersonal interactions to get over. We just missed each other.

I mentioned the last time we spoke that when my husband and daughter did show themselves, first it was as they may have looked leaving the house on the day of their deaths. Then almost instantly I saw a version of my husband as a very handsome middle-aged man, and my daughter as a young woman. They told me I could pick either version of them.

Lisa: That must have taken your breath away!

Sylvia: It did. And they enjoyed taking my breath away <laugh>. But it was also nice to know that I didn't have to pick only one option. They said, "We could be that other thing first just to get things started. But we hope you won't choose a long, slow experience of that. You know, you're not who you were that day and we're not who we were that day. We could just be who we are right now if you say the word."

They also said, "By the way, we could reminisce. It doesn't have to be right now. If we wanted to, we could all choose to go back. We could do it as a family. We could choose to have new past experiences or new future ones. But let's mostly be who we are now."

Lisa: That's beautiful. Reminiscing and the beauty of the present, I love that.

Sylvia: There was a valid thing in there. I never got to take my daughter to kindergarten. There were never soccer games or ballet lessons or mother/daughter much of anything. She was just a toddler. I had developed a few relationships with other mothers my age, and then I suddenly became childless. I no longer belonged in mom's groups.

There would've been beauty in that. So, if I feel like I was deprived of something that I would still like to do, we can circle back and include those things.

There's a freedom in it. Being kind to each other on these levels is part of how one moves from level to level. There are not bouncers at the doors forbidding you to come in because you're unworthy. It's just that the next level can only accommodate those who are well disposed to what it affords. You don't stay back as a punishment. You just stay at the most appropriate place for your development.

Lisa: And what helps you prepare for the next level?

Sylvia: More than anything: Truth. Shedding anything that is untrue. Part of what I needed to shed was my reticence to reengage. Life was so painful. I opted to spend too much time alone with my pain. So, I needed to look at the truth of that and say, "Well, there was a reason for that, but the reason no longer pertains. I'm not a widow and I'm not childless anymore <laugh>. I'm with the man I married and I'm with my daughter. We're choosing to be together, even though we're also aware that we could all go different directions and have other adventures too, if we please. But for right now, we'd like to be a unit because we missed being that. So, for right now, where one of us goes, the other two go.

Lisa: It's a beautiful freedom that you've described.

Sylvia: Well, death already did us part where marriage is concerned, <laugh>. We don't need to do a ceremony that pledges undying love and presence to one another. We can just love and enjoy each other. One thing at this level is that there are not pouty responses to other people's choices.

Lisa: Oh?

Sylvia: Like, "What do you mean you want to go without me?" Right? <laugh>. "Don't you love me anymore?" You know, <laugh>, those kinds of things. My helpers ran me through a list. It was simple. I understood that I would not choose any of these behaviors, and they said, "Well, should you want to, you would be clinging to a level below the one that you're being offered." They just wanted me to know the physics of how things work. The fact that you can ascend doesn't mean that those at the prior level are "less than." It's just that everyone moves at the pace they choose.

We don't always understand that we've made choices; maybe they were subconscious or barely conscious. Sometimes we just get into patterns or habits that we say we've chosen. Although that really doesn't stand up too well under observation. Did you really choose that, or didn't you kind of drift into it?

Lisa: Yes, yes! It sounds like you have helpers who guide and who really foster growth.

Sylvia: Of all kinds. Some of them are great wise figures with huge expertise. Right alongside them is some little somebody that they thought has a story to tell and a gift to offer. And like many, I've been brought into some of that helping work already.

And I don't mind it. I did a little bit of grief support work. There are parts of it that I didn't care for at all. Father Nathan and I have this in common: neither one of us thinks of ourselves as a shoulder to cry on. I didn't tolerate girlfriends that wanted that from me. Most of them got that message. If you need to cry about a boyfriend or broken-hearted this-or-that, I'll be happy to talk you through rational thinking. But I'm not going to commiserate.

I brought that with me. When people are in some sort of quandary here, I can be brought in to say, "Well, you can do this, or that, or that. And maybe I have a story that corresponds. I'm not an expert, but I'm somebody who has something to offer."

Lisa: It sounds like you are using the gifts of who you are and what you were given and brought forward the best of that.

Sylvia: One thing that I'm enjoying here is that however long I might have lived, I would always have been the woman whose husband and child died in a car crash when she was young. That would always have been the headline of my story.

Here nobody really cares! <laugh> When you're in a place where everyone has died already how anyone died is not very interesting. We are more than how we died.

How you or anybody died comes up and there's some recognition of commonality. "I knew somebody who went through something like what you've just described. You died in the crash of a car that left the roadway? I was once in a car, although it stayed on the road. <laugh>."

Whatever. I'm no longer that tragic woman. I don't feel like when I enter a room that I bring with me a legacy of sadness.

Lisa: I'm so glad to hear that. It sounds like you're meeting a lot of people, and you're ready to do many different things.

Sylvia: Yes, which is a bit surprising because earlier I wouldn't have called myself ready for much of anything. I approached just about everything with caution and circumspection. But that's only a part of me. And that part of me had its turn. It had its time, and now it can go away <laugh>. Now, the joyful, hopeful me is on full display.

Lisa: It sounds like you're flourishing.

Sylvia: I think so. I haven't yet found something like a purpose, vocation, or career. That's probably coming. I really liked purposeful activity. The job that I had after the accident, its main purpose became getting me out of bed. I didn't have much light and energy to give to what I was doing; it was my routine. I mean, I earned my paycheck, and I didn't short my employer. But they never knew the full-on creative force I've might have been.

It wasn't a job that demanded a lot of creativity. It had a lot of aspects to it that were rote and repetitive. That probably helped because I knew from one day to the next pretty much what I was doing, I didn't have to leave the house ready to tackle a new challenge. I knew I was going to be dealing with the same thing I was dealing with yesterday. I don't have to do that anymore. Now I'm fun to be around and excited about what I might do next. And I'm happy that maybe I'll become part of this circle of people who'll be included in your new book.

Lisa: We're so glad that you're agreeing to take part. I can't wait to see what new adventures open up for you. And I'm so grateful to talk with you again.

Sylvia: I'm almost to the point of signing off. I'm thinking of trying to be explicit for a reader: How might my story help you?

I would say don't let the worst thing that's happened to you define you. You're always more than any circumstances that befell you. You're always more than that.

And for people who had doubt or some lack of certitude about the universe, how it got here and what its purpose is, God, fate, afterlife, and all those things…you don't have to be anything that you're not. You don't have to become something else or take on somebody else's belief system. If you'll just try to live simply, truthfully, and kindly, those larger things work themselves out.

Lisa: Thank you.

Sylvia: I hope that for conventionally religious people, that doesn't sound blasphemous. I'm just telling my truth. Nobody asked me to recite creeds or prove that I was the right kind. You've had some of these stories where people died because of religious violence. Thanks be to God —and now I know there is a God — <laugh>, that I didn't have to wallow in any of that. I steered clear of that while I was there, and I don't have to do that while I'm here either. I can just enjoy the presence of all that's good all the time, in me and around me.

I think with that, I will stop.

Lisa: Thank you for that lesson.

Sylvia: I wasn't trying to teach a lesson <laugh>! On the surface of it, I was a woman still in her twenties who lost her husband and child all at once. And then got uterine cancer while still young and died of it. Who would sign up for that? But I'm a really happy person! Go figure!

Lisa: It shows. It absolutely shows.

Sylvia: Alright, well I'll leave it at that. You've got the permission you needed. If my story is included in a book, I'll be happy to be a part of the team. I understand that all the ones who've said yes to it so far think of themselves as team members.

Lisa: It's been wonderful to speak with you again, Sylvia. Many blessings to you and your family.

Sylvia: God bless you, and bye now.

(Sylvia departs.)

Nathan: This is Nathan. Glory be to the Father, to the Son, and to the Holy Spirit, as it was in the beginning, is now, and will be forever.

Lisa: Amen.

I won't try to explain Sylvia's explanations, but only highlight them.

She mentions truth as the determinant of one's afterlife level. We can all expand and ascend to the degree we allow in truth.

"We can have new past experiences." As a counselor I've helped people reframe unhappy past experiences to live peacefully and freely, but Sylvia's talking about more than that. What new past experiences would you like to have?

And finally: "Don't let the worst thing define you." Sylvia did that long enough. "But now I'm a really happy person! Go figure!"

Chapter Eight

Samuel the Clothier

Challenge: Underestimation Containing the Falsehood "I'm not Good Enough"
Value: Receptivity to Change

Three Explanations:
Helping Others Realize and Accentuate Their Beauty
Afterlife Spaces: Stained-Glass Boundaries or Flowing Watercolors
Your Next Role, "Best Supporting Actor"

Have you ever been a part of a heart-to-heart conversation? Maybe it was with a dear friend or as part of a deepening relationship. It could have been a surprising encounter with a stranger on a plane. Maybe it flowed within a conducive setting: a campfire late at night, or over a glass of wine.

Sometimes for me as a priest, these conversations have been an outgrowth of a counseling session or a confession. It's a beautiful thing when "heart speaks to heart." That phrase is the motto of John Henry Cardinal Newman, the patron saint of Catholic campus ministry centers. I've lived most of my ministerial life in such places.

In this chapter, my new friend, Samuel and I are inviting you to listen in on a heartfelt conversation that accompanied his afterlife movement. Listen to him describe his gentle heart with simple clarity. Samuel strikes me as a man who is very much at home in his own skin. Which is saying a lot, because the kind of skin he inhabited was enough to have him rejected in many circles. By way of introduction, he told us, "I was homosexual at a time when it would've been a great disgrace for that to be known."

Samuel was not a religious man. Whatever his afterlife location might be, he was unsure how welcome he would be there. When he presented himself to me in a dream, there was no spatial context. We weren't in a specific place. We were just two people talking. Samuel explains himself so well that I thought you might like to meet him.

In the session that follows, you'll hear from my own guardian angel Phillip James, and from Samuel's guardian, Amos. They are talking through me with my prayer partner, Michael.

||||||||||||||||||||||||||||||||||||||||||||||||||||||||||||||||||||||||||||||||||||||||||||||||||||||||||||||||||||||||||||||||||||||||||||||||||||||||||||||||||||||||||||||||||||||||

Nathan: I am Nathan. Today is August 1st, 2022. I'm in San Diego on a Zoom call with Michael, who is in Pennsylvania. We will be assisting a person who brought a dream story on July 25th, 2022. We've said our protective prayers asking the presence and support of the angels and saints. We've asked the Holy Spirit for gracious listening, discernment, speech, and direction.

This is the very short scene that I received on July 25th:

I was standing talking with a well-dressed and well-groomed older gentleman. Suddenly he was stricken and fell to the ground. I heard the word "clothier." I awoke.

So that's the whole of it. There was no indication of violence, although there could have been. I got only what I just shared with you. We were in a room or some surroundings without anything else in it. It was just the two of us, standing near each other. I don't know what we were talking about. He fell to the ground, and I heard the word "clothier."

I'm going to pause the recording, go into deeper prayer.

I've spent a little more time than normal in prayer. There's some ambient sound around me that's distracting me. I can feel the presence of a guardian. I'm inviting him to come and be with us and possibly give us a little background information that might facilitate our work today.

My guardian is going to come through first. He thinks maybe if he just gets things started, it will make the rest of it easier. So, you'll be hearing from Philip James.

(Father Nathan's guardian, Phillip James of the Line of Michael, emerges.)

Philip James: I don't normally use his voice. I'm assisting you in prayer always, but today it just seemed that maybe I could help get this thing moving.

Michael: Welcome, Philip James.

||||||||||||||||||||||||||||||||||||||||||||||||||||||||||||||||||||||||||||||||||||||||||||||||||||||||||||||||||||||||||||||||||

My guardian angel Philip James, PJ, is a friend of my heart. Today he was my technical assistant when noise from outside my office caused me to lose focus. He suggested within me, "Try putting on the headset. It'll cancel out the noise and help you do your work."

It did work. I could now feel and hear the approach of the guardian angel of the man we'd be helping.

||||||||||||||||||||||||||||||||||||||||||||||||||||||||||||||||||||||||||||||||||||||||||||||||||||||||||||||||||||||||||||||||||

Nathan: This angel wants to be known as Amos, A-M-O-S.

(Angel Amos emerges.)

Angel Amos: Good morning, Michael.

Michael: Hello.

Angel Amos: My role is familiar to you: to help the one in my care see how easily this is accomplished. Except that today it has not been easy, but now we're where we need to be. The one whom I assist can see that all we need is a bit of patience. You'll find him well-spoken, well-comported, and well-composed. His death was a sudden jolt to what was a very ordered, systematic way of being. The word comportment, I think, is one that describes behavior, but it has the resonance of someone who had a kind of stately bearing or sense of conduct. That was characteristic of him and still is because he's still himself.

I think he's ready to speak for himself. I will slide aside and be with Phillip James and the others whom you invited.

(Angel Amos slides aside. The man emerges.)

Man: Hello. I am now in the voice. You are Michael?

Michael: Yes. Welcome.

Man: Father Nathan is allowing me to be in his imagination and his voice. He is imagining a man called Sebastian Cabot. Do you know that actor?

Michael: Yes. He was portly...

Man: Portly! There's a certain category of the language, like the word comportment... there are words that have a kind of antiquity, stateliness, or class about them. In his [Father Nathan's] mind, this character actor, Sebastian Cabot, always played a portly gentleman. I think there was a television show when he was a child, where he played the butler of a wealthy man who was raising some orphaned children [ed. note: the show was "Family Affair."] As is often the case with character actors, once they have become The Butler, they stay The Butler from one job to the next.

I styled myself after that category as a young man. It's not pertinent to this story, but I was homosexual at a time when it would've been a great disgrace for that to be known.

It looked like there was one way of being a man in the world where I could be manly in a way that was socially accepted. I could be a clothier of men's wear.

I had taste for finer things. I wasn't raised around finery, but once I was able to go into the world and be a version of myself that I chose, I did like line and shape and color. The way a man dressed caught my eye for good or ill. So, I thought, "Well, there are people who make a living in the world helping men look their best. I could do that without giving away anything about myself that I want to be private."

Michael: I understand.

Man: I found my way into places where I might sell nice men's clothes. I could recommend tailoring and grooming products. I was always able to stay employed in that line.

I had a life that was difficult, but I made accommodations. I thought of the way that a garment, even a very fine garment, needs to be tailored to the body that it's going to clothe. There were aspects of my life that I wish were not as they were, but if they were tailored properly, my life could be pleasant.

It gave me pleasure to send a customer out the door with a positive sense of their own attractiveness and bearing. Clothes could sometimes make the man and give him confidence. Oftentimes people sought out clothing for occasions when they wanted to look their best.

Michael: Right.

Man: I was known as Sam or Sammy when I was growing up. I became Samuel as an adult because I thought it had stateliness and bearing which was all a part of the package, the way

I presented myself.

In the dream, I showed Father Nathan very little, other than the two of us talking with no sense of the surroundings of where we might have been. This was a reflection of where I came upon leaving my body. I wasn't sure about all of this. I wasn't a religious man. I didn't pay very much attention to what an afterlife might be and wondered if I would be welcome in it. I think I mostly created a neutral afterlife space.

I thought of it in terms of my chosen career. There would be something like a mannequin. There would be a beginning point. There might be a way of building from the bottom up starting with something neutral.

When a customer came in, if they allowed me to, I would say, "Would you like me to give you an assessment of your strengths and weaknesses in terms of your appearance?

I would start with positive traits and say, "You have very piercing green eyes. Anything that is in a shade of green will lead people toward better eye contact with you."

I would explain things like this and bring them along. I'd try to help them develop a sense of style that started with who they were. They weren't putting on a costume as though they were pretending to be someone whom they weren't. I'd start with something of a blank slate and then talk about a few key principles that might accentuate who they are and how they might appear.

When I got here, I felt I was something of a dressmaker's dummy. I didn't know what this place would be and whether it would welcome me because I was used to being unwelcome in certain circles and would've been unwelcome in even more had they known more about me than I allowed them to know. Here, I wasn't sure if anything could be concealed.

I was led to understand, "You can move at the pace you choose. You choose who knows what about you, but you can't tell lies if you want to stay here. And besides, you have believed some lies about yourself that need to be addressed."

The scene I presented in his dream lacked any detail, because I chose it to appear that way.

As I moved along, I made, or they helped me make, progress. They mirrored the systematic way that I helped a man who had just presented himself at the door all the way through the process of making him look and feel his very best without inauthenticity.

Michael: Right.

Samuel: I understand that I'm a little different than many people whom you assist in this way, in that I didn't die a violent death. Although I'm like others in that I died a sudden death.

I showed him…he used the word "stricken." I was never a picture of health. I was from a family line where… you called it "portly." Stocky might be another description. In our family line, stockiness came with cholesterol issues and diabetes. Ours was not a robustly healthy gene pool.

I had health issues that compounded as I got older. Perhaps mercifully I left without a lot of decrepitude. I was still upright and could tend to my own hygiene. I had the kind of work where one didn't need to retire from it completely. I could fill in when there were illnesses. I was respected as someone who'd had a long career and might possess knowledge that could benefit younger people, so I could help train others.

I'm using a lot of words to tell a short story.

I was at work when suddenly something popped. Whatever it was, something in my heart or circulation just broke. And off I went!

Michael: Did you see your guardian immediately after parting?

Samuel: I did. He presented himself as something like a grateful long-term customer. There were some men like lawyers or stockbrokers, who often got hired based on their appearance, so they needed to look successful. I had some customers who never bought clothes anywhere but from me; they had the means and they only bought things of quality. They would contact me, make an appointment, and spend the better part of a day updating their wardrobe.

My guardian presented himself as someone who had been a long-term client who was grateful for my services. He bolstered me by making me feel as though I could still have an impact. I wasn't just in new surroundings that would act upon me. Somehow, I could act upon them.

I wasn't all alone. I was with a client. There were some with whom I could share a little bit of personal life, like how I spent a holiday or something. We might at least make friendly conversation. He was able to do a bit of that.

Then one day he said, "You know, I would like to ask you if you would see me as I truly am." He did that in a disarming, trusting way. And I said, 'Well, of course I would."

At that, he manifested his…lightness. He let his human form change into the light being that he is by nature when he doesn't need to appear to be something else.

Then I knew I was in the presence of something quite different and awesome because it had only goodness and beauty in it. It was a beauty beyond anything I had ever seen or imagined, even though I devoted my life to what I thought was graceful appearance.

He let me see that for a moment. Then he said, "Now take a good look because I'm going to transform back to the way you're used to seeing me." He did something of a pirouette. He turned around and said, "See the whole of me as I come back to the way that you're accustomed to seeing me." That was quite a lot to take in.

He asked, "What did you see?" I said, "I saw beauty beyond anything I've ever seen before." Then he said, "Would you step over to this mirror?"

I was used to fitting rooms that had three mirrors. They were three different panes at different angles where a man could glance this and that way and see more of himself.

He had me look at myself and said, "For a moment, it will be like magic. You will see yourself as you have never seen yourself before, but as you truly are. Are you ready for that? Would you allow that? Would you receive it?"

I said I would. So, in a blaze of glory, I saw myself as nothing except goodness, a likeness of beauty that was true and unassailable, beyond the opinion of anyone who would like to think negatively of me.

He said, "Take a turn. Look all the way around. We'll do for you what we just did for me. You will go back to the way you're accustomed to seeing yourself, but I want you to go back differently than you came in, the same way that people came into your presence into your store and left differently without anything of fraud or concealment. You helped them leave differently than they came in: knowing themselves as beautiful, handsome."

Then, I did go back to being what I had been earlier. He said, "Do you understand that what you just saw is the true or deeper version of you that was always there?" I said, "Yes, I believe it because I've seen it. And I know it is true."

So, he said, "Well, then, you've learned all that this level has to teach you."

Michael: What a beautiful, pertinent story. In all the work that I've done with Father Nathan, this is the first time I have heard the description given of a soul being shown inherently how beautiful it is. Thank you very much for sharing. It was beautiful.

Samuel: It was, and it was fast. I didn't have to do some long, slow process. I was just given a grace. There were times when a person came into the shop and I would look at them and then a thought would come into my head, an inspiration: "Wait, just a second! I think I have something in the back."

And I would be almost led to a certain box or a certain hanger and come out with a thing that fit like a glove that looked like it was tailored. Sometimes it was delightful because tailoring was an added expense. Sometimes there were men for whom this might be the only time in their life that they'd ever be with someone like me; they didn't have much money to spend. It would be a great joy to outfit someone in the thing that looked like it was made for them! I could tell them: "You look very fine!" Anyway, I don't need to stay here any longer because I've been told it's time to go elsewhere.

As a little Catholic child, I was taught that most of us, upon our deaths, would go to purgatory, a place where we could get cleaned up so that we would look our best before entering into God's presence in heaven. Going from dirty to clean is one metaphor; another might be going from blurry to clearly focused.

Samuel told us how he was shown a version of his inherent beauty.

"Do you understand that what you just saw is the true or deeper version of you that was always there?" I said, "Yes, I believe it because I've seen it. And I know it is true."

It was clear that our work was almost done.

||||||||||||||||||||||||||||||||||||||||||||||||||||||||||||||||||||||||||||||||||||||||||||||||||||||||||||||||||||||||||||||||||||||||||||||||||||||||||||||||

Michael: Is it possible that Sebastian Cabot will be accompanying you to your next level?

Samuel: I never thought of that. I don't know the first thing about the man, other than the image that's in Father Nathan's head. I hadn't thought of him, but let's hang on just a moment. I must be still. That might be one of several options.

(There was a brief pause.)

Nathan: This is Nathan. There's another man, a different television actor, who would like to speak. He will be the guide today.

(Raymond emerges.)

Raymond: I played many roles. It was my occupation to move into another character and become that character. I'm not Sebastian Cabot. I'm Raymond. You might have known me as "Perry Mason" or "Ironsides."

Michael: Raymond Burr!

Raymond Burr: Yes. I belonged to the category that this man had in his imagination. I was portly, but I wore tailored suits. I was affable and warm with a kind of vague sexuality.

I've never done this. And I'm…I'm still marveling at it.

As the character Perry Mason, I had my devoted secretary, Della. But there was never any indication of anything sexual between our characters. Of course, the stories were all given us by the author. That author had published many books in that brand. But I slid into that character very well.

I also was a homosexual man. I was secretly partnered. It was Hollywood. I was in the television end of it, but still much of it was done in Southern California. There was widespread knowledge that many people in the industry were, in fact, gay.

I did what I could to maintain a career, which would not have gotten anywhere were I known to be homosexual. I moved in the direction that this gentleman you're working with today did, of being this portly gentleman who was authentically gentle without looking effeminate.

Anyway, I knew how to play a role onscreen and off. In my offscreen time, I maintained a slice of my life where I was not playing a role at all. I just made sure to be around people whom I trusted.

I didn't only step into a role when I went before the cameras. I did that as I left the house. But I was determined to be a happy man. And so, I did what I needed to do to be peaceful within and happy and kind. I have been passed from this plane for some time and have never been asked to do this before. But there's the first time for everything.

Michael: Welcome. It's wonderful to have you here to accompany Samuel to his next level.

Raymond Burr: Well, I don't think he needs very much from me at all, and there's probably a lot I could learn from him. But at least for today, he simply needs a bit of transport. I'm not to do anything except, say, "Let's go for a walk."

Michael: Thank you so much. And have a great trip, Samuel.

Samuel and Raymond Burr: Thank you for your help.

(They depart.)

Nathan: This is Nathan. Glory be to the Father, to the Son, and to the Holy Spirit, as it was the beginning, is now, and will be forever. Amen.

Raymond Burr was a big TV star when I was growing up. But did you notice how small his role was in this scene? He even said, "I don't think he needs very much from me at all, and there's probably a lot I could learn from him."

The acting award shows have a category for this: Best Supporting Actor. Raymond had a brief role with few lines, but he played his part perfectly. Raymond, Best Supporting

Actor, take a bow! You arrived just when Samuel needed the support you could provide.

I thought this story was so beautiful and so beautifully told that it seemed like art. I wanted to retell it if I could. So, I asked Michael if he'd be willing to go back into prayer and see if we could get Samuel's permission to share it with you. Michael's wife, Linda, was with us on that call.

Here's how that session went.

––

Nathan: I am Nathan. Today is June 17th, 2023. I'm in Tucson on a Zoom call with Linda and Michael, who are in Pennsylvania. We're about to do a permission call with Samuel the Clothier, whom we met a little less than a year ago. We're going to be asking his permission to use his story in an upcoming book.

I'm going to be still for a moment, invite presence, and see where we go.

(There was a long pause.)

All right. I've been asking quietly. Now, I'm going to ask aloud. Samuel, if you're available, could we speak with you? Would you consider using my voice to talk with us about the possibility of using your story in an upcoming book? The book would be the third in the "Afterlife, Interrupted" series. We're looking for stories where, in helping someone make their ascent or crossing, they did an exceptional job of explaining their circumstances, their sudden passing, or what they've gone through since.

As I remember your story, I think of it as having a lot of light around it. There are so many people who have not been taught their full value and beauty. Your story might help them. We're wondering if you'd let your story be told publicly.

(Samuel emerges quickly.)

Samuel: And here I am. I'm Samuel.

Linda: Welcome, Samuel. So nice to have you join us.

Michael: Samuel, about a year ago when we talked to you, Father's guardian, Philip James, was the first entity to step forward. Is he still around you?

Samuel: Yes. He is never far from Father Nathan. I had a little bit of acquaintance with him after the crossing part. A part of it involves going from here to there.

Often you see us off as though at some transportation hub, the train station, the dock, or the driveway, and we go away. That's fitting because it's at the heart of why you do what you do. You're helping us move from something that seems like a place to another, better place.

Father Nathan has allowed me to see his memories of being an art student. One of his teachers was always trying to get him to lighten up in his artistic work, but Nathan liked precision. His teacher was good at both watercolor abstraction and precision. He was trying to show Nathan that he could do both, but that he first needed to lighten up.

Nathan wanted to do something more like stained glass all the time, where the red stays in its boundaries next to the blue in its boundaries, with thick leaded defining lines. That isn't just about artwork; it's about temperament.

There are things like this at play. It's true that I left a place and moved to another place, but it's more a watercolor than a stained glass. I didn't so much cross an impenetrable boundary as I flowed across like pigment in water when a wet paintbrush glides across porous watercolor paper.

His guardian continued to be with me because he can do either one. He can be a boundaried entity if he wants to. He can take all his beingness and confine it into something like skin. But he also has an aura. He was with me even as we left without needing to be transported.

Michael: Does he want to say hello this morning?

Samuel: I would only know if we asked. I guess you've just asked.

(Guardian PJ emerges.)

Guardian PJ: This is PJ. Phillip James of the line of Michael is my formal name.

Samuel did a nice job of explaining things. I think your lady, the one who had to walk up steps to a plane in one of the books… Clare, I think is her name. [ed. note: Clare's story appears in Book Two, Ch 4.] She explained that to walk up the steps she had to make herself firmer. I will take a moment to do that.

That's one of the aspects of the state of embodiedness that these human souls whom you help must learn that they have.

Nathan was just explaining it. You already have both of those characteristics. You think of yourself as mostly a solid. In his preaching last week, he mentioned for the Feast of the Trinity that he remembered being in a third-grade classroom where the teacher taught students that they were three-quarters water.

The lesson had to do with states of matter, and that they were more liquid than solid. His point was, yes, but at the sub-atomic level, everybody and everything is energy. There's a oneness to all things. There's a distinctiveness about certain things, but the underlying truth is that all is one, good, godly, and made of God.

A thing like water can change its form according to its circumstance and be solid, liquid, or vapor. We do something similar. We have a oneness, where we're a part of all things. I don't exactly leave the room or wave goodbye at the station when one of these crossings occur. I can allow my beingness to stay with Nathan, but also to expand for a while, just to see someone off and maintain presence for a brief time.

Michael: Thank you for that explanation.

Guardian PJ: That's what we did. And that's what I ordinarily do in these crossings.

Today we're at the service of Mr. Samuel. Privately I was hoping that his story might be shared, as it could have an upbuilding or healing impact.

Those of us who are frequently engaged with humans know that one of the pernicious struggles we have with our humans is the misapprehension that they are not right or are incorrectly made. They learn very early to compare themselves unfavorably to others or to some ideal sense of who they ought to be. If that gets too embedded, a great many other sadnesses and evils can follow. One of the deepest sources of human discontent is the false idea: I am not good enough.

Sometimes that can go in directions that engage the loathing of other people. Some of it can be very deeply concealed. If you believe the thought that "I'm not good enough," then others become rivals. "We must get rid of that other kind because they make me feel worse about me. There needs to be somebody beneath me so that I'm not the one on the bottom."

Once we establish that someone's rightful place is beneath us, then we can enslave or insult or any number of things.

Michael: Sure.

Guardian PJ: I had hoped that this story, because it's told in a lighthearted way, might be included in his next book.

That's enough. I think it's time for Samuel to do his own talking. It's nice that you invited me. One day, perhaps we will have lots of eternal time to get better acquainted. But for right now, we are workers in the vineyard with jobs to do.

Michael: Okay. Thank you.

(Guardian PJ slides aside. Samuel re-emerges.)

Afterlife *Interrupted*: Book Three

Samuel: This is **Samuel**. That's the most I've heard him speak. He is a mostly silent, radiant presence. He's quite large and grand, even among his own kind.

Father Nathan was taught many years ago that his church has a language of thrones, dominions, and seraphs: different kinds or orders of angels in a hierarchy of grandeur. All are great by definition, but once that's established, there are distinctions.

Think for example, of birds. Some are peacocks and others are little wrens. They all have their own distinct beauty, but some of them have something large and grand about them. PJ has that characteristic and a simplicity about himself. He pays no attention to his plumage.

Michael: Well, we're not surprised that Father Nathan would attract a guardian of that nature.

Samuel: Or perhaps he needs one that has something extra <laugh>. The work that Father Nathan does can attract trouble. It's not just him or just priests. Almost everyone [who speaks of the afterlife, or a near-death experience] has a story of someone questioning their sanity or their good judgment. Many have family members or people in their circle who don't want to hear it. "Let's talk about sports. Or the weather or anything else." Maybe he needed more of a bouncer angel than another person might. I'm only guessing. I'm out of my depth. Let's talk about men's clothes; then I'll be in my depth.

Michael: Okay.

Samuel: You're asking a simple question: May you use my story or not? And the answer is yes. Do you need to change my name? I only gave a first name anyway, didn't I? I don't think you usually deal in surnames.

Michael: That's right.

Samuel: I don't recall anything about my story disclosing a specific location that would make me any more identifiable. In this work in which you collaborate, should that day come when verification becomes topical, I wouldn't mind being verified. But it's not timely.

It keeps coming up because he's had more success in the past year in making some inroads into academic research circles. That question arises more there than it does in simply spiritual gatherings. Although it comes up there, too. But for the present time that's not our task.

Michael: Okay.

Samuel: As you might recall from my story, my sexuality, once it was clear to me in late adolescence, that it was not a passing thing or some oddity, was something I accepted as my way of being. It's not changeable, although that remains a matter of dispute. You have circles of people who feel like if they have a homosexual young person, that they must send them to some clinic or healer or something, or perhaps beat it out of them. You at least live in a time where some of that cruelty is beginning to be called out and disallowed. I simply chose to keep my sexuality private. Sometimes that's called being closeted. I don't accept that metaphor. I'm not an object like a tennis racket or work boots that might be stored in a closet.

I never felt like I lived my life like some concealed thing. I just thought of it as a matter of personal privacy that everyone is entitled to. We can all disclose or choose not to disclose parts of our lives to other people depending upon our relation to them. I just thought, "This is an aspect of me that I prefer to leave undisclosed."

I also see the benefit of people who have done the hard work of pushing against these norms and saying, "I too can have privacy, but I can live my life out loud and have privacy too <laugh>. I can be out of the closet and have parts of my beingness that are not disclosed to others."

I knew that that was an option. I was alive during the time when some of this was becoming a movement that I could quietly applaud. But that didn't mean I had to take to the barricades. I felt like I could live a quiet life performing a service that I knew to be beneficial to at least a little clientele that found its way to my door. I could live a life of peace. And I could offer…it's from a Christmas song…goodwill toward men. Isn't there a Christmas carol that has that in it?

Linda: There is.

Samuel: I think Father Nathan particularly liked the portion of my crossing that, in his recall, had something to do with being led to looking at myself in a mirror. Do you remember that?

Michael: Yes.

Samuel: I was made to see an expanded, augmented, more beautiful version of myself than I had seen before. It was the part of my work that I think I did describe well, which is why it has stayed in his memory and made me a candidate for inclusion in his book.

I think I had a talent for looking at, but not objectifying, men. It wasn't demeaning but I could do this for a man who was interested in purchasing clothing. I was a clothier.

I was not a discounter. When someone is simply looking for something inexpensive on the rack there's a place for that. But the places where I worked... I'm using the verb tailored, because sometimes we did that. A garment almost fits you perfectly, but if only there were a nip here or a tuck there, it would fit you like a glove. So, I tailored.

I was good at the front end: having a person who was willing to be looked at and willing to have me assess what I thought were their strengths and weaknesses in terms of their physical appearance.

It was never a matter of finding anyone ugly. It was just that most of us have some little part of our body that we wish were shaped a bit differently. I was good at assessing. I'd say, "Tell me, what do you like about your appearance?" We would establish that first. Some people have a very hard time doing that at all. They've never been asked to speak out loud about physical attributes that they thought were attractive or that could be complimented.

But if I could get that out of him, I might hear that he particularly liked his hair. "Well, tell me about what you like about it." Hair is easy because it can be styled in different ways.

Next, I'd try to learn what they didn't like, that they wanted to improve. Sometimes people who are short of stature think of themselves as stumpy and would like to be more elongated. Some of that can be accomplished with good tailoring and the lines and the drape of cloth. I could show them that, and I could explain my thinking, and say, "Let's see what we can do with some simple choices and tailoring." I loved seeing a person stand in front of the mirror and look at themselves and say, "Wow, look at me. I look fine!"

Oftentimes I had clients who were lawyers or businessmen who felt like they needed to project an image of fine tailoring day in and day out. They were fun to work with, and they were really my bread and butter. Those were the clients who paid the bills.

But I also enjoyed the ones who would come in sort of sheepishly, because they'd never been in a store that had the word "clothier" attached to it. It sounds expensive. Maybe they were going to a wedding, or they got a promotion.

I would help them aspire, with their clothing, to something that gave them anticipated joy or advancement of some kind. Which is of course, where you come in. You help people advance. That's why people like me get in your line. We want to advance from one state to the next state.

I think he [Father Nathan] liked the fact that I was put through something similar. I was made to be the one who had to stand back and see himself as beautiful. I was led to continue shedding anything that might have attached itself to me about my body and my embodiedness being ugly, unworthy, or wrong. There were a lot of different ways that persons like me could despise ourselves, and there were people ready to supply more reasons why we should.

Michael: Samuel, what have been doing or learning since we talked to you last?

Samuel: One thing is quite basic. It wanted to see people I hadn't been able to reunite with at the level that I was at when you first met me.

At first, I was in something like a clinic, a healing place. It conforms well to his Catholic childhood idea of purgatory as this place of cleansing or primping, preparing oneself to be in the grander presence of God.

The simple thing is I just chose to go back. I was older at the time of my passing, and there were people I hadn't seen in 50 years. I just wanted to reconnect. At times that involved a little bit of what you might call time travel: getting to know earlier versions of a person you knew in this lifetime.

I know many people have lots of childhood obstacles to overcome, with family histories of drunkenness, abuse, poverty, wars, and such. But I had a golden childhood. I was raised in a family that treasured me. I wanted to go back and appreciate it more and see it from other points of view.

There are other things I've done, but for our purposes here, that's probably enough. There is still an eternity of other options in front of me. Sometimes I play around with what they might be.

And then there's also been service. There were service opportunities from the moment I arrived. Even if you're in the same clinic or whatever you want to call it, there's somebody nearby that one could engage with and perhaps boost a bit.

I don't think anybody here is simply on a hedonistic joyride. You might think of heaven as being this place full of toys if you're a child, or indulgences if you're a foodie. Somebody like me could have just decided that what I really want to do is go to the fashion houses of Paris. That's something thing I could do. I could get all involved in clothing if I wanted to. But for right now, I've chosen to know at greater depth the people I already valued.

Michael: That's wonderful.

Samuel: Well, thank you. You got your answer, and you got a little bit from me. Last time you did have some interaction with Mr. Burr, the actor. He was quite kind to me. We didn't pal around. I think that would have been a possible way for either of us. It is just not the way that things played out. He did his job well. If we ever circle back to one another, that's for another time.

In the moment, his presence was part of my esteeming myself better, which I needed to do. You've had a number of these encounters that involve someone with fame and celebrity serving as a helper. I think this is because some of us going through this process could use a bit of a boost. The fact that someone notable even knows you exist and then is willing to put themselves at your service, can be quite a boost. And it was.

Michael: Do you have any insight, Samuel, on what you'll be doing or where you'll be going?

Samuel: For right now, I'm happy where I am. I'm not anticipating wanting to be anywhere else or doing anything else. I know that will change. Events unfold here. Something around you shifts and brings something new into your field of vision. That creates a new calculation and a new possibility. But for right now, I don't feel like I'm in such a time. I'm happy with the status of things. When it's time for another way of being, it'll present itself and I'll make another choice.

Michael: Well, wherever your journey takes you, we wish you the greatest of blessings.

Samuel: You've been such a blessing already. Maybe when it's your turn to make your crossing, if you remember me and you want me present, just ask. It wasn't hard to invite me today. Keep me on your list.

(He departs.)

Nathan: This is Nathan. Glory be to the Father, to the Son, and to the Holy Spirit, as it was in the beginning, is now, and will be forever. Amen.

Linda and Michael: Amen.

||||||||||||||||||||||||||||||||||||||||||||||||||||||||||||||||||||||||||||||||||||||||||||||||||||||||||||||||||||||||||||||||||||||||||||||||||||||||||||||||||||

I like the part of the story, where my own guardian PJ talked about being able to contain his whole being in something like skin, or let it expand to accompany another as they make their crossing. I think it's true that on the one hand, we appear to end at the boundary of our fingertips, but there's an energy about us that goes beyond our physical limits. We do have an aura or a way allowing our energy to move out to support other people. I've noticed in obituaries or eulogies people frequently remark, "Her spirit could light up a room!"

I also liked the way that Samuel could acknowledge a person's handsomeness first, and only then say, "And with a nip here, or a tuck there you'll really shine!" It gave him such satisfaction to know that someone leaving his presence was esteeming himself well.

Thanks, Samuel, for helping us see ourselves and those around us as the well-tailored works of art that we truly are.

Chapter Nine

Ritah and Afterlife Rehab

Challenge: Drug Addiction and its Many Consequences
Value: Surprising Hope

Three Explanations:
Ritah's Life Review and the Aftermath of Brenda's Death
Effective Afterlife Rehab Clinics
Ritah's Hope for Grieving Readers

As my previous two *Afterlife, Interrupted* books have made their way in the world they've often found their way into the hands of persons grieving the death of a loved one who died because of addiction. Very often that addiction was to alcohol and drugs. Those deaths are often preceded by years of pain and frustration for all concerned. Relationships with friends and family members suffer or are broken. When death comes, exactly how and why it happened can be unclear, adding another level of painful confusion to the pile. It's not easy grieving the death of a loved one who died in addiction. And it can be difficult to imagine them having afterlife hope or peaceful rest.

We've chosen to include Ritah's story here because we're hoping it can give comfort to those who need it. Ritah reminded us that for every addict who dies there are many surviving loved ones whose suffering deepens. Sometimes people hope the end of a life here will come with some sort of meaningful closure. That just doesn't happen where addiction-related deaths are concerned.

Ritah was well educated and is well-spoken. I hope you'll benefit by getting to know her here. We first got acquainted through a dream that contained both love and sadness, and a family who tried to love her as best they were able.

||||||||||||||||||||||||||||||||||||||||||||||||||||||||||||||||||||||||||||||||||||||||||||||||||||||||||||||||||||||||||||||||||||||||||||||||||||||||||||||||

Nathan: Today is October 31, 2020. My name is Nathan. I'm in Tucson, Arizona, on a Zoom call with Michael and Linda who are in Pennsylvania. This morning we will be at the service of someone who presented a story in a dream on August 21, 2020. Here is that dream, as I wrote it down:

I was with an elderly couple and their adult daughter. The daughter had a history of addiction and had stolen from them in the past. She had been through previous rehab stays; they were fed up with her. It was in the days before Christmas. There were wrapped gifts. The parents were washing their hands of any future responsibility for their daughter. They were about to drive her somewhere. She had a Christmas gift in her hands. I awoke.

I didn't write it down, but I had a feeling I was in an urban scene; it might've been San Francisco. There were Victorian buildings, so it was a city that's been around a long time. It felt like it was highly urbanized, wherever they were taking her. She might've been able to keep a job. It seemed she was living a single's life in a high-priced city.

They were leaving what felt like an old apartment in an urban apartment building. They were driving her somewhere, but it was with a sense of frustration that they were getting rid of her. There wasn't anger as much as there was exasperation, and fatigue.

And, it was juxtaposed with Christmas presents, so there was conflicting energy in it.

I'm going to pause the recording and ask you to remind me to get it started again, because I'm going to read the story a second time.

We have said our protective prayers, and we've read the transcript of the dream a couple of times. We're now inviting a person who's in that story to come and be with us. You can borrow my voice if you'd like. You'll be talking with Michael and Linda; we're all here to help you.

(There was a stirring.)

This guardian goes by a nickname, Earl.

(Angel Earl enters.)

Angel Earl: It's good to be with you. I guard the one you will help today. The one whom I guarded took a misstep that had very far-reaching consequences. You're familiar with the perils of addiction and the pain it brings. She made repeated attempts to move against it. I did everything I could to augment what she was attempting and what others were trying to give her for help.

There were moments of brightness, but her story is one that has a lot of pain. But, as you know, she wouldn't be here today were it not for progress made after her passing. She has been able to avail herself of help, and as you know, leaving behind the body with its chemical cravings has its own advantages. There are still things of spirit and of the current way of being that are still unsettled.

She has made sufficient progress. It's now two months in your time since presenting in his dream, but she is patient, and she has a great aptitude for receiving truth. This can be difficult for people who have gotten into a cycle of addiction, because after a while, people have difficulty distinguishing false from true. But she stands out in that regard.

She can hear a true thing that's painful and difficult to hear. She can recognize that she wanted to believe that false was true and now say, "I was wrong." She has a humility that has made it possible for her to progress to this point. So, with that, I will slide to the side, and we'll see what happens.

Michael: Thank you very much.

Angel Earl: All right, God bless you.

(Angel Earl departs.)

Nathan: This is Nathan. She's moving in. She's telling me her name. It was spelled R-I-T-A-H. I think it was short for Margarita. She went by Rita, but she added the H for some panache just to stand out a little bit from anyone else who had that name.

(Ritah moves in.)

Ritah: I am Ritah.

Michael: Welcome Ritah-with-an-H.

Ritah: I had lots of counseling, so it's not so difficult for me to introduce myself and say I'm an addict. Although, in programs like AA or NA, they were very intentional about people saying I'm a "recovering" rather than a finished anything.

I'm told here that there's still growth and progress occurring. However it works, things evolve. Here there is a point at which one doesn't have to use "recovering" anymore. I don't think they even say "recovered." It seems that whole nexus of concerns gets replaced by new material.

My helpers tell me I'm ready for this day. I've progressed past of the cycle of addiction that involves self-loathing. In addition to hating myself, I hated what I did to my parents. Because of my addiction, I kept turning up on their doorstep. I think it was mentioned in the story that I had stolen from them. I made many tearful apologies, promising it would never happen again. I chose to tell the story that happened just days before Christmas.

I think it was two days before Christmas, and they had decided I was not to be in the family gathering, because it was just too painful for too many people. They had a little dinner for me, which was my little Christmas. I wasn't going to be included in the larger family gathering because I brought chaos. They were not unkind, but they were strong about boundaries because I had screwed up so often. This time, they meant it. They said, "You may come over to our house for a dinner and then a little gift exchange. Then we will take you home and wish you well." That's what that was. It was sad, but it was... I never liked the phrase "tough love," but it fits.

"We are going to have a Christmas that doesn't include your addictions." So, that was what he [Fr. Nathan] saw in his dream. I know that frequently people come in his dreams and show him car crashes and death struggles. It's enough for you to know that mine included overdose.

Michael: Okay.

Ritah: It wasn't overtly suicidal, although suicide is a common theme among addicts, because the pain seems so unrelenting. I did not decide, "I know what I'll do. I'll take enough drugs to get me out of here." I didn't do that. But I slid deeper and then took a street drug that was of course unregulated. Well, anyway, I took something that stopped my breathing and my heart. That was it.

Michael: How long after Christmas did that occur?

Ritah: It was still winter. So, somewhere in the next few months, I guess.

I used that experience of not being invited to the family Christmas as one more, poor-me story of rejection. "Nobody loves me, boo hoo." It a dark time. The weather matched my mood. I isolated. I had a job, but I was calling in sick more and more often. I was on a downward slide. Then, when I left the body... I'm going to need to pause a moment to connect with him a little more deeply.

Michael: Take your time.

(There was a pause.)

Ritah: Well, at the very end I was involved with a guy. It was some sort of any-port-in-a-storm desire for comfort. And of course, he was as druggy as I was. So, I had a story in my head about being rejected again. But in fact, he was somebody I'd only known for weeks and was just as messed up I was. Still, I was angry about being rejected. Then, [after death] I moved from something like hazy sleep, barely conscious to coming alert in a setting that was like being in a rehab facility.

I had been in three of them, residential ones, and it was like some little space where you were monitored and kept safe. And then, with different kind of therapeutics around you, different people trying to come at you from different angles to see if they could promote healing.

It wasn't very long before I noticed it was effective. That was different, because I had watched people succeed in rehabs and graduate and move on, but I was usually left behind. Even in the times when I left rehab, sometimes it was because of money and health insurance issues. There would be an attempt to put a good face on it and say, "Look at the progress you've made." There might be some sort of graduating and hoping for the best, but it wasn't driven by my state and circumstance. It always involved money.

Over here that goes away. There's no shortage of resources and there's no time constraint. You simply receive what you are able to receive. You're not shamed into thinking you're wasting other people's time and money. That was nice, not feeling shame.

So, I was able to move through. They did some things with me that you might be familiar with because I think you know about NDEs (Near-Death Experiences) and life reviews.

Michael: That's correct.

Ritah: They can show you things in a way that's almost entertaining because it's a little like watching a movie of your life. It's well-crafted and true. It shows you how this tiny little thing that happened over here began to grow. And, almost like a weed that sends spores out and plants weeds in other places, this little thing that happened over here caused this little ripple over there. And, that thing led to the next thing. And before long, you begin to say, "Wow, now I get it! That's where it started." Some of it even has to do with genetics and physical things. Some of it is just emotional stuff... For me, some of it was taking to heart unkind things that people said to me when I was a child.

One thing led to another and before long, I was struggling with addiction. So anyway, it was nice to be in a place where people weren't guessing at what your problem was. They do a lot of that in rehab because they don't know any better. But here there's just truth. Lots of it. There's nothing but truth here.

Linda: God bless you.

Here I'd like to comment on one of the things Ritah explains so well. She mentions the life review common to many Near-Death Experience accounts. While out-of-body, experiencers report being surrounded by love while being shown scenes from their life that give them truth and clarity. Often, they experience scenes from their lives where they affected another for good or ill. Sometimes they are made to see the negative consequences of their own actions on other people. But they are not shamed. They don't have their noses rubbed in it. They're just brought to truth in a loving way. They are then free to behave differently.

Jesus, whom I love and serve, is said in our creeds to "judge the living and the dead." Remember he was once judged and sentenced to death. He knows a little bit about how harsh judgment feels. I don't think he's a harsh judge. In courtrooms judges oversee a process that helps us come to the truth of something unclear. Some Christian people want to skip ahead to the sentencing phase. They want a divine judge who lowers the boom on wrongdoers. I've said repeatedly that I'm not writing doctrinal books. I'm just relaying people's experiences. I do think there's a way to think of a personal judgment that simply leads a person to the truth for their own benefit and for the benefit of all around them. Ritah has told us, "There's nothing but truth here." Her guardian told us, "She has a great aptitude for receiving truth." Jesus once said, "I am the Way, The Truth, and The Life." However it all works, Ritah's afterlife coming to truth healed her.

Michael: Ritah, was your guardian Earl with you the whole time?

Ritah: Yes, sometimes more actively than at other times. There might be a conversation with several people, for example, about parts of my story. I might say a thing and Earl would say, "That's your perception of it, Ritah. But let me tell you what happened from my point of view. It's not just an alternate opinion, it's a truth." You know how oftentimes, people here on Earth will say something very truthful, but then they'll add the caveat, "That's the way I see it." That's not necessary here when someone like a guardian speaks. They only say true things.

Angel Earl could change the course of a conversation by saying, "No Ritah, this is what happened, and this is what happened after that. Do you remember?" He's always kind, and he wasn't demeaning. He just would say, "Ritah you saw it that way, but here's how it occurred." And then I would... Because I knew he loved me, I would just say, "Oh." And then, sometimes that would be enough because there was a truth that needed to be pondered. There wasn't really a need for more talk. Sometimes it was time to be still after he would talk. Other times he would just be an observer, but his responsibility was to always be with me. He was never absent.

Michael: Thank you for that insight.

Ritah: Yeah. Well, I don't want to linger, and I don't need to go into any more detail other than I've left rehabs before. That's largely what I'm doing today, except this one has a definitiveness about it that none of the others did. I'm clearly graduating from one way of being to a next way of being.

I bet it wouldn't surprise you to know that they said, "Well, you're pretty much packed to go, but while you're still here, could you assist this one or that one?" So, I was kind of drawn into helping some of the newer arrivals.

So, my time hasn't been wasted waiting for you people to show up. They gave me good work to do. They said, "Then it will be your turn to move on to the next place. Somebody will be receiving you and doing what you're doing now. Somebody will receive you in the next place and show you around and show you opportunities and possibilities."

Linda: Ritah, can you tell us more about Earl? Earl has played such an important role in your life up until now, but now that you're graduating to another realm, will Earl continue with you?

Ritah: He's telling me yes, but that his role will shift. He really enjoys guarding souls upon Earth. The bond between the one guarded and the one guarding is love and love is eternal. His love for me will not go away but he will be distanced from me in space. I think he's going to be given some sort of angelic holiday, some bit of respite or recharge time or something where he, at the end of it, will be involved in a process of assignment to a next human soul. I think that's the way it works. But, for now it's time for a passage, and so I think that's where your skill comes in.

Michael: Okay. Is there anyone in particular, Ritah, that you would like to call forth in conjunction with your guardian and all the other supporters there, a particular person who will help you make this next step forward?

Ritah: Yes, but it requires one more bit of silence to move a little bit deeper in him, so excuse us for a moment.

(There was a pause.)

Ritah: It only needed to be a moment because I knew it would be my sister, Brenda. Brenda and I were only a year apart, she was riding a bicycle when she was struck by a car and killed when I was six. That was one of the events in the chain of things that brought unexpected sadness to my family. There was a time when my parents were so hollow inside that they only barely functioned.

I was also grieving, but I had to... I don't think people were taught in those days, how to talk about their pain. Anyway, there was a period there where it felt like I was in charge of raising myself, at least on the inside. There was clothing and food and a roof, but there was a hollowness inside. What had once been a warm and loving home, was cold and dark inside.

She left quite a long time ago, but I've been coached into this and told, "You know that everyone survives their death and that you don't have to be the same as when you arrived here. You can grow into a different version of you. Your sister doesn't have to be a seven-year-old accident victim. You and she can play at that if you choose. You could choose to be little girls who somehow move through time that was taken from you, but that'll be up to the two of you to decide how you move." But anyway, it will be Brenda, at least that's what I would like.

Michael: Okay.

Ritah: So, I'm going to be still and let it be known that I would like to see Brenda, if Brenda can come.

We wore dresses at that time; girls hardly ever wore pants. We were only small, but we were already being told what was lady-like and what wasn't. I think she was quietly deciding that when she was bigger, she would be what she wanted to be. So, she's coming on, I think you call it an off-road vehicle.

It's not a tricycle, but it's something that you would use in some wilderness where you roar about, make noise, and kick up dust. That's what she wants to present, that she'd liked to take me on a wild ride.

We're going to have to get reacquainted. I didn't know her wild side, but she didn't know a lot about me either. We're going to go for a ride at least for a little bit, and that'll get me where I need to go and then take it from there.

Michael: We hope you have a very wonderful reunion and a wonderful continuing journey into the future. God bless every step that you take along the way, you, and Brenda.

Ritah: Well, thank you, you've been very kind to me. God bless you.

Michael: God bless you.

Linda: Bye, Ritah.

(Ritah departs.)

Nathan: Glory be to the Father, to the Son and to the Holy Spirit, as it was in the beginning is now, and will be forever, Amen.

||||||||||||||||||||||||||||||||||||||||||||||||||||||||||||||||||||||||||||||||||||||||||||||||||||||||||||||||||||||||||||||||||||

It's not easy to be hopeful when you've had many failed attempts, is it? Rita told us she had three times been in residential rehab. It never worked.

I remember paying to take golf lessons once. This annoying instructor said, "Trust your swing!" I told him, "If I could trust my swing to be any good, I wouldn't be taking golf lessons from you." I can be like that. His reply was, "Well then don't trust your swing. Let's see if that helps your golf game." Instead of quitting on the spot, I tried again to trust my swing.

Is the existence of afterlife rehab clinics more than you can imagine? I've been at this afterlife work for too long to disbelieve. When we get to that part of the story, pay close attention to the way Ritah could see almost from the beginning that the therapies were working. This was different from earlier failed attempts. She was surprisingly hopeful that she would make real and lasting progress. You might say she tried again to trust her swing.

We wanted to share her story on a podcast I'd been invited onto as a guest. My sister Cathryn helped with the session where we sought her permission.

||||||||||||||||||||||||||||||||||||||||||||||||||||||||||||||||||||||||||||||||||||||||||||||||||||||||||||||||||||||||||||||||||||

Nathan: I am Nathan. I'm with Cathryn. We're in Tucson on Tuesday, January 19, 2021.

We've just read the story of Ritah. We called her story Ritah in **Afterlife Rehab**. We want to ask Ritah if we may use her story publicly on a radio show that I will be on tomorrow. So, we'll be still for a moment and invite Ritah.

Ritah, this is Nathan. We won't keep you long. We just need a yes or no answer, and either one's fine.

Cathryn: Hello, Ritah. I'm Cathryn, and you're welcome here. You're invited.

(Ritah moves in.)

Ritah: And here I am. I heard you were just reading over the transcript of my previous visit.

Cathryn: Yes, and I'm glad to hear you're doing so well.

Ritah: Well, since then, it hasn't been a long time, but obviously a new place, a new situation, and a colossal new start. For so long, maybe 20 years or more, practically my whole adulthood, I was troubled by addiction. I lived with a dark cloud of fear or worry about what might happen. That has lifted. Now I'm in a new circumstance where I'm being given all kinds of new opportunities.

Cathryn: Good for you.

Ritah: Well, I'm here because there's a question of maybe talking about or reading what you just read on a radio show.

Cathryn: Yes, that's correct. And you know we don't do these things without permission.

Ritah: Yes. I appreciate that. That's been another thing that's been so nice on this side, that there's always that courtesy extended. Nobody ever talks behind anyone else's back. No one says anything that isn't the truth. Even if there is a truth to be told, it's always shared in a charitable way. There is never some sort of indictment.

Cathryn: That's nice to hear.

Ritah: I wish people understood that better. So many people have an image of or a fear of dying because they're going to be judged and found guilty and punished. I would have had all that coming. If that's the way it had worked in my case, I could have been punished for decades of bad behavior of different kinds and the impact that my behavior had on coworkers and parents and my family. That just wasn't the way it played out. There's still a lot of reconciling to be done when people pass, but I'm told, "Look at you. They're going to get to deal with a version of you they never really got to see. They'll see it very early on. They'll get to see, 'Wow, this is the version of you that we always wished we could be around.'" So, the question is: would I mind my story being told in a public way? The only concern I would have is: Would that harm anyone?

Cathryn: Of course. If that's a concern, we can use a different name if it would make you feel more comfortable.

Ritah: Well, I added the H to Rita just to be distinctive, so that might distinguish me, but there's nothing in my story that's untrue. There's nothing of it that's unkind toward anyone else. I listened as you just read back the transcript, and even though my parents used tough love with me in a scene that I chose to put in his dream, they weren't unkind. And I didn't suggest that they were. I think I said they established firmer boundaries, is all. They explained themselves well. The fact that I felt ostracized was on me and not on them. Other people did have a right to a Christmas celebration that didn't involve my emotional baggage. I don't think that's at all unfair. So, if any coworkers recognized my story or anybody in my circle... My circle got smaller because that's the way it works when you're in addiction. Relationships get deactivated because you're just too difficult or painful to be around.

The oddity of it is what we're doing now, speaking through another person and dead people talking and all of that. I would imagine there's a certain percentage of the population that would not pay this one bit of attention because it's just too odd. There's, I guess, some who might think of it as "of the devil." I didn't pay attention to that kind of thing, but I understand being inside him that that's sometimes a concern.

Cathryn: Yes.

Ritah: I understand that the people that might listen to this... podcast, it's called? A little radio program that is sort of specific in its reach?

Cathryn: Yes.

Ritah: I understand it's like a niche magazine; only people who were interested in this very specific topic would choose to tune into it.

Cathryn: Yes, that's correct.

Ritah: Well, I just keep coming back to the fact that it's true. I can't think of any... I'm not being disturbed in the afterlife so if anyone wanted to say, "How dare they disturb her in her eternal rest," well, I think I've done a good job of explaining what my eternal way of being is. I just listened to it and it's truthful. I know you all are trying to help people broaden their imagination of what it might be like after one dies. For every person who dies in addiction, there are many loved ones left with pain, wondering what's become of her. You know that in my story, my sister was killed as a child. The pain that sudden departure caused had such a long reach, immediate and then long-term. People can make of a story what they wish, but I told my truth and I think it makes sense that life is a continuum. Even though abrupt death might seem very jarring and very, I think he uses the word "interrupted" in the title of his books—

Cathryn: Yes, that's correct.

Ritah: ... but only briefly interrupted. Then the program resumes, and life continues. I died abruptly, but I needed rehab. I don't know what it would have been like to arrive in the afterlife and been catapulted into some Disneyland. Maybe it could happen that way. There's a lot of variety here.

It makes sense to me that I continued in a kind of a rehab. The worst part of rehab on Earth was the fact that you always knew you weren't paying for it yourself. Somebody else's labor is funding this. I don't have any control over whether it succeeds or it doesn't because addiction controls. Beating it was something that, in the end, I never succeeded at, even though a lot of resources were poured into that effort. But over here that went away. Here every incremental bit of progress never has to be repeated. One never backslides.

It is always forward. Well, it wasn't very difficult to begin to get a sense of forward momentum because it was always so obviously good and productive. They could give you real goals and they didn't move the goalposts. Always the goal that was put before you, you could watch yourself get closer to it. You could meet it, reassess, and they'd say, "Now that we've done this, here's the next incremental goal." Here, everything can be shared openly. Well, maybe not everything. But anyway, the long and the short of it is, I think it could be encouraging to hear. Maybe if people who are in addiction hear it, they can appreciate the struggles of failing at rehabs and so on. It can be hard after you failed over and over, to find the will to get up in the morning and to get to a job and so on.

Here, Ritah, at her most compassionate, shares with addicted and or grieving people a message of hope based in shifting the way they might imagine the afterlife. If that's you and you feel alone in your struggle, listen up! Ritah would like to be a part of your team.

||

Ritah: Maybe there are people battling addiction that might hear this story and go, "Wow, there can be an end to it. Maybe I'll try again." And then maybe people who have lost somebody to death from addiction hear this and think, "Well, I never thought of it that way. Maybe she's getting everything she needs. Maybe we're not seeing the whole picture. We don't have to think only of her sad passing. Maybe we can..." And then maybe people who never said a prayer to somebody that's died or said a prayer for somebody that's died because they weren't taught to do that could know that it's possible for you to help in the process. Think of giving somebody a boost. You know, trying to help somebody climb over a wall, cupping your hands so that they can step into them and you can boost them up?

Cathryn: Yes, I understand.

Ritah: Something like that, where maybe your well-wish or your prayer, however you form that, as long as it comes from a loving heart, you can think of yourself as an agent who's somehow supplying something for your loved one, rather than thinking of them only with sadness. You can think of them and say, "I don't know how you're doing it in the afterlife, but I have an idea because I heard this radio show (or read this book) that you are making progress. If I can be a part of your team, I want to be." I think that would be sweet.

Cathryn: Yes. I agree.

Ritah: I've been a helper on other people's rehab teams since I've been here. Before my death, I never really graduated to the level of one of those sponsors who can be relied upon in the middle of the night. But here I've been part of people's helping team.

Cathryn: That's got to feel good.

Ritah: It does. After I made the crossing that your brother and that married couple assisted with, my helpers said, "Let's not have you do anything related to rehabs. We think you've spent enough time on that. You're free to do as you please. You've finished all you needed to do."

I'm not going to go into that any further, because it's all so new. I haven't really made up my mind what I'm doing next. For now, I'm quite happy to just enjoy being free from fears or weightiness of any kind.

My sister is quite fine and so am I, and so is everybody I'm meeting now. I won't keep you any longer. I'm happy with my story being used. That's all that I need to say.

Cathryn: We appreciate that. Like you, I think your story can be helpful to those who need a little hope, so thank you.

Ritah: Good-bye now.

Thanks, Ritah, for letting us share your story. As more people learn of you, I think you're going to find you have a widening circle of new friends. I'd like to be one of them.

Chapter Ten

Not-So-Simple Simon the Savant, Angel Shalom, and Mother Maylene

Challenge: Life as a Neurodivergent Person
Value: Determination to Seek Understanding

Three Explanations:
Compassionate Exploring
Being Convertible
Afterlife Simulators?

Have you ever loved anyone who was on the autism spectrum? If you have, is there a room in your heart for one more? If you haven't, I think you'll love Simon.

At first, I thought Simon was a man of few words. But as he said, it depended on the subject. He's quite well spoken as you'll see here.

Nathan: I'm Nathan. Today is February 25, 2023. I'm in Tucson on a Zoom call with Kim and Karen in Southern California. Kim is doing what we call a ride-along. This is her first time to be present during a crossing session.

We've already said our protective prayers, surrounding ourselves with the love and protection of many of the angels and saints.

Today, we're helping someone who brought a dream during the **night** of January 19, 2023.

The dream was one word: "Hello."
I knew in an instant it was contact: it got my attention. The voice sounded more male than female. It sounded adult, flat, metallic, and mechanical. I awoke.

This one's different because usually we get a little narrative that **might** describe the person's death. This dream was nothing but one word.

I'm going to be still and invite the person and the guardian who **attends** them to come and tell us what we can do to help. Kim, this doesn't take very long, usually just a minute or two.

(There was a short pause.)

This guardian wants to go by the name Shalom. I think they're being a clever because that means hello, but it also means peace.

(Angel Shalom emerges.)

Angel Shalom: Here I am. I've not been actively a part of this process before, but I've been made aware of it and have become a student of it, so that I might perform well in this moment. I've been in the background, watching a few of these. I think you call them crossings. I was made aware that we guardians have created our own habit of introducing ourselves with a name that we've chosen for the occasion.

We have our own identities, which you could call a name, but we don't normally use voices and speech to communicate. Things like sound and spelling are more for our interactions with humans and others who use language.

I understand we created this habit of taking a name for the day. This one only said one word: Hello. So, I just thought Shalom would be my name for the day.

It might not surprise you to learn that the one I guarded was a person of few words, who chose to do this entering into Father Nathan's awareness in sleep, without telling a story. No one yet has spoken only one word.

I'm going to go a little deeper already. There's a need for us to strengthen a wavelength or connection. We're doing that now.

The one whom I love and served in a human lifetime was a man of few words. He was an adult who preferred the company of machines to the company of persons. He was a person who was embodied in a way that set him apart from others; I think you call it "being on the spectrum." If you want to think of it as a disability, he was never fully able to read subtle social cues that other people took for granted. Everything needed to be made literal and explicit for him to understand it.

A great deal of the subtlety of human communication was lost on him. He often felt like he was on the outside looking in; he could hear the conversation inside and follow bits of it, but not be fully present to it. This was especially true in childhood. He was subject to teasing because he appeared odd. Even though he was highly intelligent, he appeared to be less so than most children in his class. This is because he comprehended differently.

His way of being made him a good student of physics, or chemistry. Mathematics. Very often there were in those fields of study people who were somewhat like him, in that they preferred to be surrounded by their tools than by other people who they found difficult to be around. No one wants to be made to feel odd and deficient in some way.

Kim: Makes sense.

Angel Shalom: He's listening, and he knows he is loved. He can give and receive love. He just does it in his own way. Some of that changed upon leaving the body, but not all of it. Some habits and patterns are well ingrained. You will see that he's ready to make a move from where he has been to where he will be, which of course you facilitate.

I have done what I need to do. His will be the voice you hear next when he's ready.

(Angel Shalom slides aside.)

Nathan: This is Nathan. His name is Simon.

(Simon emerges.)

Simon: I am called Simon. When I was a child, there was a rhyme that may still circulate, although it's becoming more remote. It was from a different place in time, but it was simple. "Simple Simon met a pie-man going to the fair." It was a nursery rhyme that he [Father Nathan] heard in childhood. When I was growing up, it became a taunt. I was Simple Simon because I was stupid.

Karen: I bet that's not true.

Simon: I didn't know, as a very young person, how one calculated stupid. Was it an F and not an A? Or was it a 50 and not 100? There were plenty of ways in a classroom where children were made to know how they ranked against other children about progress on a lesson. It depended on the kind of lesson it was as to whether I was good at it or not. For example, an English class, if it was about sentence structure, what kind of word did what kind of function in a sentence, I grasped it. I didn't always understand how to start a new paragraph. You're supposed to start a new paragraph when the subject shifts from one thing to another. But I couldn't always tell when the subject shifted. Sometimes I could, but not other times. Sometimes it was too subtle. I found it difficult to comprehend novels, the ones that involved complex human emotions. I didn't know what it was about. And then I would feel like Simple Simon, especially when others in the classroom understood concepts that eluded me.

I didn't talk much. If I was in the company of people who I thought were like me, I could speak more. But I didn't like talking to people who used humor, especially jokes. I hardly ever understood jokes, and I didn't like being around laughter because I usually didn't understand what the laughter was about.

I'm told there were biological and physiological roots to the way I operated, which are not necessarily present any longer. If only I'd been able to know what the root issues were that made me different from other people, maybe that would have been a relief.

Karen: Sure.

Simon: I'm told that I don't have to live with those limitations any longer. But the process of moving from what's familiar to what's new is gradual. I'm on that scale.

Except here they're saying, "Well, you can stay the way you are if you please. But most people here find they can try new things. You're capable of enjoying new things, but you won't know if you don't try." So, I've been trying to grow in areas that hadn't interested me before.

Karen: It takes a lot of courage, doesn't it?

Simon: I don't know what that is.

Karen: Oh, right.

Simon: I could say yes, but it wouldn't be exactly true. Does it involve a willingness to do a new thing?

Karen: That's it. That's courage.

Afterlife Interrupted: Book Three

Simon: Well, then perhaps I have at least some of that.

Karen: That's great.

Simon: I'm going to need to adjust, to go a little deeper.

(There was a brief pause.)

Nathan: This is Nathan. There's something involving electrocution. I think he died touching a live wire. I don't know the setting. I just think there was a jolt of electricity that went through him. He was experimenting using himself as a subject.

(Simon reemerges.)

Simon: This is Simon. I was aware that in a human body, we are energy. People used to think there were only several ways of being. Water could be a liquid, a solid or a vapor depending upon its temperature. People thought that there were these different states, but they were really all the same thing, behaving in different ways.

There began to be more understanding that beneath those states was a stable chemical signature. Every element was energy at the subatomic level. I was interested in that because it might help me understand why I was different from other people.

I worked in a research institute that was adjacent to a university. I had expertise which was valuable in a laboratory. I was considered an idiot savant or a prodigy. I knew these words describe somebody who was uncommon in a way that wasn't simple or stupid, although idiot is an unkind word. But savant or prodigy were words used to describe people like me.

To get to the point of our time today, I was using myself as a research subject. I was working with energy, electrical energy. There were beginning to be studies of the mechanization of human bodies that had been through an accident, maybe a spinal cord injury or something where if only we could get the circuits to reconnect, the muscle groups might respond as they once did. We were working with exoskeletons something like insects have where they could inhabit, they could be inside a skeleton rather than have a skeleton inside them. If the skeleton that's in you doesn't work anymore, could we build you a different one that you are inside of that would enable you to walk again or do other movements?

Karen: Wow!

Simon: Well, people are doing this work. I didn't have that problem. And you might have picked up by now that empathy was not my strong suit. People wrote novels about it or created music meant to stimulate empathy. I didn't understand empathy, but I could see and understand suffering. I knew what it felt like to be different.

I was doing an experiment using my own body. But I accidentally gave my body too much of an electrical jolt because I wasn't paying attention to what it would do to my heart. I was paying more attention to what it would do to my fingers. I just miscalculated the amount of electricity I allowed into my body. It stopped my heart.

I was alone because I preferred to be alone. When that occurred, I was in a lab without other people in it who might have been able to provide first aid and prevent my death.

Karen: How's it been for you since you passed? What's it been like?

Simon: I chose, to the degree that I had the power to choose, to stay alert and awake. I think when people die, they don't always get to choose. They just succumb and then awaken in a different place and are told they have died and they're now in this other place and they're well cared for. I wanted to be present to every part of the process. I made that known, and it was respected. I was still a researcher. I wanted to know what was happening. They put it to me in terms that were kind and compassionate.

They communicated to me in the language I spoke, in decimal points and data. They explained, "You knew you could introduce greater or lesser amounts of electrical energy into your body. And you knew you were going to a higher degree than you had in previous experiments. The amount of current you allowed into your system was sufficient to make your heart stop. It was just math. It was just physics. You introduced too much current for your heart to be able to continue to function."

I thought, "Well, that makes sense." I wasn't a religious person because religion used too much language I didn't understand. I didn't have a difficulty believing in a creator because the whole universe looks to me to be a created thing. So, I didn't have any difficulty with believing I was now alive outside of a body. I was told, "You were aware, even at an early age, that the body you inhabited was different from other bodies in ways that made your life more difficult."

That was undeniable. They said, "That body has ceased to function, but the rest of you hasn't. Now there's a different physics and different math that applies to you that you haven't explored yet. But you now can explore your new way of being. You were trying to find scientific applications and principles that might help a person walk who could not walk. You were trying to take the science, the math, the physics, the chemistry, and you were trying to find ways to make people's lives easier or better in bodies that had some deficiency. And now you are out of a body that had deficiencies. You can begin to move about without imagining you must compensate for a deficiency."

Karen: Right. So, you're here today to take another step where the physics is going to be different. Shalom and you have worked to get you to this place. Have you thought about someone you might like to help you make this next step?

Simon: It's my mother. She had a love for me that I understood, maybe because it was so familiar for so long. When it became evident that I was not normal according to developmental standards used by pediatricians, she just accepted it as a data point and not as a judgment. She simply got busy learning how to give me the best life I could have.

Karen: She sounds like a wonderful person.

Simon: She was. Her dying occurred when I was around 20 years old. I at least had the advantage of getting to that age with her support. She had an illness, a cancer of the uterus, that was the cause of her death. But she had time to get me ready to be without her. She did things to encourage me to go into research. She said, "You will be happier if you go where there are more numbers and there are more chemical signatures for your brain to take in to understand things." She steered me toward a career in research. She only wanted me to be at peace. Happy was not a category I fully understood. But peace, I could understand, because I knew the opposite of it: agitation, isolation, or rejection. She steered me toward a place where I could contribute in ways that were honored, welcomed, even sometimes celebrated. I think she would be a good one to point me in a new direction. She was very good at that, so I think she could probably do that again. At least she would be the first one I ask.

Karen: That would be great. Shall we see about her coming?

Simon: Yes. Here people just appear. They don't always come from a distance. They just show up. Let's see what she does.

Karen: Okay.

(There was a brief pause. Simon's mother, Maylene, emerges.)

Maylene: And I am going to borrow his [Father Nathan's] voice. My name is Maylene.
I don't need to stay long. Simon's father left us because he found it too difficult to have a son with troubles. I didn't marry again. Simon needed a very stable, consistent routine, so it was just the two of us. We were a little team.

When he was grown, I chose to relocate toward Simon's work so he could live with me, and I could provide the stability of grocery shopping and meals and laundry. I could make his life easier by just handling those things so he could focus on his research. He was not a mama's boy. He just needed someone to manage parts of his life. I chose to do that. I was content to cook and clean and provide a stable home until I had an illness that made it clear I wouldn't be able to do that for very much longer.

Karen: Your love for Simon is inspiring to us.

Maylene: Well, you know that love makes people grow in ways that allow them to share traits with their beloved. You bring to a relationship what you were before you knew them, but that person whom you love begins to change you. Sometimes you see it in old couples who have been together for a whole life, completing each other's sentences.

Karen: Sure.

Maylene: Our life moved at Simon's pace. He loved going to the planetarium. Zoos, too: he wanted to stay with one animal and understand it. He didn't want to move from place to place like people ordinarily do. He especially loved science-based museums, but he'd want to stay in one spot. I knew that, so we didn't blow past exhibits. We stayed with something that he got interested in until he felt he could understand it. Then he would tell me it's time to go to the next one. So today we're going to do that.

Karen: We're glad your team is back together.

Maylene: Well, I did everything I could to try to stay with him, even after my death. But that kind of subtlety that was lost on him. I don't know that he was ever aware of it, but I could at least bring my energy to a room that he was in. If he didn't know that it was my energy, at least it was there. Maybe it became part of what he was doing.

Anyway, now all we're doing is going for a walk. He's not exactly listening to every word, but he knows that I'm here and he can accept that as a new day or a clean slate.

Karen: Great. Thank you for talking to us. We wish you and Simon all the best.

Maylene: There's no need for him to come back into the voice. He's ready to make this movement. Thank you for your help.

Karen: Okay. Take care.

(They depart.)

Nathan: This is Nathan. Glory be to the Father, to the Son, and to the Holy Spirit, as it was in the beginning, is now, and will be forever. Amen.

Have you anything to add to the record?

Karen: I was just thinking that his whole life was about empathy. His whole adult life he felt outside the box. Then he was studying to help people who were physically challenged. In a lovely way his whole thing was empathy. That's not how he would see it. But it is how I see it.

I completely agree. Simon said, "empathy was not my strong suit." Notice the subtlety of the card-playing metaphor. Maylene said it was easier for him to understand negative emotions than positive ones. Simon saw other people suffering and got busy doing something to help.

Compassion means "to suffer with." Simon introduced electrical charges into his own body to try to help others regain freedom of movement. He is a compassionate explorer.

Kim: There were times when I wondered if he appreciated all his incredible abilities that other people didn't have. I kept hearing about the deficiencies that he perceived that he had. He did talk about being called a prodigy or a savant. There were times when I was curious. He probably had skills that I certainly don't have and I'm sure many don't have.

Karen: The impression I got was that the continuum of human praise or, it's opposite, critique, was a scale that he really didn't understand. But he understood when he was being insulted.

But in the afterlife, he'll get to a place where he can appreciate his gifts.

Nathan: Well, thank you both for your help.

Here is the permission-seeking conversation with Simon.

Nathan: I'm Nathan. Today is July 19th, 2023. I'm in Laguna Beach, California on a Zoom call with Kim, who's also in Southern California. Today we're gathered to seek permission from the one whom we called Not-So-Simple Simon. We're asking for his presence. The question we have for him is: may we use your story in an upcoming book? I'm going to be still; we'll see how this goes.

(Angel Shalom emerges.)

Angel Shalom: Kim, if you recall, I'm Guardian Shalom. When he first moved into Father Nathan's dreaming, Simon used only one word: "Hello." Even though I had not done this process before, I became a student of it before committing Simon to it. I saw how the other guardians seemed to have created a pattern of choosing a nickname just for the day. I thought since Shalom can mean "hello" I thought I'd use it for my name here. I also hope to bring peace always.

Kim: Thank you. It's great to talk to you again.

Angel Shalom: Thank you. I don't know that I have very much to offer, except that I was very pleased with how gracefully this process moved for him and the active part that his mother took in it. He hadn't had much contact with her since his passing. I don't know if it occurred to him to seek it out or ask for it. He focuses on what's right before him. His mind isn't one that roams about seeking out new possibilities. But when she arrived and spoke, he was happy to be with her again. I believe they've done some of their own interacting since then. That's probably going to be topical in the conversation that follows here.
Do you have any questions for me, or shall I slide aside and allow him to emerge?

Kim: Have you been with Simon since you were with us recently?

Angel Shalom: Good question. We're not required to be after the death of the ones we love. Our love for them doesn't die because love doesn't die. But strictly speaking, I'm off duty. He doesn't need the kind of guarding after his death that he needed earlier. I stayed with him a little longer simply because of the complexity of his psyche. I hoped that he would use his analytic skills to quickly grasp that he now was working without constraints he had become accustomed to. But when people are introduced to new circumstances, there is a learning curve and sometimes hesitancy to venture into unknown things. So, I stayed with him a little more than I might have someone else.

Kim: Okay.

Angel Shalom: But he's not at all reliant on me. He had that about him characterologically when he began as a child to understand that he was different. He was inclined towards more solitude and more self-reliance than another child might have been. He understood that "simple" meant stupid, and he prized his problem-solving skills. He learned how to do things even earlier than his same age peers, just to show to himself that he was not stupid. He can advance when he wants to. It's just a matter of him deciding and putting in the work. There's plenty of advancement that's been possible for him since the crossing that you helped facilitate.

Kim: That's great to hear.

Angel Shalom: I believe Simon will be next. He heard Father Nathan call out to him before sleeping last night and knew that this moment would be coming today. He's ready.

Kim: Wonderful.

(Angel Shalom slides aside.)

Nathan: This is Nathan. Simon is within me. He knows that he can use my voice as a machine because he's done it before, but he wants to do more than use it as a telephone or microphone. He's trying to move in the direction of emotion and subtlety. He's like circling.

(Simon emerges.)

Simon: This is Simon.

Kim: Glad to be with you, Simon.

Simon: I know that the question is: will I allow my story to be used in a book? I'm excited in my own way because it has a research application about it. He's trying to help people understand something unknown or mysterious to them. I loved doing research. The problem that I was working on, of course, had to do with helping people with spinal cord injuries. If listening to what I have to say now helps somebody think about someone they love who had a body and a way of being similar to mine, that would be a helpful thing, don't you think?

Kim: I do. Absolutely.

Simon: Do you see what I did there? I asked empathetically for your assessment of an emotional outcome.

Kim: Fantastic!

Simon: That was an attempt at humor on my part.

Kim: Haha <laugh>.

Simon: I've had some time to prepare for the opportunity to say something today that might be helpful to people here. In doing the kind of research that I did, sometimes there would be a pioneer in a field of science who had created some new theses. Sometimes they would die with work unfinished, and others would come along and wonder how would this revered person operate on the information and the data that we're working with right now? They would have to imagine how this person, were they here, would they perceive the question that we're working on? Sometimes they wished they could speak to them from beyond the grave and ask Einstein, "What do you think about this project we're working on?" That's what I mean. I have an unusual opportunity today to say something to people who are at work on questions that I cared about. I hope they will be more careful with electricity than I was.

Kim: <laugh>

Simon: That was an accident that need not have happened, but it did. There were some, I think you could call them blessings. I've heard people talk about mixed blessings. After my death, I did not incline toward self-reproach. I'm told that others might have spent a lot of wasted energy on kicking themselves. It would be hard to really kick yourself. Maybe you can kick one foot into the other foot, but that's about all. You can't make your foot kick your head. But people might want to kick themselves, like why did they do the stupid thing that caused their death? I don't do that.

Kim: It's best not to spend energy on self-reproach, kicking oneself. Our world is full of that.

Simon: Well, I learned that here. If I want to try to return to the lab and try to make my energy useful to someone in the lab, I could study how to do that. In our earlier conversation when my mother used his voice, she said that she had visited me in the lab and tried to fill the room with her energy. That was the very kind of subtlety that would often be lost on me. And indeed, it was. But I'm not limited to being only what I was before. I'd like to revisit the colleagues with whom I worked to see if there's some way that I can help.

I'm also told that there is a lot of schooling I could do. You know, I haven't been on this level for very long, and they recommended to me that I do some leisure.

That appeals to me because I didn't understand leisure very well. I knew basically that it was not work, but I would rather work than not work.

Kim: Have you been able to do much leisure?

Simon: It wouldn't surprise you to know that we began with my mother saying, "Let's explore!" She gave an example of taking me to a zoo, but then saying that I preferred to stay with one animal for a very long time until I felt like I understood it. Only then would I say, "Let's go to the next exhibit." She said, "Why don't we try that with things that are not about problem-solving or math and science? Why don't we do a little of that? Let's go to a concert."

||||||||||||||||||||||||||||||||||||||||||||||||||||||||||||||||||||||||||||||||||||||||||||||||||||||||||||||||||||||||||||||||

Watch here how Simon becomes a convertible! Convert means "to turn around." Earlier he would never have wanted to attend a concert. He took in the new information that he was no longer in a body that had trouble appreciating musical artistry. Simon made a choice to expand his experiences.

||||||||||||||||||||||||||||||||||||||||||||||||||||||||||||||||||||||||||||||||||||||||||||||||||||||||||||||||||||||||||||||||

Simon: So, we went to some musical theater and opera where the music isn't just technically sound and grand, but it's also telling a story. I'm thinking of "The Flight of the Bumblebee." It uses stringed instruments to suggest that this sound might be the musical equivalent of what's happening in nature when a bumblebee buzzes around.

My mother has been helping me with some things that are obvious to other people. She'll say, "Listen to this piece of music and then let's listen to a bumblebee." Here you can conjure up things by simply wanting them to be, which is quite amazing. All you have to say is, "I would like to hear the sound of a bumblebee in nature, please." And immediately you hear it.

Then you can say, "Now I would like to hear the piece of music called "The Flight of the

Bumblebee." You can listen to them side by side. If you want to see a graphic calibration of how the sounds look on a meter, you can do that.

Kim: Wow. How has that been for you?

Simon: Well, it's with my mother. It's pleasant because she is so loving. There was never a moment when I ever felt simple or stupid in her presence. She knew that if I had the right kind of tools and the right kind of approach and patience, that I was as capable as anyone else of understanding things. It might be remedial, but that doesn't have to mean stupid. That's from the word "to remedy, to fix." I spent a lot of time researching a remedy for other people, something that might make their life better. That's all my mother ever did; she tried to make my life better.

So, we've been having some afterlife experiences involving leisure. She knew that I didn't like mindless leisure. I didn't like to watch television comedies because I didn't understand them. But I might like to watch shows that explained ocean animals or environments. I didn't want to just listen to some laughter.

Now she's helping me understand things. The things I'm trying to understand now aren't just about science. They're about human emotions, moods, and enjoyments that make people happy and make them laugh. She uses food because I know that on one level, food is nutrition. I knew about the importance of biochemistry in eating, but I also liked a hotdog with mustard, not because of was healthy, but because it tasted good. So, she's saying, "You already were good at that. You knew about flavor. You knew you'd like to have second helpings of this, but not that."

So, we do some things; we've been to some restaurants. We didn't do that very much because a lot of restaurant experiences are not just about the food on the plate. They're about subtleties. After a restaurant meal, people might comment upon all kind of things that would be lost on me.

Kim: I understand.

Simon: She's begun to take me to some restaurants and compare them. Here there's something like those machines that are not really an airplane…

Kim: A simulator?

Simon: Simulator. That's the word I want. Here they have restaurant simulators. You can say, "We're going to the Italian restaurant, but we're going to put the setting knobs on below average."

Kim: Really?

||||||||||||||||||||||||||||||||||||||||||||||||||||||||||||||||||||||||||||||||||||||||||||||||||||||||||||||||||||||||||||||||||||||||||||||||||||||

Okay, since I was a child I've heard stories of harps, and banquets and streets of gold. But restaurant simulators! That's brilliant! I was taught in Catholic school first grade that in heaven God would provide everything we'd need to be completely happy. Restaurant simulators never occurred to me until I met Simon.

||||||||||||||||||||||||||||||||||||||||||||||||||||||||||||||||||||||||||||||||||||||||||||||||||||||||||||||||||||||||||||||||||||||||||||||||||||||

Simon: Yes. You go in, but your table isn't ready even though you have a reservation. Then they seat you near the kitchen or the bathroom in a high-traffic place, with clatter and noise. Then there's slow service about how things are ordered and delivered to the table. The grumpy personalities of servers: I wouldn't have remembered any of that. My mother helps me see what a poor-quality experience of that restaurant is. Then she says, "Do you remember all these things? Now let's do the same restaurant meal but let's change the settings at the door to excellent."

Kim: And the food too?

Simon: Well, particularly whether it arrived hot or cold. Or whether the quantity of it seemed commensurate with the price. She said, "Let's set it for below average, and then let's set it for excellent and do them back-to-back." She's teaching me how to distinguish between a below-average experience in a restaurant and an excellent one.

Kim: Wow!

Simon: Now I can see the difference. There are many other things like that. One time we were in a draft because we were seated near the air-conditioning vent. Well, that was not pleasant. The second time it wasn't doing that. There were all these small things she taught me about, like sometimes they try to take your food away from you before you're finished.

So, I'm learning how to have experiences that I hadn't been able to have before. I don't mind that they're remedial because they're remedying something. They're fixing something that was wrong. And now I'm a good student.

The next time I go to that restaurant and not just the simulator, I'll be able to do what other people do at the end of the evening and say why I enjoyed it or didn't enjoy it.

I don't know if anybody listening or reading this would think, "Why would people even need to eat? Their bodies don't need food." Eating food is something people like doing and anything that people like to do can be done here. I hope people understand that.

Kim: I think that's a great thing to convey to people.

Simon: I loved studying. I would've been disappointed if I weren't able to learn things here. They often tell me to stop because I like to keep learning and learning. That's where the leisure part comes in. I've learned that there's a learning that's not learning. There's a time when you just...I'm with him at a beach today. I can just look at the water and I don't have to wonder about its salinity or its wave motion, or the sea floor beneath it. I can just look at sparkles because the sun is hitting the tips of little waves, just little things like that.

Kim: Right.

Simon: I think I'm talking too much now. I want to say that my mother is still choosing to be with me. I don't need to rely on her to the degree that I did previously. We really like each other and like being together. We don't have to do it all the time. But when we do, we are a team, and we have a mission. She didn't get to raise me except in the presence of the deficiencies.

Now that I don't have that, it's sort of an adventure for her to get to know me, but differently. She's getting to know a me that's capable of things that she wouldn't have attempted with me before because they would've been too overwhelming.

Kim: I would like to ask you something, Simon, that I think might be valuable to the readers of this book. I know that there were certain things when you were alive here that were harder to pick up on, subtleties, emotions, laughter. But I also imagine you were more gifted than what we call neurotypical individuals. Can you still grow in the areas where you were already strong?

Simon: I think of it as on two planes. I spoke earlier about how I'm interested in the research we were doing on exoskeletons and the movement of energy through a human body. I would still like to learn more about that, especially if I were somehow able to communicate that to someone on the Earth in a way that they received it. If it became a part of ongoing medical research that would be great. I believe that has existed. I think there have been times in history where there have been advances in some human area because someone was receptive to information from this level or above it. You can probably think of some examples of people who were called savants. That was one of the kinder words that was sometimes used of me. There would be somebody who seemed to receive from out of the blue, knowledge that sent research in a new and better direction. I'd like to know if I could be a part of that. I don't know if I can or not. The other thing would be on this level, there are people who were…let me try it…neuro-atypical?

Kim: Neurotypical describes people like your mom.

Simon: But there are atypical people who've arrived here upon their deaths who I'm told are not thinking as clearly as I am. They're more confused and maybe didn't have quite the helper that I had in my mother. They are ill-disposed to seek help because they were used to trying to do everything on their own. There might be people here who'd be receptive to somebody like me helping them, where they might decline the help of other people.

That idea has been put to me as a possible new career because I loved work. They've said, "You could have a new career helping people become happier." At least within the small subset of people who were like me, I might be good at that. I'm told I don't have to commit to it. I can try it and see if I am effective and if I enjoy it.

Kim: That's a good approach.

Simon: With that, I think I'll go. Maybe I've given people who read this book something positive to think about. I hope they'll know that whatever their life is, if it's hard, don't get scared of the fact that it keeps going. Some people who are having a hard life might just want it to be over. Sometimes they take their life on purpose and hope they won't be any more.

Kim: Yes, that's true.

Simon: But here I've been around nothing but kind people. Nobody's mocking and there are resources for everything. Like I was describing earlier, all you need to do is ask for a thing and it appears. There's no scarcity or shortage of anything. I hope if there are people who find life hard that they can look forward to knowing that that won't always be true. Then maybe they can calm down and look around in their own current moment and see if there are things they overlooked that might help them be happier.

Kim: Well said.

Simon: I'm going to leave now.

Kim: Okay. Thank you so much for giving us permission to include your story and for sharing with us all the things you're learning.

Simon: You're welcome. Maybe we'll meet again.

Kim: I hope someday we do.

(Simon departs.)

Nathan: This is Nathan. Glory be to the Father, to the Son, and to the Holy Spirit, as it was in the beginning, is now, and will be forever. Amen.

||||||||||||||||||||||||||||||||||||||||||||||||||||||||||||||||||||||||||||||||||||||||||||||||||||||||||||||||||||||||||||||||||||||||||||||||||||||||

Maybe we'll meet again? Simon is now a regular in my prayer life. I'm not waiting until later. Simon might not have had a wide circle of friends here, but he has a gift for friendship, don't you think? Let's help each other out, Simon. We've got universes to explore.

Chapter Eleven

Rudolfo, The Martyred Farmworker

Challenge: Walking in the Dark Valley
Value: Un-heroic Courage

Three Explanations:
The Harsh Reality of Migrant Farmworker Life
His Post "Whack-a-Mole" Body Within a Cloud of Bodies
Mustard Seed Faith

All these encounters with souls are awesome. I've been involved in this ministry for about 27 years. My prayer partners and I have done several hundred of these sessions. When the person we're assisting arrives it's normally quiet and low-key. Not this time. The energy around this one was very strong, very joyful, even dizzying. I wasn't sure why.

What I didn't know at first was that we were being approached by a whole cloud of witnesses. It makes me think of that lyric, "How I want to be in that number, when the saints go marching in!" They were ready to party because an important moment had arrived for their new member, Rudolfo.

Nathan: I am Nathan. Today is May 12th, 2023. I'm in Tucson on a Zoom call with Karen and Kim, who are in Southern California, and Dave, who is in Buffalo. We have said our protective prayers inviting the presence and protection of the angels and saints. I'm about to relate a story that came in a dream during the night of March 28th, 2023. It's brief.

I was standing next to a small truck. People were singing Happy Birthday as they stood in the back of it. Someone shot several of them from behind. I awoke.

(There was a pause.)

We've been still, gone into prayer, and read the little story a second time. I just commented that I thought I could hear in my head the Spanish version of Happy Birthday. Maybe that's relevant and maybe it isn't.

We'll be still and invite a guardian to give us some clarity to help us out.

This guardian is going by the name Adele.

(Angel Adele emerges.)

Angel Adele: Good morning. It's only been a few years since that name was made famous by a singer. It has been around before that. He [Father Nathan] is thinking of "The Farmer in the Dell." The word comes from a field, especially one in a valley.

I mention that because we were in a field; these people were field workers. They did speak Spanish as their primary language. Some also spoke English. They were migrant workers. There were some who chose to stick together and move from place to place at the same time. Some of it depended upon whoever did the hiring. There could be all kinds of variables about these things.

They had hard lives. Some people rise above that and find joy where they can. One of those things was, on this day, celebrating the birth anniversary of one of their members. They were doing that at the end of a working day.

The overseers were gone. The workers were about to be transported from the field to the place where they would sleep. They didn't all live in the same housing or neighborhood, but there was to be a party at the home of the one being celebrated, or at least in the street near it. Not everyone would be able to go there. So, before they parted for the day with some of them not to be seen until the next day, they decided to sing "Happy Birthday" to the honoree, whom I guarded.

But there had been a darkness. There was one man who thought of himself as the owner of some of the women. He felt he was entitled to some of their wages, because he had gotten them the job. He had been a part of a network that helped them do an illegal crossing of the border and he felt that they owed him. It wasn't sexual trafficking, but this man believed he was always owed some portion of their pay.

They were complaining about this to some fellow workers, men who then offered to stand up for the women and protect them. But the man had an assistant, a kind of a weaker person, who did his bidding. The two of them chose this moment to try to reclaim their property.

Karen: Like to scare them?

Angel Adele: It was more than that. They intended to murder them, one in particular. The one they targeted happened to be standing with others in the back of a truck. The workers were all packed together in a truck, and others were hit by bullets. But he was the target.

Karen: It all sounds very cruel.

Angel Adele: Well, it was a hard life that got much harder for a lot of people that day. The one I guarded died very rapidly. And with that, I think I should slide to the right and let him take it from here.

Karen: Thank you for your help, Adele.

Angel Adele: You're welcome. Thank you for yours. We won't take much of your time, I think.

(Angel Adele slides aside. An unusually large, warm energy began to emerge.)

Nathan: This is Nathan. His name is Rudolfo, and he's very large or very energetic. There's lots and lots of energy around this one. There's a very, very strong warmth. He's about to speak.

(Rudolfo emerges.)

Rudolfo: My English was not very good, but today I don't have to use it anyway. I can just form my thoughts and they come out of his mouth in English.

I will be a little unlike many you have helped in that I'm already surrounded by the ones who will take me across. You don't need to prompt me to that decision.

I was a Catholic and I loved the parts of the Jesus story that were with poor people. And so many of them were. He was in the fields with people who barely got enough to eat.

One of the things in those stories that I liked that I don't think always got enough attention was the way that men treated women badly. Jesus refused to be a part of that. Sometimes he was given trouble because someone didn't like the fact that he included this woman or that in his circle. Or he touched a woman who shouldn't be touched or went across a border and talked to a woman whom others hated for whatever reason. We had all crossed borders. We knew what it was like to not be wanted in a place except for your back-breaking labor.

We knew the cruelty and the injustice of being wanted only to do work that others wouldn't do. But then, it's like, "Get the hell out of here!" you know? We knew the receiving end of cruelty. And of course, cruelty doesn't know boundaries. Anyone who chooses to be cruel can do so. It hasn't to do with wealth or poverty, the language you speak, or the country you're from. Sometimes even though I and the ones I worked with were already poor and already had very hard lives, there would be someone like the man who shot me, who would make our lives even worse by deciding to prey upon us if he could get away with it. And he had been getting away with it.

Maybe you are familiar with "coyotes" who help people cross the border for a fee, often a very high fee. Sometimes they will behave like kidnappers and threaten families. Many of these people, might be as poor as can be, but they spend what money they had on a cell phone so they could try to stay in touch with other relatives. But these cruel people made poor migrants phone back to their homes and demand ransom monies. The one that shot me was allied with people like that. They were building out their business. Rather than just taking money to get someone across the border, they would continue to extract money from them. They threatened them if they didn't pay up. It wasn't exactly slavery, but it was close to it. It was believing that you own a percentage of what another person worked for.

Karen: It's very cruel, isn't it?

Rudolfo: Well, these women had been used to such cruelty. They were cowed into being stolen from. They complained about it because they worked in the fields alongside others who got all their pay, and nobody took it. "But then we're different from you because there's this man who takes part of our money." And they didn't like that.

He knew that they were mixed together, but he continued to encircle the ones who were under his thumb. I just decided to take their side. It's not that I didn't think that there could be a bullet with my name on it, because these people are violent. Anyone who would behave like that toward another person is someone that you have reason to be concerned about.

Kim: Rudolfo, that was just very brave and kind for you to try to advocate for these women who were being cheated of their hard-earned wages.

Rudolfo: We had so little to lose. None of us had much of anything to our name. If they were going to take my life, I thought, "Well, I'd rather wake up in the morning and live the life I want to live rather than be under the shadow of someone who wants to make my difficult life even more so."

When I came toward him [Father Nathan] today he felt such warmth, power, and grace. He thought it might be that I was some sort of exalted being or higher version of something. But what he was feeling was what you might call the presence of the communion of the saints.

By God's grace, they included me among the martyred ones all the way back, centuries back. In his church…I too am Catholic…there's a special category for when the mass is said. The priest wears red on the feast day of a martyr. There are prayers that are only prayed for a martyr. I think after the 12 apostles, the next in rank are the martyrs.

I didn't know I was going to be raised up in that way. I only know what I know, but in this little area that I occupy, some of it flows according to those principles. I know the universe is much larger than one religion or one way of ordering things. But I've been accompanied or included in the company of martyrs. There is a Bible verse: "They have washed their garments in the blood of the lamb." Somehow, I have an exalted state because I'm in this group.

Karen: We all see that you deserve that!

Rudolfo: Well, it's funny because it was about these women deserving their livelihood. They worked for this money; they didn't deserve someone stealing it from them by threatening them. But I don't think of myself as deserving anything. I'm just always learning things. Today I'm about to learn something new.

There's a phrase, "the cloud of witnesses." Until we decide to be firm, we are maybe more like a cloud. We can choose to be firm like the Earth below the clouds. Or at least I can. I know how to make myself be firm, but I must choose to do it. And if I don't, I'm more of a cloud. I'm in this cloud of witnesses until I decide to become…maybe it's like raindrops. They go from being a vapor to a liquid and maybe to ice. I know how to become firm without being a block of ice!

Karen: Well, as Kim said, we are in awe of you being a champion for the women. We really appreciate you. And here you are today and ready to move on.

Rudolfo: Yes. The wind blows the clouds around the sky. I think the wind of the Holy Spirit is just about to blow. It will blow us from here to hereafter. I'm going to be carried along.

Karen: Wonderful!

Rudolfo: Wasn't that easy? You had to do almost nothing!

Karen: Right! We're just happy we got to meet you.

Rudolfo: Well, I'm finding that I haven't had to do very much. I was so used to such hard work. And now it's not as though I am asking anyone to peel me a grape or fluff my pillow. I don't have to ask anybody to be my servant. But neither do they ever ask me to work <laugh>. All I do is float about. And today I'm floating from where you found me to a higher realm or a better place or something. Beyond that, I don't know what will be next. I only know that it will be better.

Karen: I'm happy that you're free.

Rudolfo: Well, me too. My death was recent enough that some of the people who were my companions are still toiling away amidst hardship. I feel like I got this instead. I didn't deserve it or earn it. I'm just in it. But I wish you all well, and I will move along.

Karen: We'll be praying for you.

Rudolfo: Thank you.

(*They float away.*)

Nathan: This is Nathan. Glory be to the Father, to the Son, and to the Holy Spirit, as it was in the beginning, is now, and will be forever. Amen.

Psalm 23 is loved by both Jews and Christians and is probably vaguely familiar to many others. Its first four verses echo down the centuries:

The Lord is my shepherd; I shall not want.
He maketh me to lie down in green pastures:
he leadeth me beside the still waters.
He restoreth my soul:

he leadeth me in the paths of righteousness for his name's sake.
Yea, though I walk through the valley of the shadow of death,
I will fear no evil: for thou art with me;
Thy rod and thy staff they comfort me.

Rudolfo will explain his thinking more clearly in the conversation still to come, but this much is clear: he knew that in standing up for these women he was creating powerful enemies. He said that he knew "there could be a bullet with my name on it." He lived with that knowledge day in and day out.

Rudolfo sometimes went to church and took part in religious activities. He didn't think of himself as extraordinarily religious. But he did listen to the gospel stories and knew Jesus spent a lot of time with poor people in the fields.

When he decided to oppose the men who were stealing from the women, he'll tell us he didn't do so primarily on religious grounds. He just chose to do what's right. He didn't need to summon extraordinary courage; the ordinary courage available to all of us was all that was needed.

The four of us prayer partners in this first part of Rudolfo's story belong to four different parts of the larger Christian world. One belongs to the United Church of Christ, one is Methodist, another Episcopalian, and I'm Roman Catholic.

In the following session I didn't wait until I could get all our schedules to coincide. Dave is retired and was available on short notice. Our task was simple enough: we wanted to ask Rudolfo if we could include his story in this book. Here's how that went.

|||||||||||||||||||||||||||||||||||||||||||||||||||||||||||||||||||||||||||||||||||||||||||||||||||||||||||||||||||||||||||||||||||||||||||||||||||||||||||||

Nathan: I am Nathan. Today is August 19th, 2023. I am in Durango, Colorado on a Zoom call with Dave, who today is in Seattle. We have said our protective prayers inviting the angels and saints to surround us and keep us safe.

We are about to invite Rudolfo whom we met earlier this year. He was shot to death because of his defense of some women who were being maltreated. We'd like to know, Rudolfo, if you would be with us, and if you would be willing to allow your story to be shared in a book that I'm writing.

I'm going to be still for just a moment and invite Rudolfo.

(There was a pause.)

This is still Nathan. Rudolfo is here. I think he's gone to some trouble to power down some of his energy. When he came the last time, it was with lots of energy. Today he is trying to make himself a little smaller or something, more compact.

(Rudolfo emerges.)

Rudolfo: And this is Rudolfo. Good morning to you, sir.

Dave: Good morning, Rudolfo. Nice to hear your voice again.

Rudolfo: You know, because you recently reread the transcript of our earlier conversation, that my English was poor. But it doesn't matter because I can simply form my thoughts. Even though I'm still somewhat new here compared to a great many who have been here for ages and ages, I'm still learning different ways of communicating and presenting myself to others.

The last time I was here I was escorted by other martyrs. In the Roman Catholic Church there's a list called the Martyrology. I think from the earliest days, the church was so impressed with the witness of the martyrs that they had attempted to remember the names of each one. Even if people were martyred in a group there was some attempt made to make sure that the ultimate sacrifice made by some seemingly insignificant person was noted.

I was a field worker so I could be thought of as insignificant. But I'm not insignificant here, nor is anyone else. But there seems to be, at least in the company I have been associated with so far, I'm accorded a great deal of respect. That's uncommon for me.

Today I did ask some advice. "I know I'm going to be invited by these men into a conversation. Can you help me not overwhelm them with too much energy when I first arrive?"

And so, they showed me. "It's quite simple, just do this." There's a way in which you take all of who you are, and you compact it. I don't know that I was ever in my life on Earth around a famous person, but you see it on television all the time where some queen or president visits a school. Maybe they sit on the tiny chairs the children sit on and they play a game or something.

Even people who have very large personas and power know how to get down on the floor and roll around with the dog or how to talk to a child or how to visit a sick person in a hospital. It's not that different. It's just a matter of taking who you are and making a very concerted effort to be this version of yourself for this person in this time.

Dave: That makes sense.

Rudolfo: You must have done that with grandchildren or something. You set aside your credentials and your impressive... whatever it is <laugh>... that you have that's important and powerful, and you simply read a story or feed a child.

Dave: I just did that last night.

Rudolfo: Okay. Enough of that. Here I am. I understand the question is: May you use my story in a book? The short answer is yes.

I understand that he [Father Nathan] is choosing stories that he thinks have an uncommon capacity to explain something to people who, like you, have an uncommon interest in what happens after we die.

Dave: And that's why we picked you, because you explain yourself very well.

Rudolfo: Well, if I did, it was only incidentally. I was busy with the purpose of our being together, moving me from one level to another. I think I was easier for you than some others because I had this cloud of witnesses, the martyrs, helping me on.

I'm anticipating that even this conversation could well find its way into the pages of a book that would potentially make this conversation immortalized.

Dave: Yes.

Rudolfo: Once it gets in print, it's there for the long term, so I'm not approaching this conversation casually. I've been trying to form my thoughts to say, "What do I think I have that could be read into the record that might explain something to Father Nathan's primary congregation?" The people who populate his dream stories and whom you as prayer partner assist, almost all have died violently and suddenly. There are also a few who had some traumatic event that occurred in their lives from which they didn't recover and carried it to their grave.

Dave: That's correct.

Rudolfo: I died by gunshot. My murder was not a random act. It also had about it some predictability. I knew the men who were stealing some of the women's wages were part of a criminal network that was related to the cartels. Sometimes people call them drug cartels because that's really where they got their start and where they still make the most of their money. It gives them the power over the police and even some regions in Mexico. Whoever the governor is, is not as important as the *jefe*. But they had broadened their reach because they could, like a lot of legitimate corporations are known for first making toasters, and then they end up making jet engines or something.

They were not just doing drug manufacturing and distribution anymore. They saw all the money involved in helping people cross the borders illegally. Even though these refugees seem so poor that they put themselves in such vulnerable states to cross a border, they still are connected to somebody who has money.

They began to have kidnapping rings. The price of having a coyote help you cross the border was knowing that you're under their thumb and that they could kill you if they please. Sometimes they would extort money from anybody who had it. I think in our earlier conversation I mentioned how it might surprise some people to think of people as poor as field workers, especially ones who don't have documentation, owning cell phones.

Dave: Yes. You did mention it's commonplace.

Rudolfo: I think in the United States, if you look closely at your homeless population who appear to have nothing but a shopping cart and a sleeping bag, they'll have a cell phone.

Dave: Yeah, I saw that yesterday.

Rudolfo: I'm trying to be conscious that I'm not just having an idle chat, that this can find its way into a book. I want to confine myself to saying only things that really need to be said. I knew that opposing these men could cost me my life.

I didn't make a big deal out of the decision to side with the women. Maybe one of the advantages of being relatively poor is you have less to lose. Maybe the decision would've been harder if I had wealth. I was a poor man with less to lose than others.

When I learned of the women's plight, it made me angry. I was Mexican and Mexican American. I knew that there are many beautiful things about our culture, music, and traditions and so on. But I also knew that within our culture was too much machismo. There was too much domination of women, including domestic abuse. I wasn't going to look at that and just say, "That's the way things are, and they can't be any other way."

Dave: You stuck up for these ladies. It was the right thing to do.

Rudolfo: They were right in front of me. I'm trying to say that I don't think of myself as somebody who led this exemplary life. I could walk past a needy person the same as anybody else. "That's just more than I can handle." But this one landed at my doorstep. It was right in front of me in a way that just seemed unavoidable.

It didn't feel like much of a choice. This one was simple: "Are you going to do what's right or are you going to do what's wrong?" I chose to do what's right. It's not that I did that every time I was faced with a similar choice, but this time I just thought, "I'm not going to stand by and watch these women bust their backs to do this hard field work, only to have these jerks come behind them and steal some of their pay."

Dave: That's one of the reasons why we think your story should be in the book.

Rudolfo: Well, what I want to say is: the choice that I made to stand up for these women is a choice that's within the power of whoever reads these words.

I didn't have heroic courage. I just made up my mind to help them. I might not be able to right every wrong in the world, but these women don't deserve to be treated this way. I know their names, and I know these men who are stealing from them, and I could stand between them.

I did for a time without being murdered. But then, one day, I was <laugh>.

It was easier than I would've thought. Bullets do their job well. I guess I could have been shot in a way that paralyzed me for decades or something. There could have been a lot more suffering involved in being the target of these men. Can you say it's a blessing that they were good at what they do? <laugh> They at least finished me off, and off I went!

But that's really the takeaway. If anybody reads this and wants to find inspiration in it, make up your mind and stand your ground. I was kind of religious. I'm talking through a priest right now, and I know that you also are a man of faith. It wasn't always in the forefront of everything I did. Sometimes I might say a quick prayer over a cup of coffee in the morning and then start my day or review the day in prayer at the end. Or I might join in if there were things happening around me like some festival. Our Lady Guadalupe was a major force among the people that I lived and worked with. So, if there were some procession or rosary or something, I could fold into it.

I'm trying to say I wasn't a person who thought of their religion all the time. But I liked the clarity of the Jesus stories. He was threatened. In one of them, he was threatened while he was a baby. And then when he's a young adult, he does things that are obviously compassionate and kind, like healing somebody with a withered hand or a blind person. There would be other people standing right there criticizing him. And sometimes not just criticizing him, but threatening him, kicking him out of a synagogue or a temple. They let him know that he wasn't welcome in their town. He even told his followers, "I know they're going to kill me, but let's go." He didn't have some dark death wish. He just treated people as we all ought to treat each other.

Dave: So even though you call yourself only kind of religious, you were using Jesus's principles?

Rudolfo: Well, I did go to mass. I'm just saying… you know, I didn't spend a lot of time around churches. I was there for a service, and then I went home. But I liked what I heard: simple truths about people being worth even dying for.

Dave: Right.

Rudolfo: And not just Jesus, but sometimes the Old Testament ones. There was one I liked. I don't remember, it was one prophet. Maybe you remember it, because you know some of these stories, it's a conversation among people that are grasping at money. They're complaining, "When is the Sabbath going to be over so that we can put our goods back in the marketplace? You know, let's get this Sabbath over with so that we can get back to making money and we can sell the poor for a pair of sandals."

Dave: I don't think I remember that one.

Rudolfo: Well, if you went to look for it, you'd find it quickly. Even back then people could be treated like commodities that are bought and sold. [Ed. note: It's from the Jewish prophet Amos, Chapter 8, verse 6, "Let us buy the poor with silver and the needy for a pair of sandals."]

And I saw how it wasn't just individuals. It was cultures. It was whole societies, a whole world of inequality that people just seem to think is all right. It's all right to allow poor migrants through leaky borders. All these people who own those fields, they needed somebody to work in them, and they couldn't find enough people. Sometimes those same people at election time would raise a clamor about protecting the border and then turn around and hire illegal workers. I saw all that around me. I knew I couldn't do everything about everything, but then it landed at my doorstep. These women, I saw how hard they worked. Then to have somebody come along and think he had the right to steal from them: I couldn't stand that.

Dave: Yes. Here again, that's why you need to be in the book.

Rudolfo: All right. Well, I don't have another message other than to say to people, if you think of my voice as one that has anything important to say to you, it's, "You don't have to be heroic to do what's right. Can you just do what's right?"

I don't think I did that in prayer. I don't think I went to God or Jesus or Holy Spirit and said, "Give me the strength to make this decision." I think maybe they were in the background, probably because they're always everywhere. Maybe I was more impacted by my religious training than I thought in the moment. But I didn't think of myself as being some champion of the faith who's going to stand up for these women, because it's the godly thing to do. I just did it because it was right, and because I was angry that anybody treated these women that way.

And if you want to kill me, well, that's beyond my control.

I was shot while folks were singing happy birthday <laugh>.

Dave: That's right.

Rudolfo: And in his church, my church too, if you become a saint, the day of your death becomes the day of your official feast day because it's your birth into eternal life!

For ones like me that get called martyr, it's ironic because the day you take a bullet, <laugh> is the day you get promoted and exalted! While your body's falling to the ground, you're being elevated! Isn't that fun! It's built into the universe!

Maybe that's one more potential takeaway. There's probably lots of saints that wrote this way. I think his [Father Nathan's] friend Saint Paul, who died a martyr, said something like, "In my weakness, His strength is made manifest," or something like that. Don't get discouraged if you get put down.

Do you know the carnival game Whack-A-Mole?

Dave: Yes, I do.

Rudolfo: Well, I got whacked <laugh>, but I popped back up! I think that's the whole, Good Friday to Easter Sunday thing.

Truth and love don't die. The truth doesn't die. We might have to move through a temporary dying, but it gives life to something even better. And for people who might read these books, they could be people who are grieving the death of their children, or a spouse. They might not be reading it just because they have a vague interest in the topic. They might be reading it through the pain of deep loss.

Maybe Whack-a-Mole is a way to think of it. Can you find the irony or humor in terrible things? These guys who thought they were so powerful that they could take a gun and put a bullet through me? Well, they did. And now I'm praying for them because they're as valuable to God as the women they were stealing from. They must have their own backstories. How did they go from being newborn babies to murderers?

Dave: Yes. Right.

Rudolfo: There's got to be a long story of wrong turns and sufferings, and fear in that. And of course, people in a network like that are always under the thumb of the ones above them. The money they took from these women, somebody above them probably took a cut of that. That's the way those systems work.

So that's enough. I'm a happy man. I'm grateful that you think my story might belong alongside those of others that will be in this book.

Dave: It's been great talking to you.

Rudolfo: Well, God bless you as you go on your way. Maybe we'll meet up again.

Dave: We might.

Rudolfo: We haven't really gotten to know each other because we've been at work on our tasks. And we got the job done. But maybe after you make your way here, we look each other up.

Dave: I'd like that.

Rudolfo: Well for now, adios.

Dave: Adios amigo.

(Rudolfo departs.)

Nathan: This is Nathan. Glory be to the Father, to the Son, and to the Holy Spirit, as it was in the beginning, is now, and will be forever. Amen.

Rudolfo did not set out to explain the mysteries of the universe to us. He was just telling us about his own experiences here and hereafter. I'm choosing here to highlight several things I thought he explained well.

Rudolfo knew plenty about the harsh realities of migrant farm workers' lives. He saw suffering and injustice on such a large scale, problems too large to solve. He didn't just blame one kind of person for the situation. He knew that we're all capable of being indifferent or cruel. He pointed out the hypocrisy of landowners who decried illegal immigration at election time but then turned around and hired undocumented workers. But he also saw how low-level cartel members, themselves poor, could be cruel to someone even poorer. Rudolfo said he was as capable as all of us of walking past someone in need. But this time the problem landed at his doorstep, and he felt he needed to act. I wonder if his story can move any of us from indifference to compassion.

I liked the way Rudolfo spoke from his own experience about getting used to the new kind of body he has. He knew that when he first showed up with us that I felt lots of warm energy. He prepared for his second visit by learning how to compact himself. He spoke of clouds being a vapor that can become a raindrop or even ice. Religious people and I suppose lots of other people wonder about what form we have in the afterlife. Grieving people want to know if they will see and recognize their loved ones later. Some people experience something like ghostly apparitions of loved ones who've died. Rudolfo didn't go on about the forms he could take; he just made the effort to be with us.

Finally, I think of Rudolfo as having what Jesus called "mustard seed" faith. Mustard seeds are tiny. But built into it is this superpower to break open and grow into something large and beautiful. Rudolfo did that. He broke open to become something large and beautiful. Not that he was trying to do that: he was only trying to do what he knew was right.

At the end of our conversation as he spoke through me to Dave, Rudolfo essentially said to Dave, I hope we will later be friends. Let's look each other up. Well, Rudolfo I'd like to start now. Please keep me in your heart. I know there's lots of room there.

Chapter Twelve

Tony, "The Floating Anthonys" and Tinkerbell

Challenge: Crafting a life that was interrupted
Value: Practical common sense

Three Explanations:
Finding humor in his death story
Hopeful change in family dynamics
Tony's advice: fast track your grief

Has anyone ever said to you, "I've got good news and bad news. Which would you like to hear first?" Imagine someone saying, "I've got bad news, worse news, and horrible news. Which would you like to hear first?"

In the moments just before his violent death Tony saw three different fatal options. He never told us precisely what his cause of death was because it didn't matter. His guardian angel spared him the worst of it and assured him, "You're safe now with me."

Tony was a young adult still finding his way in life. He saw some career opportunities in family businesses that he knew he did not want to take. He was working in a short-term job on the day he died. That's where our story begins.

Nathan: I'm Father Nathan. I'm with Lisa via Zoom videoconference. Today is June 4,

2020. We're going to start with a prayer.

In the name of the Father, the Son, and the Holy Spirit, we call upon Saint Michael the Archangel and ask for your gracious protection. We call upon Raphael, Gabriel, Holy Mary and Saint Dominic, Saint Joseph, and Saint Mary Magdalene. We call on Maximilian Kolbe, all the Holy Ones in our family lines and, Lisa, any whom you'd like to invite.

Lisa: Yeah, Saint Catherine, Saint Teresa of Avila, Saint Gerard, and the guardian angels who are present. And any of the people that we have spoken to in the past who want to be present in this conversation today.

Nathan: We ask this through Christ our Lord. Amen.

Lisa: Amen.

Nathan: All right. I received this dream on Easter, April 12, 2020.

I was a young man in the middle back seat of a van. We were a work crew. We had been detoured to an unfamiliar road. In the distance were oil refineries and a tank farm. A fire had started. Thick black smoke was filling the sky. There was a big explosion and fire. I said, "These plants are old." The driver decided to reroute our trip to avoid going in the direction of the explosion. We were next to a waterway with several ships. Our van began to totter on the driver's side as we were backing up. I thought, "If we fall into that water, there'll be no getting out of here". We leveled out, but the driver kept backing up. We tilted more and I awoke.

Nathan: I'm going to pause the recording. I'll read the dream again slowly to let this person's story sink in.

(There was a pause.)

Well, the scenery in that dream brings back my childhood because I grew up around oil refineries. My dad was a harbor pilot in coastal shipping. When I got my driver's license at age 16, I had to go inside the refineries, down to the docks where the public never went and to the waterways to pick Dad up after he docked a tanker. Now those plants are old. My hometown was evacuated not too long ago when an explosion at a refinery sent a tower shooting up like a rocket.

I'm going to be still as we invite the person who brought this story on Easter to come and be with us and tell us how we can help.

I'm Nathan and I'm with my friend, Lisa, through a conference call on the computer. There's an angel present. They're all joyous, but this one, I think, is sort of giddy.

(The Guardian moves in.)

Guardian: And this is the guardian. It's funny that he would pick up on that so quickly. We all are joyful, but among my own, I'm sometimes teased good-naturedly for being overly sunny or bright. I think if I were gendered, I would be thought girly and giggly. You know his love of words. He likes the word *enthusiasm* because it means "to have God inside," and all of us do. It's just that today I'm particularly excited because this has been a long time coming; or at least there have been moments when it felt that way.

We're confident because the one I was given to accompany through his life has been very studious about this. Upon his abrupt leaving of his body, once he was able to command his imagination and consciousness to focus, he wanted to approach this in a very businesslike manner. His temperament is different from my own. He asks intelligent questions, pushing back a little bit about, "How could that be?" or pondering what might be the implications of this or that. I don't need to give it all away. I'm just talking a little overmuch so that he can see that it's easily done. He's observed others doing it and I believe he's ready to step up to the mic as I slide to the side. You'll enjoy him. The next voice you hear will be his, so blessings to you.

Lisa: Thank you. Same to you.

(The guardian moves aside.)

Nathan: This is still Nathan. There's something about her that's like Tinkerbell at the beginning of the television program, The Wonderful World of Disney. There's like a contrail of rainbows and glitter, something like that.

Okay. Now focus.

(The young man moves in.)

Young Man: Anthony is my name. I went by Tony. I believe I can do this without a lot of anxiety. I was Italian and I'm not ashamed of crying. I liked that about my family. Other guys that I was friends with were all up in their heads and cut off from their emotions. I liked the way we could shout at each other and hug and cry and laugh. You heard from the one that was just here. She's kind of a handful. Some of the time with her, well, flightiness…they all fly. They don't have wings, but they dart about like sparks. But she's been very faithful to me.

You heard the story I left with him on Easter. Coming on Easter wasn't planned, but the sequence of it worked out that way. And that's kind of a nice touch, the death and resurrection. You know that everybody lives after they die, even if they die in a way that was horrible and sudden and all of that?

Lisa: Yes.

Tony: I was a young man still starting out. I had tried college. Many of my cousins, uncles, and aunts had small businesses of one kind or another that needed delivery people or somebody to work in the back or warehousing or sometimes upfront customer service. There was always work available. I had worked from a young age, doing odd jobs, because that's the way a family business works. Everybody pitches in. Then as I got into high school and just beyond it, I did summers in different ones where they were testing me out to see if I might take to any of these lines of work and want to go into it as my own job.

I was still playing around with that, but there was a little bit of pressure in that family to take up sides. They quarreled a lot. Somebody would say something at a wedding reception or Thanksgiving. Or somebody skipped out on Nana's 90th birthday party and other people were pissed off about that. As much as we loved each other, that drama was a lot to take. I certainly didn't want to commit to a lifetime of it. It was one thing to observe the way that the two generations ahead of me did this stuff. But then when they invited me to go to work for them, I just thought, "Yeah and you're going to invite me into all of your quarrels. I'm not so sure I want to commit to that." And as soon as you committed to one thing, the other one was annoyed, you know?

Lisa: Right.

Tony: So, I got a good paying job in oil field work. Some of it, occasionally, was offshore. Much of the time it was in oil and gas fields. It involved traveling from place to place because it would be wherever there was a drill site. My crew was not unskilled, but we were kind of nonspecific. We did what needed to be done right away and we could be mobile. Sometimes we'd all be thrown into the cheapest motel they could find. But I didn't mind it. I was making good money and it occupied my time. I was with people who were kind of fun to be around. We worked so hard and were tired enough at night that there wasn't carousing or heavy drinking. I'd seen all that in high school and it just wasn't appealing to me.

I didn't want to work so hard and then blow my money on drinking or drugging or anything. So, I had a life that I was enjoying. It wasn't going to be my future, but it was my right now. I was saving some money and trying to see if there was a way in the world that I might be an adult in my family on my own terms, without having somebody always questioning everything I did and wanting to know why I didn't do it a different way. That was just part of the family script. But then, there was this explosion.

It didn't have anything to do with us except we were kind of near it, but far enough away that all we needed to do was figure, "Well, let's go back the other way. This doesn't pertain to us exactly. We're probably going to need to get on the radio and hear if our work order has just been changed. There's obviously an emergency." I was a young guy in my early 20s sitting in the middle of the backseat. I was not the driver that day. I was just somebody being delivered to a job site.

Lisa: Sure, I understand.

Tony: But then, when we started to turn around, we were next to a waterway. The roads were partly paved but the shoulders were just gravel. The guy who was driving wasn't used to driving a big passenger van. The place where he went to turn around wasn't very wide. There wasn't much traffic inside a plant, so he just figured he could maneuver and make the U-turn that he needed to make. Once he got into it, he was sort of committed to it. It wasn't as safe as he thought it might be.

Then there were a whole bunch of backseat drivers. People were telling him what he ought to do. There was too much noise and distraction and stuff. I began to think, "What the hell, if he does topple this thing over, I'm sitting right in the middle, not near a door or a window. I'm right smack dab in the middle of a box that could be tumbling into a river, and a nasty river, too, inside of an oil refinery." But there wasn't anything to do except hope it didn't turn out that way. It looked like for a minute maybe it wouldn't. You've probably seen movies where somebody was dangling on the edge of a cliff, and they show a closeup of a spinning tire that maybe it's going to grip and maybe it's not.

Most of the time in cliffhangers like that it all turns out okay and that story goes on another way. Well, this one, it just didn't. We did tip over and we rolled. You know how it is inside a van, hardly anybody puts a seatbelt on. We were all like rag dolls being thrown every which way inside it. It rolled down an embankment and into water. There was screaming… and I've told this story enough times now that at the places where I used to break up and cry… I'm pretty much…you only have so many tears and I've pretty much cried them already.

Lisa: I understand. It's certainly a scary, difficult thing to go through.

Tony: Well, it was. I couldn't really be mad at the driver. He just was a guy who made a mistake. I wasn't going to get hung up on that.

I was always curious about how things worked. That's part of why I didn't want to commit too early to a job that I would do for the rest of my life. I wanted to have some different experiences. Then I wondered sometimes, when I would go to a funeral or when I'd hear that somebody's got cancer or whatnot, how the body worked and what happens when somebody dies. Some of the older women in my family were devout. Sometimes they talked to the saints. You did a bunch of praying to saints when this started, right?

Some of them had different ones that they talked to or had little pictures dangling from the rear-view mirror of the car or little statues and stuff. They acted like the saints were part of the family. Some of them talked to their dead mother or their grandmother or whatever. They'd talk to the patron saint of the town that the family was from in Sicily.

Anyway, I've done all the talking. I haven't let you get a word in.

Lisa: I'm happy to listen. It sounds like you are a reasonable, intelligent person. You've thought about a lot of different things and just found yourself in a difficult circumstance.

Tony: Well, if anybody cares to know, when accidents happen and especially when young people die… for me, by the time it was done, the van went off the road, rolled, then caught fire and landed in water. I mean, it was like you had several different ugly ways to leave here all in one episode. And so, you could end up wondering if you someone you love went through that, "Oh my gosh, what were his last moments like?" Some of it was tumbling and screaming, but on the other hand, little Tinkerbell did a nice job of getting me up and out of that in a hurry.

She was kind of authoritative, like a schoolteacher. Maybe not like your mom, but maybe an aunt that you paid attention to, or a schoolteacher, or some woman in charge. She just said, "Now sit right here. You can either look at that or look away." I kept wanting to look at it. She said, "You were in that, but you're not now because you're over here. Your body is in there, but you're not in it anymore. And you're safe over here. Your body did the best it could to carry you as long as it could, but it couldn't carry you through that."

She made me listen. "Do you understand that you're not in your body anymore, but you're safe and I'm with you? I'm not going to leave you. We're going to just sit here until you tell me you're ready. Then I'm going to take you somewhere better, but we're not going anywhere until you say the word." I think I said the word quickly and then we were in another place. Then, well, there's a whole lot of other stuff involved that I don't need to go into. But mostly I stayed awake. I rested some, but they told me that the others… I didn't go with the other people, the other guys that were in the van. People might wonder about that. "Did you all go in a group?" Maybe that was an option, but it wasn't the way it worked for me. She took me off to my own self and then brought me to a place.

There were people there who were not shocked about hearing stuff like this. I was in the care of human people who once worked in ambulances; they were first responders or people who were not horrified by these things because it was in their line of duty. They were very sensible and professional about it. They wanted to kind of debrief me, "Tell us what you heard, what you saw, anything that you want to talk about and any questions you have." They made sure I was okay. You don't have to eat, but you can do it anyway because it's comforting and familiar. It's a way people extend themselves as a kindness. You know, "Mangia! Mangia!" So, there was something like snacks or a kind of leisure where you could enjoy a drink and sit and talk.

Then before I knew it, there began to be a little knock at the door. "Someone's here to see you. Would you be receptive to a brief visit?" It was mostly relatives who had died who just said, "Well Tony, what the hell are you doing here? You're too young to be here."

We chatted about what happened, but they were just joking to break the ice. They'd say, "You're going to like whatever it is you end up choosing." Anyway, they were nice. We joked a little bit about how I was still trying to figure out what I wanted to do, but I'd wanted to avoid some of the family pitfalls.

They said, "You're really going to like it here, because those go away." Everybody here moves at their own pace and must own up to being too bossy or having feelings that were too easily offended and all of that. Because the whole family had to do it, nobody was having their nose rubbed in it. But it was like, "Now it's time to be the grownup version of our family. We're not going to torture each other for all eternity, being petty about foolish things." So, I learned that there was already that going on and that made me happy.

|||||||||||||||||||||||||||||||||||||||||||||||||||||||||||||||||||||||||||||||||||||||||||||||||||||||||||||||||||||||||||||||||||||||||||||||||||||||||||||||||||||||||||||||||||

I'm calling this out as one of the things Tony explains so well. Imagine every single member of your family being someone who has made positive changes.

Imagine all the hurtful behaviors, even very serious ones, being a thing of the past. Imagine everyone living peacefully in the truth. Even you. Imagine everyone who ever lived choosing to take part in humble healing. That gives me joyful hope.

|||||||||||||||||||||||||||||||||||||||||||||||||||||||||||||||||||||||||||||||||||||||||||||||||||||||||||||||||||||||||||||||||||||||||||||||||||||||||||||||||||||||||||||||||||

Tony: I don't think I need to tell you anything more. It's just that I got to the point where they're ready for me to move along and they said, "It's your time."

Lisa: Yeah. Well, I'm so glad to hear about those experiences. It sounds like you were brought into circles who welcomed you out of a difficult circumstance. There were people who encircled you with warmth, care, and love. It sounds like you were given just what you needed.

Tony: Yeah. When I look back on it, I didn't break somebody's heart. I wasn't married, and I didn't leave small children. I had family that loved me that of course was grieving my sudden death, but it might have been worse for other people than it was for me. I was a young unattached guy who just left unexpectedly. On the other hand, here they were happy to have me. They were careful both to welcome me and suggest, "If you wanted to hang out with us, come this way, but for right now, you do what you need to do." They were welcoming, but they were also trying to make sure I understood that there wasn't the kind of, I don't know, peer pressure to do something here the way that I had been raised with.

Lisa: And you have so much. There's still so much for you to embrace and discover.

Tony: Well, I'm already seeing somebody showing up and it's ... I don't know. There's something like ... do you know those families or groups that do acrobatics at circuses, The Flying Wallendas?

Lisa: Yes, yes. What are you seeing?

Tony: This is like "The Floating Anthonys." We had too many Anthonys in our family. One of them was Anthony of Padua, the saint in a brown robe. You know, "Tony, Tony come around, something's lost and must be found," or something like that. I think he's just having a little fun. He's the one that started all these Tonys and Antoinettes and Tonettes. We had to take that name, Anthony, and do every little version of it that anybody could think of so that everybody didn't leap up when their name was called. There's a whole bunch of them. He's out front because he's kind of like the star.

So, I'm going to go off with a big crowd of Tonys and Antoinettes to God-knows-where… whatever the next thing is. My little Tinkerbell is going to come along. She has another name, a real angel name, but I just started calling her Tinkerbell because I thought it kind of fit her.

I won't take any more of your time because you've helped us do the thing we need to do. I'm in good hands. I think they're eager to get me to a party.

Lisa: Oh, I can imagine it's going be a beautiful, welcoming. You have such good people around you.

Tony: Well, there'll be a lot of food I'm told. Food and laughter and stuff. We did all that stuff on a big scale. *"Mangia! Mangia!"* All right. I'll be on my way.

Lisa: So nice to meet you, Tony.

Tony: Thank you, Lisa, for your help.

Lisa: Thank you. God bless you and all your adventures with the Floating Anthonys.

(Tony, Tinkerbell, Saint Anthony and all the others depart.)

Nathan: Glory be to the Father, to the Son, to the Holy Spirit, as it was in the beginning is now and will be forever. Amen.

Lisa: Amen.

Nathan: This is Nathan. Let's do a little debrief. Do you have any comment to share?

Lisa: The energy around his guardian angel was remarkable. A warmth and a joy. All the people who were there to help him were just what he needed. I loved all the Tonys, the love, laughter, and food. The very best of who he was, was brought to meet him. That was profound. It sounds like he processed a lot after going through a difficult death.

Nathan: Yeah. He didn't talk about physical pain. The thing he remembered feeling was fear, but not pain. He was pulled out of it before any of that.

Lisa: Right. It was much more of the emotional stuff. He sounded very adventurous, but also reasonable, thoughtful, young man.

Nathan: His family tended to be reactive and maybe volatile. But he preferred stepping back, thinking, and considering possibilities. He was happy to hear that he could enjoy, in the not-too-distant future, the happier parts of his family dynamic without the downsides. He said they all must act like mature adults. They can't behave like bratty children and annoy each other for all eternity.

Lisa: That's right. And they must be forthright about what their shortcomings were. They all had to be forthright about being mature adults and say, "All right, we're going to put this or that pettiness or that defect behind and be upfront in order to come together."

Nathan: That's a positive message for anybody that felt in a bind in a family that they both loved and hated. Hate is maybe too strong, but sometimes people find their families exasperating. Even though they love them, they can only take them in small doses. They must pick their spots about which things to get involved in and in which ones to stay clear of.

Lisa: Yes. There's also a message that it gets easier, right? It gets easier.

Nathan: Well, I've enjoyed, in all these encounters with people who have passed, that at least in this portion of the afterlife that we've been invited to deal in, there are no new affronts. People have to work through pain that they've already caused other people, but there's no new offending.

Lisa: It's such a beautiful thing.

Nathan: Yeah. You can heal without further injury, which is nice.
All right, good job, Lisa. I think our work here is done.

||||||||||||||||||||||||||||||||||||||||||||||||||||||||||||||||||||||||||||||||||||||||||||||||||||||||||||||||||||||||||||||||||||||||||

I've assigned a value to Tony: practical common sense. At a young age he had weighed the pros and cons of working in a family business and made a practical decision. He endured a horrible death but didn't dwell on it. He called it "a very bad day." In a bit you'll hear his advice on how to deal with your own trauma. But he's humbled about it too. "He said we're all different, but if you want my advice here it is." And it's practical.

||||||||||||||||||||||||||||||||||||||||||||||||||||||||||||||||||||||||||||||||||||||||||||||||||||||||||||||||||||||||||||||||||||||||||

Nathan: This is Nathan. Today is Friday, April 21, 2023. I'm in Phoenix with Lisa. We're asking if we could speak with Tony. We've called his story, "Tony, Tinkerbell and the Floating Anthonys." <laugh> He's from an Italian family. Lisa helped with that one almost three years ago. We've said our protective prayers and will be inviting Tony to be with us.
So, Tony, this is Father Nathan and Lisa; do you remember us? The reason we're at your door today is we're wondering if you would allow your story to be told in a book I'm writing. We want to know; would that be okay with you?
I'm going to be still and see if you'd like to borrow the voice.

(There was a pause. Tony emerges.)

Tony: This is Anthony. Yes, I remember you both well. I don't expect that you would remember me necessarily, because you do a great many of these.

It's an honor to be considered. Since going through this process with you, I made it my business to find out more about all of it. I'm aware of the books and have met some of the people whose stories are in them. All of them have the element of violent death, or at least a violent trauma event earlier in the life.

I think one part of my story is the perilous moments before the van accident. If you remember, I was in a work van. I was in the middle of it, not near a door. No one uses seat belts inside a van. Like when you park at the airport and you're in the shuttle, hardly anybody bothers. I could tell that if this thing tumbled, I could die any number of awful ways. It could burst into flames on the way down. I could drown in this nasty water inside a chemical refinery. I could die from blunt force trauma.

All of it was... <laugh> I'm imagining a cartoon, called "The Far Side." There was a drawing of the Crisis Center? It was in "The Far Side." Do you know this cartoon?

Lisa: Sure, I remember "The Far Side."

Tony: The cartoon was a simple drawing of a building with the sign "Crisis Center" on it, <laugh>. But the building was on fire, floating down a river, and it was about to go over a waterfall! Anyone inside it was in a world of trouble! There were all kind of crises going on at the Crisis Center!

He [Father Nathan] remembers me as having a lightheartedness about my sudden death that he thought might be uplifting.

How could anyone's violent death be uplifting? I love and serve the crucified and risen Jesus the Christ. He didn't dwell on the awful details of his death. He forgave everyone with one of his dying breaths. Tony can see humor in the predicament he was in in the moments just before his death. I want to be like that.

Tony: And the big Italian family component of my story might ring a bell. It might be familiar to some people who've grown up in a large Catholic family.

Can you use my story? Well, the short answer is yes, of course. And thank you for asking.

Lisa: That's wonderful. Is there any update or message you might like to add to this story?

Tony: Well, before I move into that, one consideration would be, "Would the telling of this story reopen a wound?"

Would anyone feel like the family's honor or privacy or anything like that was disregarded? I should speak to that at least.

These people are asking my permission, and it is my story. It was my death. And yes, it's true I had a big family. But it is my prerogative to say yes or no. And I'm saying yes.

If you recall my story, my family argued about just about everything, which was part of why I didn't want to go into a family business. I saw that a pattern was too well set. I would be drawn into one drama after the next. I just saw enough of that at a young age to know that I wasn't going to make my livelihood in a family business.

The only concern I have here is: would the telling of this story hurt anybody? And in the books that he's written so far, he never uses last names, and has even changed a person's name if that's what they wanted.

Lisa: Right.

Tony: He [Father Nathan] has asked God from time to time about whether he's supposed to do this verification thing that people sometimes push him toward. He's not been given the green light or the urge to do that, at least not yet.

But you asked a different question. Let me be still for a moment and get us linked up for that question.

(There was a brief pause.)

Well, I met St. Anthony, the real dude.

Lisa: Oh, you did?

Tony: Yeah. Well, I wanted to. He was such a force in the family and some of the old grandmas had a love for him. I wasn't too surprised to find out that he's very real. And relatable. I started out saying, "Yeah, okay, you're a priest and a Franciscan and a saint. I know how those stories are told. Those plaster statues make everybody look alike. Goody-goodies, all just perfect and whatnot." He shared how lived his life and things about himself that would never be in a book about holiness. I don't mean that he had some wild side that he hid from everybody, but he just shared that he was a regular guy. He thinks it's important to show that he could be a regular guy.

Lisa: Of course.

Tony: And among Italian men, that's important. A lot of them don't want to go to church because they feel like the priests, or the church women want to take from them some of the parts of their life that are the most fun. They think that if they're going to be a real Catholic, they must be careful not to curse, or never tell a dirty joke or something. Anyway, he's let me see him as a well-rounded, full human being, and not just the little snapshot you get on a holy card or in a stained-glass window.

Lisa: That does sound relatable.

Tony: Well, I had a lot of counseling from a lot of people. But he acknowledged me. He said, "I know you've done a lot of work on getting through the way your life ended. And good for you!" Most of that was already in the past. By the time I met you people, I knew it was just, you know, wrong place, wrong time. I wasn't angry at the driver or at anybody else. It was just a really bad day.

Lisa: Right.

Tony: If my story does get included in the book, here's my chance to say something that might get remembered.

I don't know that it would be profound. In an Italian family, we were not ones to go to counselors. It's not that we didn't have our troubles. Any one of us could have gone on the psychiatrist's couch and kept them busy, but it just wasn't the way we did things. And even though I lived a short life and didn't have profound sufferings before the day of my death, I really would like to just say, "Get on with it however you do it."

Push against long, slow processes if you can. Maybe some people need to do the slow and steady thing. But I would just say, "Turn up the heat. Amp it up. Go for it. If you do, the helpers show up. You don't have to think, "Oh my God, I can't expend any more energy than this. I need to go slower."

If you say, "I want to go faster, I want to go deeper, I want to work harder," before you know it resources you didn't know existed start showing up. You don't have to be a standout. You don't have to be the gold medal winner. You just have to say, "I want to go faster."

Part of it is to get over your own stuff. Anybody who has been wounded wants to be healed of what has wounded them. But you can also make yourself more useful, too. This version of me that's still limping along because of trauma can still be helpful. You can be a wounded healer. What you might want to say is, "What I'd really like is for the universe to get the best of me and I want to be the best of me to give it."

You can make your own healing process be not just your private little workout regimen or something. You can say, "I want this to be for the good of everybody who runs across me, that I want to go faster and further."

I don't know if I have very much more of that left to do. Really. I mean, I was young, and as I said before, I wasn't married, I didn't leave a grieving wife and little kids.

It's been long enough ago now that most people who remember me can also remember that I was a lot of fun to be around. My memory doesn't have to be a horror story about my death unless people want to do that, because you can't stop people from being the way they want to be. But get over it <laugh>. Go faster, reach higher! The sky's the limit! Something like that.

I would just say, set your intention that, "I want to be the next great version of myself and not let the way that I died weigh me down." The boss, Jesus, is the icon of that. That's why there are crucifixes all over the place because he's the one who went through hell and back and didn't take but three days to do it. It doesn't have to be long and slow. It can be fast if you ask for the right help. At least it's one option. There's no shame if you opt for a different way, because not everybody's the same.

Lisa: True.

Tony: That's what I would say: "Get over it. Hurry up!" Something like that. If you wanted any advice of mine, then that's it. I'm only me. I'm only one Tony among all the Tonys. But now I'm somebody who can be enlisted as part of a team. If anybody felt like they read about me and connected with what they heard and wants me to be on their team, I'd be available in an instant.

Lisa: Aw, that's a very kind, very inspiring.

Tony: Well, I grew up a Catholic and I knew about calling on the saints. I knew a little bit about purgatory, although I thought of it more like a jail. I know I can help people; I was helping people while I was here. I've helped people since the last time we spoke. And I could help people even if they only meet me because my story is in the book, if it ends up being there.

So, I'm done here. I don't need to stay any longer. I guess I'm kind of establishing myself as this guy on the go. <laugh>. So, If I'm that guy on the go, I really should go <laugh>.

Lisa: That sounds like great advice. Thank you for that. For us living now and upon our passing. Thank you.

Tony: Bye-bye.

(Tony departs.)

Nathan: This is Nathan. Glory be to the Father, to the Son, and to the Holy Spirit. As it was the beginning, is now and will be forever. Amen.

"Amp it up. Get over it!" That doesn't mean don't feel your pain. But I believe it's true that if you ask for help doing what feels beyond your strength, you'll be strengthened in ways you couldn't have imagined.

I love Tony's take on Jesus' death and resurrection. "The boss, Jesus, is the icon of that. That's why there are crucifixes all over the place because he's the one who went through hell and back and didn't take but three days to do it. It doesn't have to be long and slow. It can be fast if you ask for the right help. At least it's one option. There's no shame if you opt for a different way, because not everybody's the same."

Tony knows he's been a helper here and hereafter. Did you hear him offer to be on your team? Hey, Tony, I'd like to take you up on your offer. You did "make the cut." Your story deserves to be told in this book. If there's room for a Nathan in that sea of Anthonys, count me in. Godbless.

Chapter Thirteen

Abraham's Family and
Our Lady of Rwanda

Challenge: Genocidal Betrayal
Value: Forgiveness

Three Explanations:
Universal Belonging
Afterlife Childcare
The Saints' Eye for Detail

Many of the stories I've shared in these books are about an individual who experienced a violent traumatic death. This story is different. In the dream, I was brought into the life of a small family. Their violent deaths were a part of a very much larger event, a genocidal one.

I remember the Rwandan genocide of 1994 primarily as a long-ago news event. I hadn't given it much recent thought until I received a short dream that looked more like a snapshot. I met Abraham and his family and, upon meeting them, met Charles and Mother Mary as Our Lady of Rwanda.

I am a member of IANDS, the International Association for Near-Death Studies. I regularly attend our annual convention. In 2019 I was invited to be a presenter on a panel. So was Michael Quinn. We each had about 15 minutes to describe our contribution to the field of Near-Death Studies and related topics. Afterwards, Michael and I had lunch together. He showed a lot of interest in the ministry my prayer partners and I share. I asked him if he would like to take part in a session. He agreed right away. Here is the story of our first prayer session together.

||||||||||||||||||||||||||||||||||||||||||||||||||||||||||||||||||||||||||||||||||||||||||||||||||||||||||||||||||||||||||||||||||||||||||||||||||||||||||||||||||||||||||||||||||||||||||||||||||

Nathan: I'm Nathan. I'm with Michael. We're in Philadelphia, at the IANDS conference. We've said our protective prayers. I'm uncertain about this, but here are my notes from a dream I had on August 13, 2019:

I saw a group of three African people. I think they were a family. There was a young man in his 30s who was smiling, a woman who might have been his wife, and a child who might have been between 10 and 13 years old. All they did was look at me, and the man smiled. I awoke.

I'm wondering if they're in need of the kind of help that we might be able to provide. I'm going to go into prayer for a moment and see if they do.

(There was a pause.)

Someone is going to speak who will clarify what this is about. Do you know the name Charles Lwanga? I don't know him very well, but he's a Ugandan saint. I think he was martyred in the 1880s with a group of people. They're known as St. Charles Lwanga and Companions. He wants to greet you with the sign of peace.

(Charles emerges and extends his hand to Michael. They shake hands.)

St. Charles: This is new for me, doing this. But I live in the Kingdom of God and always am open to surprises. I'm here only to provide a little help.

I was a martyr along with others who were martyred. I was one of the first African martyrs to be recognized by the universal church. I have a fondness for the people of my continent, particularly people who died a violent death, especially if it was involving the faith. I'm given to know, the Spirit is speaking in my ear explaining, that this man [Father Nathan] has been for decades following a Spirit-guided process. These people who peered into his dreaming recently are operating a little differently from many who preceded them. I'm here just to give assurance that this is in the Holy Spirit. These people came in a little unconventional way, but they've arrived with you.

They looked as though they were peering through a window because they were looking for safety. They died in hiding. These were people who died in the Rwandan genocide.

There came a mass hysteria where people who had for decades lived side by side in peace but were of different tribes were whipped into horrific violence.

This family had to run to safety. They sought sanctuary in a Catholic church. It proved not to provide for them the safety they had hoped it would. They did die together, although their dying was horrific. They need some comfort, guidance, and direction that you two have been enlisted to help supply.

So that's my role. I am to come and provide some assurance that, yes indeed, this is something the Holy Spirit has invited you to help with. Have you any questions for me before I slide to the side?

Michael: Have you already been working with them in preparation for this moment?

St. Charles: Only as a member of a larger team, as something of a chaplain or someone who might be at the front of the room giving a talk, not in the close one-on-one work that you're about to do. Others have helped them become ready to cross. The smile that the father showed him in the dream was an attempt to indicate willingness and hope.

So with that, I will recede. Next you will be speaking with Abraham.

(St. Charles slides to the side; Abraham emerges.)

Abraham: I'm Abraham. I am most grateful for your willingness to help me and my family. You are on the Earth still and have not died, but you belong with a team, some who were human and who died and are now souls. We were taught that they were the holy souls or the souls in purgatory. My family has been Catholic for three generations. The animist, or the native religions that preceded our ancestral baptism line, had already a reverence for the ancestors and a sense of praying for their good. So, when the missionaries came and spoke of the souls and the connection between the ones who had died and the ones still here, that made the Good News easier to embrace because it seemed familiar.

The man who was just here, Saint Charles, was revered by us because there are not very many canonized Africans, and especially ones more recent. There are some very old ones, like Monica and Augustine, and Benedict. Some of the North African desert folk were less black, maybe browner, and looked a little more as Jesus might have, more Palestinian. They were still of our continent, but we particularly revered Charles Lwanga and Companions because they looked like we did and were from a land very near where we lived. It's been an honor to have him come to us.

We have been schooled in how to take what happened to us and move ahead in a graceful way. But what happened to us was so appalling for several reasons.

Michael: Excuse me. When you say "us," are you talking about just your wife and child or are you talking about a group of you?

Abraham: All of us. I'm going to get specific to my wife and child, but all of us endured the collective madness of what happened in our countries.

Part of it aligns with the story of Our Lord of having companions who, when he most needed them, betrayed him. We were devout Catholics. They've been reminding us that the colossal betrayal that happened to all of us, where our neighbors took machetes to hack us to death, has a place in the heart of Jesus. Part of what Jesus endured was not only the pain of the cross, the nails, and spear, but also the pain of betrayal. To move through it, he needed to compose himself to the Father's will, and trust in the Father's love. So here we've recently been on something of sacred retreat to adopt this way of being.

I'm highlighting forgiveness as an exemplary value Abraham displays. He has a horrible experience he can replay; he simply chooses not to. Listen as he describes how the process of forgiving can move. Also, note his sense of universal belonging, even after having been singled out and rejected violently.

Abraham: The group we have been in were particularly devout Catholic Christians. There were other kinds too: Lutherans and Anglicans. We've been in a smaller subset because it felt most comfortable to us, and we have needed to feel comfortable. One of the things that we suffered from was the perception of differentness, that we were the wrong kind and therefore to be killed. So, for a short time, we wanted to be with our own kind because it felt safest. Later, we'll move out because this very idea that we have only one kind is a distortion. But for right now, it's best that we be in a safe group. Our own kind will later move. They've taken me aside as husband and father and given me a bit of coaching about how to help my wife and our child to ascend or move.

I simply came in his dream and, as a mercy, opted not to show pictures of machetes, screaming murderers and people being hacked, because that's what the experience was. I hoped I could simply peek in a window.

You asked already if we had been prepared, and, yes, we have. Others have assured us: "You and your family are indeed safe and are ready to move to a new home that you're going to recognize, even though you think you've never seen it." They've said, "You will likely experience a coming home to a place you haven't been." So, it's one of those mysteries of life and of faith.

I have been told that my wife and my child don't need to be part of an active conversation, and I felt relieved. They've suffered enough. I've been assured that I can speak for all of us, and I can. You are a father, are you not?

Michael: Yes.

Abraham: Sometimes men, in cultures, are told that we are the head of a household. Even in cultures where there's very strong masculine bossing of women, in such places, right below the surface are the women running everything and making you know that they're the hidden boss. So, I don't have pretensions that I am the male head of the household and the chieftain who will take my little family across. My wife is a very strong woman; she proved it in the ordeal of our passing. My daughter is her mother's daughter, so we were a household of three chiefs. But for now, I'm grateful that I can be the one to do the steering of whatever this is and let them simply try to move as calmly as possible into the next realm. That's what you're helping us do.

Michael: Also, just to add a little bit of the beauty of your connection with your beautiful family, yes, I have a son. But in a few weeks, I'm going to have a grandchild for the first time.

Abraham: That's good! I had the grace of fathering a daughter. I was a catechist. Even though I didn't get to be a father for as long as I would have liked, or a grandfather, I'm told the truth that we're all brothers and sisters in Christ, not only Roman Catholics, and not only Christians. We're told, "You've known this already. But you're going to begin experiencing it in ways that are new. We won't shock you with all of it at once, but you're going to see unfolding before you how much you belong to everyone and everything. Some of that will take you into the heart of the crucified Christ who had to love the ones who crucified him. We want you to know that on your future task list, will be the forgiving of the people who committed this atrocity." I knew that already, and I'd said some of those prayers, but I think that is ... it's a stubborn stain. It will take more scrubbing. I believe that's what purgatory is, a cleaning place. I'm hoping to be cleaned more deeply. I know it's beyond my power. I can't clean myself that cleanly. So, I know that there's some of that to be done. Perhaps my wife and daughter have it to do in some way, too.

I've also been told that I had already been chosen and had responded to the call of leadership. And that if I'm willing, I can both undergo this process and turn around to those a little bit behind me and guide them into the part that I've just become familiar with, that I might be some sort of a peer counselor, servant, something. That feels very comfortable to me. They use the word "comfort" a lot here because we've been in much need of comfort and comforting.

So, I don't think I need to talk any further. I think it's clear that we are to move. We just need transportation. We need a mode: we need a guide or a cab, or something. That's what we were told: that when we get with you it will be made clear.

Michael: Did Saint Charles or anyone else give you any indication of what form that assistance might take?

Abraham: We were told that it would be as creative and vast as the jungle and the sky, and that there wasn't only one way in which it would appear. God's great creativity demands that there be many specific, sweet ways in which this might take place.

Michael: Just to clarify, were you asking for this assistance for yourself and your family? Or are there others?

Abraham: For right now, I think you are being asked only to help us three.

Michael: Okay. But you talked about so many other magnificent ways of doing this I thought maybe you were encompassing others.

Abraham: I think we're being observed. It's not our business to turn to others and say, "Come this way." I think we're simply to undergo whatever this will be for the three of us and perhaps it will encourage or inspire others who are watching.

I believe I am to invite helpers now. I think I'm to close my eyes and be still. Father Nathan and I are to connect more deeply; then something will be made manifest.

(There was a pause.)

It is as sweet and delightful as we had been prepared for. She is Our Lady of Rwanda.

When we taught the children, one of the things we had to do to enculturate the faith was to begin with the images that the Belgians, and the Germans, and the British brought us. All the statues, and the paper pictures, holy cards, all of them looked white. Some of them were a little more forward-thinking and were able to say, "You understand that these were our artists who created these depictions of what the Holy Family might have looked like." They didn't look at all Middle Eastern. They looked British. Some of them said, "It will be for you, your people, and your own artists to begin to take the seed of the faith and help it become Rwandan or African."

One of the things we used to do with children ... Well, I'm thinking of this one. Corn was a staple for us. It grew abundantly. We were not disposed toward waste, so everything got used. Even before the stalks and the roots could be ground up to be put back to enrich the soil, we would take the dry husks of the leaves, and those became fabric for toys, and art objects. It was abundant and cheap.

If you were careful with it and you dried it in just the right way, and perhaps put it under a rock or a book, something heavy that would make it flat, it began to be something like paper. Then, you could use it in a classroom. One might take the scissors and the paste and make objects of it. The children could play with it. We taught them how to make Madonna and child dolls with bits of fabric that would be dyed black, scraps of fabric that could be put in a dye bath to become dark so that the skin of the mother and child looked like we did. Then, they could adorn their creation. They would perhaps wrap the fabric around a bit of some fluff, anything that made it round, and then create some sort of a veil and some wrapping for the child to be in.

We called this Our Lady of Rwanda. It's not that she appeared [in physical form] as she did in Portugal or France. There was not a pilgrimage site that people visited. We simply created an image that we venerated as Our Lady of Rwanda because we were inviting her to live in our homes. A moment ago, when he and I closed his and my eyes, this is what I saw. Our Lady of Rwanda would like to come and to take us to her. So, I think I'm to be still one more time and see how she will do that.

Michael: Good.

(*There was a moment of stillness.*)

Abraham: We will ride on sacks. When anything that came in a large sack, beans maybe or fertilizer or something, we didn't throw the sack away. It found some other use. The use that it was often put to ... it didn't tear easily. The fabric was strong. You could poke holes in it and tie string or cord with another longer string that an adult could hold on to and it became a toy to drag children. You could have small ones sitting on the bag and the adult would pull it with a cord. It became a toy to pull them along a road or a field.

She's coming, and she's going to pull us. We're going to sit down on a rather large sack for two adults and a child who's nearly our size. Given another year, she might've been taller than us both. So, Our Lady is apparently strong enough to pull three at once! She's going to pull us to the next place. I thank you for your help. We don't want to keep Our Lady waiting.

Michael: Have a wonderful journey!

Abraham: Thank you. God bless you.
Before she goes, she would like a word with you, to say, "I'm now what they just referred to as Our Lady of Rwanda."

Michael: Good.

(Our Lady of Rwanda emerges.)

Our Lady of Rwanda: It's amusing to me that I'm Our Lady of so many things. Lakes, and mountains, and waysides. People can make me "the star of the sea" or "the rose of something." I have a great many titles. This one is particularly dear to me.

Michael: It's beautiful.

Our Lady: It is, isn't it? They know me as their mother. Their family life is strong and very sweet. They lived as I did with very little materially. When they spoke of taking every scrap of everything and turning it to a creative use, I did that for a lifetime. Even though I can now be called "Queen of Angels" and "Queen of Heaven" and many of the depictions of me are with royal dress and crowns and such, that's all very sweet and it's honoring me. But my real way of being was saving every scrap and finding a new use for it.

These people felt like they were scraps. And in fact, they were cut and hacked. They are going to find that they are now the raw material for beautiful creations. Not just once, but many times, because it's eternity. They're going to find that every bit of them, every scrap of them has a holy application. They are going to be the media of art for many creative projects because they've made themselves so trusting. They have every reason not to be very trustful, and yet they've overcome it. They have a sweetness that's extraordinary.

(Our Lady departs.)

Nathan: Glory be to the Father, to the Son, and to the Holy Spirit. As it was in the beginning, is now, and will be forever. Amen.

||||||||||||||||||||||||||||||||||||||||||||||||||||||||||||||||||||||||||||||||||||||||||||||||||||||||||||||||||||||||||||||||||||||||||||||||||||||||||||||||||||||||||

In the past when I have requested permission to use someone's story, it was because it was going to be included in a book. This time we were asking permission to tell this story before a live audience at the 2023 IANDS conference. We were asking the Holy Spirit if it was prudent to do this.

I was on a Zoom call with Michael and Linda Quinn on January 6, 2023.

This story included a visit from Saint Charles Lwanga, then Abraham, and finally Our Lady of Rwanda. It seemed like we should have the permission of all three. The conversation we had that day included several others but here I'm limiting myself to only mentioning these three. We said our protective prayers, then sat in silence for a bit. Here's how pieces of that conversation went. Our Lady spoke first.

Nathan: This is Nathan. We are going to hear from Our Lady.

(Our Lady emerges.)

Our Lady: And this is she. Hello.

Michael: Welcome, Our Lady.

Our Lady: I'm delighted that you have this idea of sharing the story of Abraham and his family. I never was a schoolteacher, but, late in life, I had the role of being something of a mentor to young men and women whose lives were imperiled by doing the thing that Jesus, the risen version of him, asked them to do. Most of them died violently because somebody was offended at their way of being and their message. None of us moved through that period without grief.

However, we knew very well the joys of serving the One who later was called the Risen Christ. We simply went about our business with as much peace as we could muster. And when we couldn't muster sufficient peace, the Holy Spirit would supply some.

You've lived long lives. You know that one must cultivate inner peace. It's not a given for anybody.

Linda: Certainly. Thank you.

Our Lady: And if telling this story causes Nathan trouble, he has many helpers. So, we needn't concern ourselves with that. And for heaven's sake, if you needed to edit anything I said, I was just speaking in the moment. I was just saying what I felt in the moment.

Michael: Sure.

Our Lady: It's a lovely story, and Abraham's family are lovely people. It's a little different than most of the stories that Nathan has been invited into. I'm thinking of the category of genocide. You're familiar with a variety of traumatic stories that come his way. But a genocide story…this one stands out.

He [Father Nathan] has already told you his thought process that's evolving has to do with people who explain well what has happened before, during, and after their passage. I think it's a lovely idea.

Mine is not the last word on permission giving, but I would be a part of the cast. So, it's appropriate to ask me if I want to take part. And my answer is yes. Absolutely.

Then it would be up to Charles Lwanga and Abraham and his family. There was no one else named.

All right. I think Charles should be next, or perhaps Abraham. So, God bless you. I won't go far.

(Our Lady slides aside.)

Nathan: This is Nathan. Is this going too fast for you? Do you feel like you need a breath?

Michael: No, no.

(St. Charles emerges.)

St. Charles: This is Charles. I will be brief. I was brief when I came into this story the first time. I'm not very well known. Where I'm known, it's mostly by Roman Catholic people because I did rise to the level of having a day on their calendar.

The people at your conference probably will never have heard of me. But you can at least introduce the story. It would be he [Father Nathan] giving me voice as he did before. Should this occur, I will occupy the voice and, without drawing attention to myself, be in it. I recall very fondly the first time we did this.

Michael: In the many sessions we've had with Father since then, you were the only saint to shake hands with me. Do you remember that?

St. Charles: Yes, I do. And Father Nathan only read it a short time ago. I think he referred to it as my wanting to share a sign of peace. I think that your custom of the shaking of a hand had its origins in showing that you were unarmed. For the people in that story that was important. It would've been nice to meet someone who was unarmed extending their hand.

There's nothing I said when I was with you that I would not want said aloud. I didn't have a very large role in it to begin with, other than to make an introduction. I didn't stay long. I'd be happy to be an active part of this project.

Michael: Thank you so much.

St. Charles: One day we'll be good friends. Maybe we can have adventures together. But this presentation can be one adventure that happens on these two planes in the meanwhile.

Michael: Nice! We'll look forward to it.

St. Charles: I didn't leave a body of literature like some others, but, if it ever interested you, you could probably find stories and tales about me that might have some truth in them. <laugh>. You could get to know me a little better if you wanted to do that.

Michael: That'd be nice. Thank you.

St. Charles: All right. I think, I now will once again introduce Abraham because he's the next logical one in this sequence of things.

(St. Charles slides aside. Abraham emerges)

Abraham: This is Abraham. We were becoming less tribal, I think, right at the time that these tribal divisions reared and caused all the damage that they did. The nation states, those lines that Europeans drew all over Africa sometimes didn't serve us well. That had a great deal to do with what happened in that genocidal madness. I'm talking about tribe because we had ways in which we would make someone an honorary member of the tribe. Most tribes had some way in which they acknowledged that even though this person was not of our bloodline, we've made them an honorary member. And I think of the two of you as honorary members of our family tribe, because you made yourselves available to us at a moment when we most needed kind support.

Michael: Abraham, in the story three years ago, Our Lady came. You were transported to another realm on sacks. Even though you keep time differently than we do, how has your time been spent?

Abraham: Well, that would take a great long time to describe. We've kept the sacks here. <laugh> They're artifacts that you wouldn't want to discard.

You know, we don't have such scarcity of materials to make us want to hang on to every bit of a thing. And here there's no waste anyway. A thing might cease to be because it's not needed any longer. There's not a need for landfills. I guess it would be more like recycling. Whatever is lasts long enough to serve its purpose. And if it's no longer needed, it stops being. I'm speaking of artifacts, things not persons.

The short story would be that once we passed as a group, the three of us did different things.

We understood already, but it was made clearer to us that we were a unit, but we were also individuals. There are things that we would be best advised to do together and others that we would be best advised to do individually.

We were also told that we were always in charge of our own processes. Decision-making was always up to us.

Michael: Okay.

Abraham: My daughter was already asserting herself at 12 years old. The culture was beginning to take on more western habits. Children were getting freedoms that their parents didn't have, or the grandparents certainly didn't have. My daughter was ready to assert herself here and go off on her own in good company to pursue things and then kind of report back.

I didn't get to raise my daughter to adulthood. But, since her movement here, I don't feel responsible for her safety, which I couldn't provide in the end anyway.

That phrase, "It takes a village" comes to mind. The village has done a great job with her. We see her when she wants to be seen. She has her own…I hesitate at the word independence, but it's at least somewhat appropriate.

Michael: Sure.

Abraham: I don't feel like I have a lot of healing left to do. Or a lot of laborious, forgiving left to do.

Michael: What about your wife?

Abraham: Well, let me finish with me first. I just want to read that into the record because you're recording the conversation. It might be important for people to know that when you've been involved in something on such a colossal scale, it might just seem like you'll never be finished with the forgiving part.

At least for me I don't think that's the case. I think forgiving can be like other things. When you do enough of it, you get used to doing it sort of second nature. You don't have to give it a great deal of time and thought. You just do it.

Why would I want to not forgive? I've been able to be with some people who went through that same genocidal event who are much more hung up on the cruelty of specific times, persons, and places.

Michael: I see.

Abraham: Some folks get so embedded in a story about what happened that day or the day before. They had no idea that the neighbor who babysat their child was now the one to betray them. Some of those stories are so vivid, and the detail of it is so appalling that as much as people might like to forgive, they still are working through the colossal betrayal of it.

I had such stories. Maybe I was just given an extraordinary grace. Maybe it wasn't so much any attribute that I brought to the topic. However it happened, I sometimes can help others with that to the degree that they allow themselves to be helped.

And then other times I'm directed, 'You've had enough of genocide. Let's go somewhere else.' Sometimes just the fact that you went through a thing like that doesn't mean you need to focus on it, in what you call the afterlife. You can assist with it without it being your principal occupation.

They've told us, "You had such a rough go of it that we think that some of the amusement park aspects of the afterlife might be really more fitting. Go have some fun and don't feel like you have some obligation to stay in places in the universe where there's lots of laborious work to be done. You can always come back to that."

I won't go on more about how I've done that. You asked a question that I deflected about my wife. For this purpose, we're going to stick with the format. Since she didn't speak earlier, she's not going to speak now.

Michael; Okay.

Abraham: Let me be still.

(There was a pause.)

This is still Abraham. She's saying it's kind of you to inquire. The thing that I was just referring to about our daughter choosing a significant amount of her energy to be on her own or apart from our supervision, has afforded my wife the opportunity to take up new interests.

She's supplying this, but it's been my experience too, that sometimes we're used as exemplars. We're being shown as an example. "Here are people who went through what you went through, who mostly are finished with it, and with its effects,"

Some people conform to the idea that their murder is so appalling and dark that they'll just never get to the end of it. Sometimes we have been used to say, "Oh, please don't think that way. In fact, here are two people who would say the opposite. You don't have to be defined by any part of your history to the exclusion of the whole person you are. Please don't do that. Don't let yourself become this horrific story. It's just a thing that happened."

My wife would have liked to have had more children. That just never happened for us. She miscarried several times. She is participating in childcare. There are little ones who came here before their parents. There are people who love caring for small ones. And there's much to be gained by the maturation process that we go through on the Earth, even if we die as little ones. People might wonder about that. You know, what happens when a toddler dies? Do they stay that age? Do they instantly become adult? How does that work? It doesn't have only one way of working, but let's just say my wife has continued in a maternal role and is enjoying it.

⸻

Have you heard of a grace note? In a musical composition it's a tiny flourish that adds beauty to the main theme. In sheet music it's a little note like an apostrophe above and coming before the main melody note.

Abraham's wife loved motherhood. Her daughter, now a teen, wanted more time away from her parents. In her afterlife, Abraham's wife found a place to share a mother's love where it was needed. It's incidental to the main storyline of this chapter, but I found it worth noting.

Abraham: [For those who died while still learning to speak] there is something like the acquisition of speech and comprehension, not exactly of human languages like on the Earth, but something like it where you do have to learn how to form thoughts and communicate them to others, even here. And that involves some coaching by people who already know how to do it.

There are people who lived chronologically adult lives on the Earth who felt robbed of a childhood because of traumatic abuse that made them feel robbed of their innocence. They are given the opportunity to revisit childhood. "If you feel cheated that you didn't get to have an innocent childhood, would you like to have one now?"

There are helpers who are there to be the teacher or the band leader, providing what might have been part of a normal childhood. You get to move through some of those things that you felt deprived of. My wife does some of that.

Michael: We appreciate the insight.

Abraham: I love her more than I ever loved her. We've opted to spend a fair amount of our time as a couple. We're free to do that. There's that one place in scripture that sometimes people refer to where Jesus says, "In heaven, there's no giving or taking in marriage."

It's a ridiculous story. People who were angry at him and who didn't believe there was an afterlife at all, told a stupid story. "There was a woman who buried seven husbands. Jesus, in this stupid afterlife idea of yours, who's going to be the husband of her? Is there going to be some brawl of seven men claiming her?" Because that was the way that men thought: women were their property. In that story Jesus says something like, "There will be no such giving and taking in marriage in heaven." And so, some people take that as proof that there will not be marriage in heaven because it says so in the Bible.

Okay. I've said enough. I should be still and see how this concludes.

Michael: Thank you. Thank you so much.

(Abraham slides aside.)

Nathan: This is Nathan. St. Dominic would like a word.
(This was a surprise to me that day. Saint Dominic founded our order. I've lived as a Dominican for 44 years. I pray with him often, but today was special.)

(St. Dominic emerges.)

Michael: Hello?

St. Dominic: I can be brief.

Michael: Oh, we have all the time in the world.

St. Dominic: Well, yes. You're generous with your time.

Michael: Thank you. It's wonderful to have you here.

St. Dominic: Well, I'm never far from Nathan and his projects. I'm grateful for all the support that you've given him in recent years in the growth of this work. Thank you for helping him laugh and be at peace with what he's been given to do, which he's willingly taken up. I once shared with him that I was hated during my lifetime for being a reformer, because always that means upsetting someone. Changing the way things are done is never universally acclaimed. You can do that with all the love you have to bring but that doesn't mean that others won't find fault.

Michael: That's right.

St. Dominic: Your concern about the outlandishness of this process, of getting in front of a group and saying, "Oh, yeah, Mary talked with us." Well, she talked to me too. She just does that.

If this comes to pass, at this conference you'll at least be in front of a group of people who have their own experiences. Each one can turn to the one next to them and tell a story as outlandish as the previous one. If anyone were to say, "Well, that's ridiculous," or "It's blasphemous that he's purporting to say or do such a thing," he knows very well that the motto of our order is "Veritas," which is truth. And he's only telling the truth.

The reason you've engaged us all in conversation today is to point out, "Yes, but not every truth necessarily needs to be broadcast." You're doing this with discretion and forethought.

You've already gotten the permissions you've sought. I don't need to stay any longer and neither does anyone else. I think we've sufficiently covered the territory. All right. Adios.

Michael: God bless. Thank you.

(St. Dominic slides aside.)

Nathan: Glory be to the Father, to the Son, and to the Holy Spirit, as it was in the beginning, is now and will be forever. Amen.

This is a very Catholic story. The Story of Abraham and his family is full of Catholics. Three Catholic saints, Charles, Mother Mary, and Dominic show up. Abraham is a catechist, a Catholic leader. Their deaths occur on the property of a Catholic Church and the story is moving through me, a Catholic priest.

At our best we Catholics are more than just a denominational subset of the larger body of Christians. Our name means universal. At our best we offer universal blessings that you don't have to be Catholic to receive. When Saint Charles Lwanga first speaks through me he says, "This is a new thing, me doing this. But I live in the Kingdom of God and am always open to surprises." No matter how well you think you know yourself, God, and the universe, leave room to be surprised.

It's possible to grow in the capacity to forgive and even to excel at forgiving. Abraham did that. He knew he had still more forgiving yet to do. He called being hacked to death with a machete "a stubborn stain," but he trusted that he could finish forgiving those who did this to him and to his family. He even taught this to others. "You don't have to give it a great deal of time and thought. You just do it."

And how do you explain something as beautiful as Mother Mary using something leftover, a scrap of a bag turned into a kind of sled, as the vehicle to move this little family along? It's such a lovely detail that had unique meaning. Abraham was told to anticipate that his family's movement "would be as creative and vast as the jungle and the sky, and that there wasn't only one way that it would appear. God's great creativity demands that there be many specific, sweet ways in which this might take place."

I'll end with this. Mother Mary added this insight: "These people felt like they were scraps. And in fact, they were cut and hacked. They are going to find that they are now the raw material for beautiful creations. They're going to be, not just once, but many times, because it's eternity, they're going to find that every bit of them, every scrap of them has a holy application. They are going to be the media of art for many creative projects because they've made themselves so trusting. They have every reason not to be very trustful, and yet they've overcome it. They have a sweetness that's extraordinary."

Should you ever feel reduced to just scraps of your former self, remember that divine creativity as vast as the jungle and the sky. If you'll allow it, the scraps of you might be on the way to becoming new and beautiful.

Abraham, thanks for choosing us to be part of your family's crossing. I hope that many who hear your story will be inspired by it and will find a place in your family's hearts.

SECTION TWO

Introducing Jimmy Akin:
This Isn't Rocket Surgery!

Once, I was watching a stand-up comedian doing his routine when a joke fell flat. The audience didn't get it. He scolded his silent audience and said, "C'mon, folks, this isn't rocket surgery!" Then they laughed. He taken those two references to very complex themes, rocket science and brain surgery, and mashed them together. Get it?

Some people comprehend very detailed, precise things. They become scientists, lawyers, accountants, surgeons, and computer repair technicians. I'm always grateful that these folks exist when I need their services.

When I began writing my *Afterlife, Interrupted* books, I was told by Christopher Fadok, OP, my provincial superior, that I really ought to get in touch with Jimmy Akin. For whatever reason, that advice went in one ear and out the other. I just didn't get it. At least not at that time.

It was Jimmy Akin who, years later, got in touch with me. He invited me to be a guest on his podcast, "Jimmy Akin's Mysterious World." I appear as a guest on many podcasts but was unprepared for what awaited me. This host had read both of my books cover-to-cover and was easily conversant in the various stories in them. He footnoted and cross-referenced my writings with the official Catechism of the Catholic Church and Old and New Testament scriptures. Our very long interview became two episodes of his podcast, which has an audience of over 100,000 listeners.

With skillful precision, Jimmy Akin explains that I am not doing something dark and forbidden. Jimmy has changed my world.

I don't know what he knows, but in the essay that follows he explains his reasoning so clearly that you'll be smarter when you're finished. Jimmy calls himself "a Catholic apologist and paranormal investigator." I think of him an advocate, which means "one who speaks up for."

That's a title Christians give to the Holy Spirit.

Jimmy, you've been a gift in my life and work. I'm grateful to the Holy Spirit that you've developed your gifts and talents and put them to work for me. Thanks for contributing your expertise here in Section Two. I hope this book is the first of many projects we work on together.

Helping Souls Versus Necromancy

By Jimmy Akin

Jimmy Akin is an internationally known author and speaker. He is a senior Catholic apologist with more than 30 years of experience defending and explaining the Faith. His Jimmy Akin's Mysterious World *podcast can be found in standard podcast apps, at Mysterious.fm, and at YouTube.com/JimmyAkin.*
Copyright © 2023 by Jimmy Akin.

"What a fascinating ministry Fr. Nathan Castle conducts! Catholics and other Christians have long prayed for the deceased to help them on their way to heaven, and history contains many accounts of souls reaching out to the living for help. However, most people have only a few such encounters, at most. Fr. Castle reports being contacted by souls on a weekly basis, suggesting a special calling to this work. While verification still needs to be done on his experiences, they are suggestive of a rich and complex afterlife in which 'Love thy neighbor' is an enduring principle and in which love—and help—can reach across the barrier."

— Jimmy Akin, host *Jimmy Akin's Mysterious World*

The most famous English-language Bible is the King James Version. Prepared for the Church of England in the early 1600s, it has had a profound impact on believers in many groups beyond the Anglican community, including other Protestants, Catholics, Jews, and even English-speakers with no specific religious affiliation.

One of the subjects it discusses is necromancy, and in the King James translation of the Old Testament book of Deuteronomy, we read:

> There shall not be found among you anyone that maketh his son or his daughter to pass through the fire, or that useth divination, or an observer of times, or an enchanter, or a witch, or a charmer, or a consulter with familiar spirits, or a wizard, *or a necromancer*. For all that do these things are an abomination unto the Lord (Deut. 18:10-12a, emphasis added).

With a powerful warning like that, believers have been very wary of necromancy, but what actually is it? For many, the term is unfamiliar, and many others have only a vague sense that necromancy involves contacting spirits—such as the souls of the departed or even demons. Based on this, some have asked whether the ministry that Fr. Nathan Castle reports conducting to help souls might be a form of necromancy. Given only the fuzzy descriptions of necromancy that most people have heard, this question is not unreasonable. But we must be careful, because the Christian theological tradition has understood necromancy to be something **very specific**, and—as we'll see—not everything that involves spirits involves necromancy.

What Is Necromancy?

Let's begin by looking at the phrase that the King James version translates "a necromancer." In the original Hebrew, it is *doresh el ha-mettim*. The word *doresh* can mean a few things. It is commonly translated "one who inquires," though it can also mean "one who makes requests." The word *el* is a preposition that, in this context, means "of." And *ha-mettim* means "the dead." So, a *doresh el ha-mettim* means a person who inquires of (or makes requests of) the dead.

This gives us a basic understanding of the kind of people the ancient Israelite community were forbidden to have in their midst. In Christian times, the concept of necromancy continued to be discussed, and it meant basically the same thing, although it took on a few nuances.

One of the contributions of Christian theologians was to classify necromancy as a form of divination. This raises a new question: What is divination? Here we are helped by St. Isidore of Seville (c. 560-636). He was an archbishop and a scholar, and he wrote a famous work known as the *Etymologies*. It was basically a combination of an encyclopedia and a dictionary, with entries organized by keywords, whose origin and meaning Isidore would explain. The *Etymologies* was a standard reference work in the Middle Ages, and so it gives us a good understanding of how words were being used at the time.

When it comes to diviners and divination, Isidore says:

> Diviners (*divinus*) are so named, as if the term were 'filled with god' (*deo plenus*), for they pretend to be filled with divine inspiration, and with a certain deceitful cunning they forecast what is to come for people (*Etymologies* 8:9:14).

So, diviners *forecast* what is to come. In other words, divination involves predicting the future (by some improper means). This was the standard understanding of the concept, and the great medieval theologian St. Thomas Aquinas (1225-1274) agrees. He defines divination this way:

> Divination denotes a foretelling of the future (*Summa Theologiae* II-II: 95:1).

Divination thus involves predicting the future, and necromancers are the kind of people who do so by asking the dead to tell the future. In explaining this, Isidore goes back to the word's Greek roots—*nekros* (dead person, dead body) and *manteia* (prophecy, prediction, oracle). He writes:

> Necromancers (*necromantius*) are those by whose incantations the dead, brought back to life, seem to prophesy, and to answer what is asked, for *nekros* means "dead" in Greek, and divination is called *manteia*. The blood of a corpse is applied for the crossquestioning, for demons are said to love blood. And for this reason, whenever necromancy is practiced, gore is mixed with water, so that they are called more easily by the gore of the blood (*Etymologies* 8:9:11).

St. Thomas Aquinas agrees and cites Isidore's explanation:

> All divinations seek to acquire foreknowledge of future events... Sometimes they employ apparitions or utterances of the dead, and this species is called "necromancy," for as Isidore observes (*Etymologies* 8) in Greek, *nekron* "means dead and *manteia* divination, because after certain incantations and the sprinkling of blood, the dead seem to come to life, to divine and to answer questions" (*Summa Theologiae* II-II:95:3).

We thus see that necromancy has classically been understood as predicting the future by means of consulting the dead, though Isidore also mentions one other party that might be involved: demons. He notes that many ancient forms of necromancy involved the ritual manipulation of blood and observes that "demons are said to love blood." St. Thomas concurs, stating:

> When the demons are invoked openly, this comes under the head of "necromancy" (*Summa Theologiae* II-II:95:3).

Necromancy thus involves a spirit other than that of a living human. A necromancer could call upon (or think he is calling upon) the soul of a dead person or openly ask for a demon to reveal the future to him.

This remains the basic, core concept of necromancy, but in recent times, some authors have slightly broadened it. For example, in a 1909 volume of the *Catholic Encyclopedia*, Edward Graham defined divination as "The seeking after knowledge of future *or hidden things* by inadequate means" (s.v. "Divination," emphasis added). On this broader understanding of divination, one might not only seek knowledge of the future but also hidden things, such as the location of a lost object or buried treasure. With an expanded understanding of divination to include gaining knowledge of the hidden, necromancy could involve this, too.

This expansion nicely captures what was happening in ancient Israel. An inquirer of the dead (*doresh el ha-mettim*) was a person who would consult the dead on behalf of clients who wanted information that had practical value to them. This could be something hidden—like the location of a lost object—but it often concerned the future—such as who would win a coming battle. In fact, it was a desire to know what he should do with respect to a coming battle with the Philistines that motivated King Saul to seek out the famous medium or "witch" of Endor (1 Samuel 28:3-25), who happens to be the basis of the character Endora on the 1960s TV program *Bewitched*.

Clients also had to *pay* inquirers of the dead—it was part of how they made their living—so the information that the client was seeking needed to have enough practical value to him that he was willing to pay for it. The orientation of necromancy—like other forms of divination—was thus directed toward helping the client, providing him the information he wanted. It was not oriented toward helping a departed soul.

Fr. Castle's Ministry

Viewed in this light, it is easy to see how Fr. Castle's description of his ministry to souls *does not* involve necromancy. He is not calling upon the dead in order to get knowledge of the future or hidden things for the benefit of a living client. Instead, the focus is on helping a departed soul. In a sense, this is the opposite of necromancy. The focus is not on helping the living but on helping the departed.

Fr. Castle also avoids the classic subject matter of necromancy. He does not ask the departed to foretell what is going to happen in the future. Neither does he ask about hidden things, like where a lost object or a buried treasure can be found by the living.

Both in terms of his ministry's fundamental orientation and its subject matter, this simply is not necromancy as the Church understands it.

Still, some might ask how Fr. Castle's ministry fits with other aspects of historic Christian teaching and practice, so we will look at that.

Apparitions

Some people have the idea that we should not have any communication with the spirits, but this is not the attitude we find in the Scriptures. In fact, they reveal that God frequently sends spirits to communicate with living people. Most commonly in Scripture, God uses angels to do this—like when the angel Gabriel appeared to the Virgin Mary to tell her that she would be the mother of Jesus Christ (Luke 1:26-38)—however, God sometimes has the souls of departed humans appear also.

For example, the second book of Maccabees—which was written about a century before Christ—tells a story of how the military leader Judah Maccabee encouraged the men under his command by relating to them a vision he had received in a dream:

> He armed each of them not so much with confidence in shields and spears as with the inspiration of brave words, and he cheered them all by relating a dream, a sort of vision, which was worthy of belief.
>
> What he saw was this: Onias, who had been high priest, a noble and good man, of modest bearing and gentle manner, one who spoke fittingly and had been trained from childhood in all that belongs to excellence, was praying with outstretched hands for the whole body of the Jews.
>
> Then likewise a man appeared, distinguished by his gray hair and dignity, and of marvelous majesty and authority.
>
> And Onias spoke, saying, "This is a man who loves the brethren and prays much for the people and the holy city, Jeremiah, the prophet of God."
>
> Jeremiah stretched out his right hand and gave to Judas a golden sword, and as he gave it he addressed him thus: "Take this holy sword, a gift from God, with which you will strike down your adversaries" (2 Maccabees 15:11-16, RSV).

In this dream, Judah Maccabee receives what is known as an apparition. An *apparition* is when a spirit *appears* to someone. The person may *see* the spirit—as Judah did in this dream—but apparitions also can involve voices or engage other senses of the living.

Here, Judah experiences apparitions of both the deceased high priest Onias III (2nd century before Christ) and the deceased prophet Jeremiah (sixth century before Christ). The two delivered a message of comfort and encouragement to Judah, and Jeremiah gave him a sword as a symbol of future victories in battle. Jeremiah thus gave him information about the future.

Yet this was not necromancy. From what we are told, Judah did not seek these apparitions. He did not call upon the spirits of Onias and Jeremiah. Instead, God allowed him to see a vision of them while he was asleep. And it was perfectly fine for Judah to receive this message—including the information about the future—as long as it was on God's terms. God took the initiative by sending the vision to Judah. Judah did not go to an inquirer of the dead.

After the Christian era began, we see a similar attitude toward contact with spirits. Christians were not expected to avoid all contact with them. For example, in 1 Corinthians, St. Paul writes:

> You know that when you were heathen, you were led astray to mute idols, however you may have been moved. Therefore, I want you to understand that no one speaking by the Spirit of God ever says, "Jesus be cursed!" and no one can say "Jesus is Lord" except by the Holy Spirit (1 Corinthians 12:2-3).

Here the apostle indicates that not every message from a spirit should be believed. Instead, he provides one kind of test for discerning the kind of spirit that is speaking—based on the message it brings. Later, he describes how a worship service that incorporates prophecy should be conducted, and he says:

> Let two or three prophets speak, and let the others weigh what is said. If a revelation is made to another sitting by, let the first be silent. For you can all prophesy one by one, so that all may learn and all be encouraged; and the spirits of prophets are subject to prophets. For God is not a God of confusion but of peace (1 Corinthians 14:29-33).

Here Paul emphasizes orderliness in worship services, but he also indicates discernment: When one prophet is speaking, the others should weigh what is being said to see whether it is really a message from God or not.

St. John is even more explicit. In his first letter, he writes:

> Beloved, do not believe every spirit, but test the spirits to see whether they are of God; for many false prophets have gone out into the world. By this you know the Spirit of God: every spirit which confesses that Jesus Christ has come in the flesh is of God, and every spirit which does not confess Jesus is not of God (1 John 4:1-3).

We thus see that both St. Paul and St. John expect Christians to test the spirits that communicate with them—not to run away and have nothing to do with them. Rather than forbidding any communication with spirits, the New Testament *expects* Christians to have contact with them *and* to test them, because not all spirits are truthful.

In context, the spirits that Paul and John are envisioning are most likely the Holy Spirit and angels (or, in the case of deceitful spirits, demons), but Christian history has revealed that God also allows the souls of departed humans to appear in apparitions—just as he did in the time of Judah Maccabee. The apparitions have been widely reported in Catholic, Eastern Orthodox, Oriental Orthodox, and Assyrian churches, and apparitions of saintly humans are also accepted in some Anglican and Pentecostal/Charismatic circles.

For its part, the Catholic Church accepts that some of these apparitions are genuinely from God, and in 1978 the Vatican's Congregation for the Doctrine of the Faith (now the Dicastery for the Doctrine of the Faith) published a document to guide bishops in "testing the spirits" and discerning which apparitions are genuinely from God. In 2011, it was published on the Vatican web site (Vatican.va; see "Norms Regarding the Manner of Proceedings in the Discernment of Presumed Apparitions or Revelations").

When one studies the history of Church-approved apparitions, the saints that God has allowed to appear to the living may reveal information about the future or other hidden matters. For example, when the Virgin Mary appeared to the three shepherd children in

Portugal in 1917, she stated that the current war (World War I) would be ending but that a worse one (World War II) would break out in the future if people did not repent.

Yet this did not constitute necromancy because the children had not summoned the Virgin Mary for purposes of finding out this information. Just as Onias and Jeremiah had come to give Judah Maccabee an important message that included information about the future, so the Virgin Mary had come to give the Fatima children such a message.

And it is acknowledged by historic authors that this is possible. In a 1911 volume of the *Catholic Encyclopedia*, Charles Dubray wrote:

> The Church does not deny that, with a special permission of God, the souls of the departed may appear to the living, and even manifest things unknown to the latter (s.v. "Necromancy").

We thus see that whether God takes the initiative in sending a message or whether one is inquiring of the dead for practical, personal benefit makes a great deal of difference. The former is receiving information God wants you to have, while the second is necromancy.

Helping Souls

What about helping souls that are still on their journey to God in heaven? Over the course of this life, God works with us to help us grow in holiness, but few of us are completely holy at the end of life. Yet we know that when we are with God in heaven, we will be completely holy—no longer burdened by disordered desires and temptations to sin. We will be perfectly free of these bonds and able to experience God's love to the fullest.

Jews and Christians have therefore recognized that—between death and heaven—there must be a final purification from all our remaining flaws to fully and freely liberate us from the bonds of sin. Christians of all kinds refer to this purification as beginning during life, where it is empowered by the Cross of Christ and referred to as "sanctification" (the process of being made holy or saintly). Catholics refer to the final purification at the end of life as "purgatory."

We don't know much about purgatory, including how long it takes. For those who still need purification when Christ returns, it will undoubtedly happen "in the twinkling of an eye" (1 Corinthians 15:52). However, both Jews and Christians have recognized that they are able to help those experiencing purification by their prayers. This practice predates the time of Christ. At one point, Judah Maccabee and his men found the bodies of comrades who had fallen in battle because they had engaged in superstitious practices, and so:

> They turned to prayer, begging that the sin which had been committed might be wholly blotted out... He also took up a collection, man by man, to the amount of two thousand drachmas of silver, and sent it to Jerusalem to provide for a sin offering. In doing this he acted very well and honorably, taking account of the resurrection.

For if he were not expecting that those who had fallen would rise again, it would have been superfluous and foolish to pray for the dead. But if he was looking to the splendid reward that is laid up for those who fall asleep in godliness, it was a holy and pious thought. Therefore, he made atonement for the dead, that they might be delivered from their sin (2 Macc. 12:42-45).

Similarly, Jewish people today still customarily pray for their departed loved ones for eleven months after their death. The prayer is known as the Mourner's Kaddish, and it extols God's greatness in the expectation that he will bless and help the departed loved one in the afterlife. Christianity inherited this practice of praying for the dead, and Catholics, Eastern Orthodox, Oriental Orthodox, and Assyrian Christians all pray for the departed. Even many in the Protestant community pray for their departed loved ones. They may not always have a theological explanation for this, but the love they have in their hearts tells them to engage in this beautiful practice.

We thus see abundant evidence in the Judeo-Christian tradition for the practice of trying to help souls as they make their way to their final destination with God in heaven.

Ghosts

What happens when these two things—apparitions and helping souls—come together? Christians have historically recognized that God doesn't just allow the saints in heaven to appear to the living but also those who are still being purified. In fact, this is the historic understanding of what ghosts are.

The term *ghost* just means "spirit" (that's why the Holy Spirit is also called the Holy Ghost). And it was understood that human spirits—human ghosts—that manifested to the living were the spirits of those who had not yet arrived in heaven because they still needed prayers or were being held back by unfinished business from life.

Theologians thus recognized that the spirits of humans being purified might appear to the living (e.g., Aquinas, *Summa Theologiae* III-Supplement:69:3), and Christian history is filled with numerous accounts of them doing so and asking for the living to help them, such as by praying for them and by having Masses said (the modern equivalent of what Judah Maccabee did by having a sacrifice offered for the souls of his fallen comrades).

According to *The Life of St. Thomas Aquinas* written by his younger contemporary, the Dominican bishop Bernard Gui (c. 1261-1331), St. Thomas himself was visited by the soul of his departed sister:

> On another occasion, at Paris this time, his deceased sister appeared to him as he was praying, and said that she was in Purgatory and needed Masses and prayers; which he was quick to arrange that she should have. Sometime later, Thomas being now at Rome, she appeared again to say that she was now in glory, because of

this help. He took the opportunity to ask her about the state of his two deceased brothers, the lords Landulf and Reginald. Landulf, she replied, was in Purgatory, but Reginald already in the glory of God. Then Thomas asked about himself and got this answer: "You are in a good state, brother, and you will soon be joining us; but to receive a greater reward than ours because of your labors for the Church of God" (*The Life of St. Thomas Aquinas* 20 in *Saint Thomas Aquinas: Biographical Documents*, Kenelm Foster, ed., tr.).

Here Aquinas's sister sought his help and also—at his request—gave him information about his deceased brothers and his own future.

Fr. Castle's Ministry Again

All of this establishes a framework for understanding Fr. Castle's ministry to souls. It is not necromancy, for he is not contacting the dead to obtain an oracle or prophecy from them. He is not seeking information about the future or buried treasure. In fact, he is not seeking anything for the benefit of the living, which is what necromancy involves. Instead, he is seeking to help departed spirits.

Like in the case of Judah Maccabee and the apparitions of the saints and other human souls in Christian history, he waits for them to make contact, which in his case happens in dreams. He then responds to the messages, just as those who received apparitions did. This responsive rather than summoning nature of his ministry is another reason it is not necromancy and, instead, fits with historic Christian practice.

The specific souls that he reports contacting him are those seeking a form of help—as is common in historical Christian accounts of ghosts—and Fr. Castle seeks to provide this help, as Christians have historically done.

What is distinctive in Fr. Castle's case is that he doesn't just respond by praying for the spirits—although he does do that. He understands his dreams as requests for further communication, and in responding to this request, he and his prayer partners provide what sometimes amounts to a form of counseling to help the souls move past remaining attachments that have kept them from further progress.

This specific form of help is uncommon, but it is easy to see that it is different than necromancy and that it fits within broader principles that Jews and Christians have used for millennia. It certainly has not been condemned by Church teaching.

What a fascinating ministry Fr. Nathan Castle conducts! Catholics and other Christians have long prayed for the deceased to help them on their way to heaven, and history contains many accounts of souls reaching out to the living for help. However, most people may have only a few such encounters, at most. Fr. Castle reports being contacted by souls on a weekly basis, suggesting a special calling to this work. While verification still needs to be done on his experiences, they are suggestive of a rich and complex afterlife in which "Love thy neighbor" is an enduring principle and in which love—and help—can reach across the barrier.

For More Information

For further discussion and analysis, see Episodes 269 and 270 of my podcast *Jimmy Akin's Mysterious World.* In Episode 269, I interview Fr. Castle and describe his ministry, and in Episode 270, I conduct an extensive analysis of how his ministry comports with Catholic teaching. You can access the episodes by going to Mysterious.fm/269 and Mysterious.fm/270.

Jimmy Akin's
Mysterious World Podcast

SECTION THREE

Prayer Partners

Cathryn Castle Garcia

Cathryn has been Father Nathan Castle's baby sister her whole life. She's also his editor/ publisher and feels blessed to be one of his prayer partners. Cathryn loves words and water and wild places. Together with her husband Capt. Gui Garcia she owns C2G2Productions, a multimedia production company specializing in wildlife and underwater filming. She is the co-author of *Ocean Metaphor: Unexpected Life Lessons from the Sea.*

Linda and Michael Quinn

Linda and Michael Quinn have been hospice volunteers for 20 years. Their work is a part of their ordained journey to awaken us to the reality that we are all beautiful, sacred souls, loved beyond measure by God. They perceive their work with Father Nathan Castle as affirming the value of transforming our lives now, while we are still alive. Serving as Father Nathan's prayer partners has deepened their commitment of service to the dying and celebrating the reality that our journey is not about death at all, but about the next step in our life. [ed. note: *Linda died unexpectedly on December 6, 2023, as this book was being readied for publishing. Father Nathan dedicated it in her memory.*]

James and Jeanne Marie Rachal

James and Jeanne were both born into families of strong Catholic faith. They attended Catholic schools through high school graduation. They met Father Nathan during their high school years at Bishop Byrne High School in Port Arthur, Texas and have remained close friends. During their adult lives, they have worked in several parish ministries. They were leaders in the Catholic Youth Organization for over 20 years. James has been in the Knights of Columbus for over 40 years and has worked on his parish ACTS retreat team. They have both volunteered in their parishes and have served on parish councils. Their Catholic faith and friendship with Father Nathan drew them to help him with his ministry.

Karen Saliba PsyD, MFT

Karen is a psychoanalyst, working with couples and individuals who want to live in healthy harmony with one another, their families, and their communities. She believes that we can be healed from our Earthly life hurts by engaging in dynamic and compassionate relationships. As a prayer partner with Father Nathan, she has learned so much about love, spirituality and how we are never alone. Her husband and two daughters support her endeavors to inspire hope for those in this life and afterwards. Her relationship to athletics and pickleball is also very close to her mind, body, and soul.

Kimberly Sharp, LMFT, DTM

As a psychotherapist, Kim loves helping people connect with the deepest part of themselves, which can promote joy, peace, and relief in their lives. Working from a mind-body-spirit perspective, she has witnessed how when we do our own inner work, it can lead to a deeply meaningful and fun life! Working as a prayer partner with Father Nathan, Kimberly has been amazed at the benevolence, kindness, and creativity the heavenly helpers on the "other side" use to support souls on their journey in the afterlife. Kimberly enjoys spending time with her husband and family, good friends, and volunteering with Toastmasters International and in her home parish of St. Peter's Episcopal Church in San Pedro, California.

David Monroe Wright

David Monroe Wright is a retired fourth-generation dentist. Early in life, as a depressed teenager, he discovered that his way to happiness was to be of "service and love" to mankind. Throughout his adult life he has volunteered his dental skills in poverty-stricken areas like Appalachia, Indian tribal lands in North Dakota, the Dominican Republic and at a free clinic in on the east side of Buffalo, New York. God gave him his next assignment when he was introduced to Father Nathan and prayer partner Karen Saliba. In his free time, David paints, studies the Bible and volunteers as a visitor to hospice patients in Buffalo.

Lisa Armijo Zorita, Ph.D.

Creating avenues of possibility is Lisa's passion. For over 28 years she has engaged in multiple levels of community mobilization. She is a skilled researcher, community needs assessor, evaluator, trainer, and community developer. Dr. Zorita works with people at all levels of government, business, and non-profit organizations to design and implement programs and processes to maximize effectiveness. She is a third order Dominican and finds great joy as a wife, mother, and she is a lifelong friend to people from all walks of life. Lisa enthusiastically believes in the resilience of the human spirit.

And Toto, Too

Toto brings a uniquely canine perspective to this work with human souls who have been through trauma. Early in his life he spent much of his time caged and neglected. Rescued by his companion and friend, Father Richard, Toto often sits calmly in Father Nathan's lap as souls move through and make their passage. Toto loves rides, walks, treats and watching sports with his human friends. He loves to dance and can cross the room on his hind legs in pursuit of a treat. One of the angels referred to Toto as "a great champion of the good."

About the Illustrator

Stefan Salinas is a liturgical and studio artist, author, and illustrator, whose works adorn the interior and exterior of several churches, as well as the University of San Francisco. His books and webcomic address matters of psychology, spirituality, Catholicism, and interfaith relations. He was awarded a Xeric grant to publish his first graphic novel. Born and raised in Houston, he now lives in San Francisco. Learn more at stefansalinas.com.

Acknowledgments

When I am presiding as a priest at mass, at one point I lead the congregation in praying a creed. It's simply a list of some of our most important beliefs. In the Nicene Creed we affirm that we believe in "all that is seen and unseen." That includes all those *who* are seen and unseen.

My prayer partners and I constantly enjoy the support of many who are unseen. The mostly healed souls that get in our line and move through our process have been helped by many saints and souls whom we haven't seen. One fine day I believe we'll see you all.

I want to give a shout out to all of you who have made financial donations in support of my ministry and to my Dominican brotherhood. A few of you make monthly gifts that are so reliable. I'm talking about you, Ed, Julie, Sally, Rob, Pat, John, Karen, Peaceful Hiker, and Guy.

My assistant, Chontell, has been an answer to prayer. Is there anything you can't do or figure out how to do?

Some of my volunteers do their work so quietly I don't even know about it. Lisa and Lori, I do know you've put in many hours on one project or another. Thank you.

I'm always grateful to my brother and provincial superior, Christopher. I couldn't do this work without your unfailing support.

Doreen and Stefan, you're at it again, bringing a new, beautiful book to life.

This past year "The Joyful Friar" podcast has made its way in the world. I'm grateful to the team that dreamed TJF into existence. And to all my guests, listeners and viewers: I'm praying for you.

Some of you take the time to bring some problem or concern to me by email via my website. I've been honored to be a part of your journeys.

Jack Canfield, Patty Aubery and team, you've been so kind to me. I always value your advice.

To my local Dominican community in Tucson and to the Castle and Monks families, thank you for being there for me.

Cathryn and Gui, having you nearby, even for a while, has made this joyful friar even more joyful.

Richard, congrats on 40 years of priesthood this year. Your people love you. So do I.

Toto, thanks for dancing for joy every time I enter a room.

And Friend of my Heart, thanks for creating and loving me and all of the above.

Nathan G. Castle, OP
November 2023

About the Author

Nathan G. Castle has been a Catholic priest of the semi-contemplative Dominican order since 1979. Father Nathan has served as a campus minister at Arizona State University, the University of California, Riverside, and Stanford University. Currently, he lives in a community of Dominican men and women serving the University of Arizona in Tucson.

Father Nathan has prayed for deceased souls since childhood and has helped "stuck" and not-so-stuck souls cross over for nearly 30 years. This is his third book on his afterlife ministry. He has used his first book, *And Toto, Too: The Wizard of Oz as a Spiritual Adventure*, as the basis for healing of trauma retreats for spiritual groups and survivors of natural disasters. He is an active member of the International Association for Near-Death Studies and is the host of "The Joyful Friar" podcast.

Available for speaking engagements and retreats, Father Nathan can be reached through his website, nathan-castle.com and on various social media outlets.